ROUTLEDGE LIBRARY EDITIONS:
WW2

Volume 33

SPECIAL OPERATIONS

SPECIAL OPERATIONS

Edited by
PATRICK HOWARTH

LONDON AND NEW YORK

First published in 1955 by Routledge & Kegan Paul Ltd

This edition first published in 2022
by Routledge
2 Park Square, Milton Park, Abingdon, Oxon OX14 4RN

and by Routledge
605 Third Avenue, New York, NY 10158

Routledge is an imprint of the Taylor & Francis Group, an informa business

© 1955 Routledge & Kegan Paul Ltd

All rights reserved. No part of this book may be reprinted or reproduced or utilised in any form or by any electronic, mechanical, or other means, now known or hereafter invented, including photocopying and recording, or in any information storage or retrieval system, without permission in writing from the publishers.

Trademark notice: Product or corporate names may be trademarks or registered trademarks, and are used only for identification and explanation without intent to infringe.

British Library Cataloguing in Publication Data
A catalogue record for this book is available from the British Library

ISBN: 978-1-03-201217-9 (Set)
ISBN: 978-1-00-319367-8 (Set) (ebk)
ISBN: 978-1-03-207377-4 (Volume 33) (hbk)
ISBN: 978-1-03-207378-1 (Volume 33) (pbk)
ISBN: 978-1-00-320661-3 (Volume 33) (ebk)

DOI: 10.4324/9781003206613

Publisher's Note
The publisher has gone to great lengths to ensure the quality of this reprint but points out that some imperfections in the original copies may be apparent.

Disclaimer
The publisher has made every effort to trace copyright holders and would welcome correspondence from those they have been unable to trace.

Special Operations

By

*Peter Fleming, C. M. Woodhouse, W. Stanley Moss,
David Walker, Julian Amery, Anthony Quayle,
Basil Davidson, Hugh Seton-Watson,
Xan Fielding, George Millar, Peter Churchill,
Christopher Sykes, Bruce Marshall, Maurice Buckmaster,
Francis Noel-Baker, John Connell,
F. Spencer Chapman, J. H. Williams, Richard Usborne*

EDITED BY PATRICK HOWARTH

Routledge and Kegan Paul
LONDON

*First published 1955
by Routledge & Kegan Paul Ltd
Broadway House, Carter Lane, E.C.4*

CONTENTS

	Page
ACKNOWLEDGMENTS	ix
INTRODUCTION	xi
AN AMMUNITION TRAIN IN GREECE *By Peter Fleming*	1
BLESSED LITTLE VIRGIN *By C. M. Woodhouse*	8
THE CAPTURE OF THE GENERAL *By W. Stanley Moss*	19
CHRISTMAS '40 *By David Walker*	33
INVITATION TO ALBANIA *By Julian Amery*	40
PARTISAN LIFE IN ALBANIA *By Anthony Quayle*	59
THE COST *By Basil Davidson*	79
RESISTANCE IN EASTERN EUROPE *By Hugh Seton-Watson*	88
ARREST IN FRANCE *By Xan Fielding*	114
DESCENT TO THE MAQUIS *By George Millar*	131
SEMNOZ *By Peter Churchill*	142
WOMEN OF THE FRENCH RESISTANCE *By Christopher Sykes*	151

		Page
HOW YEO-THOMAS WENT TO FRANCE		158
By Bruce Marshall		
THE TRAINING OF AGENTS		171
By Maurice Buckmaster		
FLOOD IN THE DESERT		181
By Francis Noel-Baker		
ARAB RADIO STATION		189
By John Connell		
NIGHTMARE JOURNEYS		198
By F. Spencer Chapman		
THE GREAT ELEPHANT TREK		210
By J. H. Williams		
OUR SECRET SERVICE		224
By Richard Usborne		
BIOGRAPHICAL NOTES		232

LIST OF ILLUSTRATIONS

	Facing page
Patrick Howarth	32
Peter Fleming	32
C. M. Woodhouse	32
W. Stanley Moss	33
David Walker	33
Julian Amery	33
Anthony Quayle	48
Basil Davidson	48
Hugh Seton-Watson	48
Xan Fielding	49
George Millar	49
Peter Churchill *Photo by Mark Gerson*	49
Christopher Sykes	160
Bruce Marshall	160
Maurice Buckmaster	160
Francis Noel-Baker *Photo by Basil Shackleton*	161
John Connell *Photo by Howard Coster*	161
F. Spencer Chapman	161
J. H. Williams	176
Richard Usborne	176

ACKNOWLEDGMENTS

The publishers, the editor, and the Special Forces Club most gratefully acknowledge the kind permission of the following publishers to include without any payment extracts from the following works:

Batchworth Press Ltd., Maurice Buckmaster, *Specially Employed*.
Bedford Books Ltd., Basil Davidson, *Partisan Picture*.
Chapman & Hall Ltd., David Walker, *Death at my Heels*.
Wm. Collins, Sons & Co. Ltd., Christopher Sykes, *Four Studies in Loyalty*.
Constable & Co. Ltd., Richard Usborne, *Clubland Heroes*.
Evans Bros. Ltd., Bruce Marshall, *The White Rabbit*.
Evening News, John Connell, *Late Extra*.
George G. Harrap & Co. Ltd., W. Stanley Moss, *Ill Met by Moonlight*.
Rupert Hart-Davis Ltd., J. H. Williams, *Elephant Bill*.
William Heinemann Ltd., George Millar, *Maquis*.
William Heinemann Ltd., Anthony Quayle, *Eight Hours from England*.
Hodder & Stoughton Ltd., Peter Churchill, *Duel of Wits*.
Macmillan & Co. Ltd., Julian Amery, *Sons of the Eagle*.
Methuen & Co. Ltd., Hugh Seton-Watson, *East European Revolution*.
Martin Secker & Warburg, Ltd., Xan Fielding, *Hide and Seek*.
The 19th Century and After, C. M. Woodhouse.

They are also most grateful to the B.B.C. for permission to reproduce without charge talks given by Peter Fleming and Francis Noel-Baker.

INTRODUCTION

THE organization known as S.O.E. or the Special Operations Executive, was one of the great creations of the second world war. The history of this extraordinary essay in improvisation has been recorded and filed, but it remains unpublished. Indeed it is only in the last year or two that the initials S.O.E. have come to have any meaning to people who were not in some way personally connected with the organization. During the war the general public were given as little information as possible that a central body existed for the purpose of developing resistance in occupied territories, and so far as the matter was considered at all, the body in question was generally assumed to be some part of the secret service. The various cover names under which S.O.E. operated were designed to add to the public confusion.

S.O.E. grew up from a number of different roots. It was in part a temporary offshoot of the regular British secret service, whose function is the obtaining of secret information and whose existence is permanent. It was partly the creation of a number of bankers and businessmen, who had both international connections and the gift of foresight. In its early years it attracted to it patriotic British subjects whose occupations kept them abroad as well as soldiers, sailors and airmen who had novel ideas about the prosecution of war.

The task of S.O.E. was to fight the enemy away from the acknowledged battlefields. Simultaneously it waged economic warfare with the war of the spirit, and its strategy was continuously offensive rather than defensive. The modern invention of which it took particular advantage was the parachute, and in time the parachute became S.O.E.'s unofficial symbol.

S.O.E. had to exploit both the ruthlessness and the weaknesses of enemy occupation, and as the grip of the enemy occupying powers was loosened, much of the organization's activity took the form of direct support of open guerrilla warfare. The way in which S.O.E. extended its scope from the planning of clandestine acts of sabotage to the supply, by air, of equipment for partisan armies was one of many examples of its remarkable flexibility.

The brain-child of a few far-sighted men, who shortly before war broke out had recognized the need for some such organization as S.O.E., grew in fact into a new service—a secret service yet not an intelligence service—a service whose contribution towards the winning of the war was without parallel in earlier times. As a contribution towards the extension of British prestige it can at least be said that one reason, among others, why London was for so long the capital of the free world was that patriots of so many nations, who strove for the freedom of their countries, could find the help they were looking for in Baker Street.

Resistance in occupied territories had, of course, to be considered not only as a military problem but also as a political one. As the end of the war drew near and the political differences between the Eastern and Western allies, which had always been large, grew steadily more apparent, the political responsibilities of individual S.O.E. officers increased greatly. Young men, who in some cases had originally been dispatched to occupied territories primarily as instructors in elementary forms of demolition, suddenly acquired consular or even ambassadorial responsibilities without either diplomatic experience or diplomatic amenities. In meeting these responsibilities they too, in the overwhelming majority of cases, showed the flexibility and adaptability which accounted for so much of the success of the whole organization.

In the twentieth century—in Britain at least—the influence of the young in public affairs has seldom been strong, but the

INTRODUCTION xiii

operations of S.O.E. provided an exception to this prevailing rule. Colonel Woodhouse, Lt.-Col. Maclean and Lt.-Col. Deakin, when they undertook their remarkable military and political tasks in Greece, Albania and Yugoslavia, were of an age which might have qualified them for important military or naval tasks under the younger Pitt, but which in most walks of life today would be considered appropriate only for a junior executive under instruction.

S.O.E. not only achieved great results; it also attracted great spirits, and these great spirits were, above all, individualists. It is arguable that in a war such as that of 1914–18, in which the defence continually held the advantage over the attack and the opportunities for diversion, movement and surprise were limited, some of the gayest and most successful of the S.O.E. individualists would simply have been misfits swallowed up in the general slaughter. Whether this would have been so or not, it is certain that between 1939 and 1945 S.O.E. provided a number of young men with opportunities which they would not have found elsewhere, and the manner in which they took advantage of those opportunities is now recorded in history.

So readily did persons of originality and strong individualism find their way into S.O.E. that it is not altogether surprising that the organization contained, or developed, a high proportion of people whose profession is today that of author. There are, of course, leading figures in many other professions who are the products of S.O.E. In such diverse fields as dress-designing and politics, the musical stage and broadcasting there are Mr. Hardy Amies and Miss Pat Hornsby-Smith, Mr. Eric Maschwitz and Mr. Lionel Hale—to mention only a few familiar names—who are all graduates of S.O.E. in the war. But since the war it is in the writing of books that members of the organization seem to me to have gained the most varied and continual distinction; and that is the main reason why this anthology has been produced.

The origin of the anthology is to be found in the finances of a club and a benevolent fund. There is near Knightsbridge a club known as the Special Forces Club, whose members served in S.O.E. during the war. Associated with it is a committee which tries to give such help as the money available allows to the dependants of certain members of S.O.E. who lost their lives during the war. Both the club and the benevolent fund are suffering from serious financial difficulties.

It was because there are a considerable number of us who served in S.O.E. and who have subsequently published books that the suggestion was put forward that an anthology should be produced wholly for the benefit of the club and the benevolent fund. The suggestion was accepted by the committee of the club, who asked me to act as editor.

It was originally proposed to include works by as many professional authors who had served in S.O.E. as possible. But several writers of distinction have never touched on the war in their works, and the publishers felt, no doubt rightly, that an anthology produced along the lines first suggested would be too much of a miscellany. It was therefore decided to include only contributions related directly to the war of 1939-45 and to S.O.E. as an organization.

The authors who were invited to contribute were asked to make selections from their own published works, and my part as editor has therefore been a small one. It was hoped that the authors who contributed would waive any claims to reproduction fees and that the publishers concerned would be equally forbearing. These hopes were wholly fulfilled. The generosity of the authors, of the publishers, to whom acknowledgments are made on page ix, and of the agents who also gave their services gratuitously, is truly appreciated.

This book is therefore launched as a charitable enterprise. At the same time it is my hope, as editor, that those who read it will find that they have encountered in its pages some of the more remarkable spirits of our time.

London, 1955   PATRICK HOWARTH.

AN AMMUNITION TRAIN IN GREECE

By Peter Fleming

I FORGET which of us it was who found the ammunition train. There were two of them, as a matter of fact, lying forlornly in a railway siding outside the town of Larissa. Larissa, in the great empty plain of Thessaly, was our main supply base in northern Greece, from which, in April 1941, we were withdrawing under heavy German pressure.

The town had been bombed by the Italians, then it had been badly damaged by an earthquake, and now it was receiving regular attention from the Luftwaffe. It was an awful mess. The Greek railway staff had run away and it was pretty obvious that the two ammunition trains had been abandoned. I knew that we were seriously short of ammunition further down the line so I went to the Brigadier in charge of the base and asked permission to try to get one of the trains away. It was given with alacrity.

I don't want you to think that this action on my part was public-spirited, or anything like that. My motives were purely selfish. We wanted a job. We were a small unit which had been carrying out various irregular activities further north; but now the sort of tasks for which we were designed had become impossible, and we were in danger of becoming what civil servants call redundant. We felt that if we could get this train away we should be doing something useful and justifying our existence. Besides, one of us claimed that he knew how to drive an engine.

This was Norman Johnstone, a brother officer in the Grenadier Guards. One of our jobs earlier in the campaign had been to destroy some rolling-stock which could not be moved away. Norman had a splendid time blowing up about twenty valuable locomotives and a lot of trucks, but towards the end we ran out of explosive. At this stage a sergeant in the 4th Hussars turned up, who was an engine-driver in civilian life. With Norman helping him, he got steam up in the four surviving engines, drove them a quarter of a mile down the line, then sent them full tilt back into the station where they caused further havoc of a spectacular and enjoyable kind.

These were perhaps not ideal conditions under which to learn how to drive an engine, especially as the whole thing was carried out under shell-fire; and all we really knew for certain about Norman's capabilities as an engine-driver was that every single locomotive with which he had been associated had become scrap metal in a matter of minutes. Still, he is a very determined and a very methodical chap, and there seemed no harm in letting him have a go. So early in the morning we made our way to the railway station, just in time for the first air-raid of the day. Except for occasional parties of refugees and stragglers from the Greek army the station was deserted. There were two excellent reasons for this. First of all there were no trains running, so there was no point in anybody going there anyhow. Secondly, the station was practically the only thing left in the ruins of Larissa that was worth bombing; we had ten air raids altogether before we left in the afternoon, and they always had a go at the station.

The first thing we had to do was to get steam up in a railway engine. There were plenty of these about but all except two had been rendered unserviceable by the Luftwaffe. We started work on the bigger of the two. After having a quick look round, Norman explained to us that one of the most popular and probably in the long run the soundest of all methods of making steam was by boiling water, but, he said, we might have to devise some alternative formula as the water mains had been cut by bombs and there was very little coal to be found. However, in the long run we got together enough of these two more or less essential ingredients, and all was going well when one of the few really large bombs that came our way blew a hole in the track just outside the shed we were working in, thus, as it were, locking the stable door before we had been able to steal the horse. Greatly disgusted, we transferred our attention to the other sound engine.

There were more air-raids, and it came on to rain, and two Greek deserters stole my car, and altogether things did not look very hopeful, especially when somebody pointed out that there was now only one undamaged and navigable set of tracks leading out of the battered marshalling yard. But the needle on the pressure-gauge in the cabin of our engine was rising slowly, and at last, whistling excitedly, the ancient machine got under way. It was a majestic sight, and it would have been even more majestic if she had not gone backwards instead of forwards.

It was at this point that a certain gap in Norman's education as an engine-driver became evident. The sergeant in the 4th Hussars had taught him how to start a locomotive and how to launch it on a career of self-destruction; but Norman's early training in how to stop an engine had been confined entirely to making it run violently into a lot of other rolling-stock. We trotted anxiously along the cinders, hanging, so to speak, on to Norman's stirrup leathers. 'Do you know how to stop?' we shouted. 'Not yet,' replied Norman, a trifle testily. But he soon found out and presently mastered the knack of making the engine go forward as well as backwards, and we steamed rather incredulously northwards towards the siding where the ammunition trains lay.

We chose the bigger of the two. It consisted of twenty-six trucks containing 120 tons of ammunition and 150 tons of petrol. It was not what you might call an ideally balanced cargo from our point of view, and nobody particularly wanted the petrol, but the train was made up like that and we had to lump it.

It really was rather a proud moment when we steamed back through Larissa with this enormous train clattering along behind us, and out into the broad plain of Thessaly. Norman drove, the stoker was Oliver Barstow—a young officer in the Royal Horse Artillery who was killed a few days later—and Guardsman Loveday and I, armed with our only Tommy-gun, prepared to engage any hostile aircraft who might be so foolhardy as to come within range. It was a lovely evening, and we all felt tremendously pleased with ourselves. Driving a train, once you had got the beastly thing started, seemed to be extraordinarily easy. No steering, no gear-changing, no problems of navigation, no flat tyres, none of those uncomfortable suspicions that perhaps after all you ought to have taken that last turning to the left. There's nothing in it, we told each other. I am afraid we were suffering from what Stalin once called 'dizziness from success'.

Almost as soon as we had left Larissa we had begun to climb up a long, gentle slope; and we had only done about five miles when the needle on the pressure gauge began slowly but firmly to fall. We stoked like mad. Norman pulled, pushed and twiddled the various devices on what we quite incorrectly called the dashboard. Pressure continued to fall, and the train went slower and slower. At last it stopped altogether. 'We'd better get out,' said Norman, 'and have a look at the injector-sprockets.' He may not actually have said 'injector-sprockets' but anyhow it was some technical term which meant nothing to us and may not have meant a very great deal to him. It was at this point that we realized that the train had not merely stopped but was beginning to run slowly backwards down the hill. The thought of free-wheeling backwards into Larissa was distasteful to all of us. In the hurry of departure we had had no time to organize our ten brakesmen, who were all confined in the guard's van instead of being dispersed along the train so that they could operate the brakes on individual goods wagons. There was only one thing to do. I leapt off the engine and ran back down the train as fast as I could, like an old lady running for a bus: jumped on the back of the nearest goods van, swarmed up a little ladder on to its roof and feverishly turned the wheel which put the brake on. The train continued to go backwards, but it seemed to have stopped gathering speed and at last, after I had repeated this operation several times, it came reluctantly to a stop.

We were really getting a great deal of fun out of this train. We had got a tremendous kick out of starting it, and now we were scarcely less elated at having brought it to a standstill. But we had to face the facts, and the main fact was that as engine-drivers, though we had no doubt some excellent qualities—originality, determination, cheerfulness, and so on—we were open to the serious criticism that we did not seem able to drive our engine very far. A run of five miles, with a small discount for going backwards unexpectedly, is not much to show for a hard day's work. At this point, moreover, it suddenly began to look as if we were going to lose our precious train altogether. As we tinkered away at the engine, the air grew loud with an expected but none the less unwelcome noise, and a number of enemy bombers could be seen marching through the sky towards us. We were a very conspicuous object in the middle of that empty plain and I quickly gave orders for the ten men in the guard's van to go and take cover five hundred yards from the train. In point of fact there was no cover to take, but they trotted off with alacrity and sat down round a small tree about the size of a big gooseberry bush in the middle distance. We couldn't very well leave the engine because the fire might have gone out (or anyhow we thought it might) and we should have had to start all over again.

But if we had our troubles the enemy, as so often happens, had his too. The bombers were obviously interested in us, but it soon became equally obvious that they had no bombs, having wasted all theirs on the ruins of Larissa earlier in the day. They still, however, had their machine-guns and three or four of the aircraft proceeded to attack us, coming in very low, one after the other. But they all made the same mistake, which they might not have made if we ourselves had taken evasive action and left the train. They all attacked the engine, round which they could see signs of life, instead of flying up and down the twenty-odd wagons full of petrol and H.E. and spraying them with bullets, which could hardly have failed to produce spectacular results. They concentrated on putting the engine out of action; and the engine, as we ourselves were just beginning to realize, was out of action already, all the water in the boiler having somehow disappeared.

We used the engine in much the same way as one uses a grouse-butt. Whichever side the attack was coming from, we got the other side. The flying-machine, making a terrible noise and blazing away with its machine-guns, swept down on us and as it roared overhead—much bigger, much more malevolent but not really very much higher than the average grouse—we pooped off at it with our Tommy-gun, to which the German rear-gunner replied with a burst that kicked up the dust a hundred yards away or more. It got rather silly after a bit. I am quite sure we never hit the Luftwaffe, and the only damage the Luftwaffe did to us was to make a hole in a map somebody had left in the cab. And one of the things about driving a train is that you don't need a map to do it with. They gave it up quite soon—it was getting late anyhow—and went home to Bulgaria. We climbed back into our engine again and as I looked at our only casualty—the map, torn by an explosive bullet and covered with coal dust—I couldn't help rather envying the Luftwaffe, who almost certainly believed that they had succeeded in doing what they set out to do. It was only too obvious that we had not. Night fell, and it was fairly cold.

Then, all of a sudden, out of the darkness, another train appeared. It was full of Australian gunners whose guns were supposed to have come on by road. They towed us back to the next station. Here we picked up a good engine with a Greek driver and set off for the south. It was ideal weather all next day—pouring rain and low cloud—and we never saw a German aeroplane at all. Forty-eight hours after we had started work on this unlikely project we reached our—or rather the ammunition's—destination. It was a place called Amphykleion and here I formally handed over the train—26 coaches, 150 tons of petrol, 120 tons of ammunition—to the supply people. Everyone was delighted with us. 'This really will make a difference,' they said. We felt childishly pleased. The sun shone, it was a lovely morning. And this marked improvement in the weather made it comparatively easy for a small force of German dive-bombers, a few hours later, to dispose of the train and all its contents with a terrible finality.

So you see this is not a success story. Nor is it a story which can have—from me, at any rate—a moral; for the only possible moral anyone can draw from it is that human endeavour is always likely to be futile, that it is better to leave ammunition trains in their sidings. And I hope the nonsense I have talked here has not included anything as nonsensical as that.

BLESSED LITTLE VIRGIN

By C. M. Woodhouse

WIPING his damp brow, staring unhappily out of the window at the flies that buzzed across the blinding sunlight, the lieutenant compared the instructions he had been given four days before. His commanding officer had advised him to let everyone have his say without interruption: then there could be no complaint of partiality whatever the outcome, even if it took a fortnight. But the adjutant, whose experience of the country was longer than the colonel's and ten times as long as the lieutenant's, and more than a little bitter, had advised him to cut the cackle and keep the bastards to the point. *That* was the only way to hold an enquiry in *this* country.

'And the *point*,' he had added with the finality of justified scorn, 'is just what you make the point. If you leave it to *them*, there'll never be any point. . . . What I always say about about these people is,' he had concluded, turning away from the lieutenant to others better equipped to appreciate what he always said, 'that after a week you think you know them inside out; it takes a year to find out that you don't know the first thing about them, and another ten years . . .'

The well-remembered tones faded from the lieutenant's recollection before the stifling reality of the crowded schoolroom. So far he had allowed two and a half days to pass in reaching the point by the colonel's way, and he wondered if it was enough. If he was right in thinking that he had found the point, it seemed to be the murder of the priest of the hill-girt village of Neokhori. But if he was wrong in identifying this as the point, how was he to keep the witnesses to it? It was too late to ask the adjutant that question without confessing failure. Even the local telephone, running uneasily down liberated barbed-wire from tree to tree, from exchange to exchange, down the parched hills from Neokhori to the plains, to civilization and battalion headquarters, would certainly be inadequate to the disentanglement of so subtle a dilemma.

The torrential babble of the witness confronting him across the table came to an end, and the interpreter at his side wiped his ragged grey moustache, cleared his throat, spat and said in the adopted accents of Brooklyn: 'Dis guy, he say dey killed him, dem Bulgarians. . . .'

'Bulgarians?' said the lieutenant, suspecting that something had been lost in the condensation of seven minutes' outpouring into nine words.

'Reds—bandits—Communists—Russians—'

The lieutenant caught the eye of the schoolmaster and flushed. The schoolmaster, the recognized leader of the village's left wing, sat among his henchmen against the wall on the lieutenant's left, watching him disdainfully with a cold glint through horn-rimmed spectacles. Although the schoolmaster was openly accused of being the ringleader of the murder, he showed no embarrassment: he treated the enquiry with detachment, and the lieutenant with the polite tolerance due to foreigners, leaving his adversaries, who crowded the opposite wall under the leadership of the priest's surviving brother, to veer awkwardly from the outbursts of abuse to uneasy defensiveness. It was as though they themselves were on trial, and the lieutenant with them; and when from time to time the schoolmaster intervened to put a question, the whole conduct of the enquiry seemed to pass under his dignified control.

'I suggest,' he said frigidly, addressing the witness and the lieutenant simultaneously, 'that this is no way to refer to our gallant allies who helped to liberate our country from the tyranny of the fascist beasts...?'

The lieutenant had no alternative but to agree warmly, knowing that he was himself assumed in the nature of things to be at one with all fascists. At his hasty gesture of dismissal, the witness shrugged and withdrew, and another replaced him.

The new witness who pushed his way through the crowded doorway of the schoolroom was the owner of the mule that had carried the priest to his death: so said the priest's brother with a note of special triumph in his voice, explaining that the murder had taken place half an hour away from the village, and the priest was bound hand and foot. The muleteer was known to be a sympathizer of the schoolmaster's faction, but a quarrel had sprung up between them, because he had not been paid the hire of the mule for the occasion. Consequently his evidence was expected to be biased, one way or the other, but none could say which; and both parties watched and waited cautiously, to see whether what he had to say would call for their support or challenge. The muleteer smiled nervously at the schoolmaster, and stared in puzzled silence at the lieutenant's invitation to tell his story. Then with a sudden flash of understanding he exclaimed: '*É*, what happened, you wish to know?' and plunged into it.

When he had reached, in a frenzy of illustrative gesticulation, the point at which the murderers had carved slices out of the priest's back and rubbed salt into the wounds, the lieutenant interrupted him to ask if he could identify the murderers. The deep ruts of his grey, unshaven face wrinkled in amazement at the question, and he replied: 'Of course! Everyone knows them: this one—' he indicated the schoolmaster—'and those ones—' his arm swept comprehensively round the room, including most of the schoolmaster's accusers as well. 'Who else?' he added thoughtfully in conclusion. 'Are they not all of the party?'

'Did you see *all* of them take part in the murder?'

'All, all!' replied the muleteer vigorously; 'with the difference that I did not *see* them.... They would not let me.... How should they let me, after all? They left me with the mule at the spring while they took him up the ravine. '*Och, my blessed little Virgin!*' he cried as they took him, and again when they cut his throat: '*Och, my blessed little Virgin!*' It was what he would always say when he was in an embarrassing position, so to speak.... Ah, he was a good man, after all....'

'So you did not actually see what happened? You only heard?...' The muleteer nodded in admiration at the foreigner's miraculous comprehension, and the lieutenant went on: 'So what did you do?'

'What did I do? I waited: what else would I do? The beast was tired and thirsty, and the water is good at the spring, the best water in Makrovouni, with the difference that the spring at Prophet Elias is better; but *that* a man cannot reach six months in the year on account of the snow.... Besides, they had not paid me...'

'And when they came back, what happened?'

'Nothing! They paid me nothing—*dip!*' The muleteer's head jerked back, his chin shot up, and his right hand beside it, palm forward; his tongue clicked twice, and he repeated emphatically: '*Dip! Dip-kata-dip!*' The interpreter could not translate, but it was unnecessary. Even the schoolmaster smiled with a pitying wince.

'But the priest was not with them any more?'

'*Bah!* Where would he be? They said he had gone to the Place.... They said the moon ate him.... They told me to plug my mouth, but as for paying—never mind!'

'That's all?'

'That's all... with the difference that I can tell you where they buried him. . . . I saw the earth, freshly turned, and the mule kicked as he passed it, marry the brute! He kicked *me*, you understand, and there is *another* it would have been better he kicked: *another*, you understand? May an evil time be his. . .!' he concluded, glaring at the schoolmaster.

'That's all?'

'That's all. . . . What more do you want? As if it were not enough!' He was ushered out, reproachfully muttering: 'What more? As if it were not enough to hang them all, bad factors that they are. . . . They want stick. . . . They want stick and hanging, beyond discussion. . . .'

There was no doubt which side he was on when he withdrew: he had convinced himself. The schoolmaster watched him go with a bitter smile, which turned to a look of icy triumph as the next witness came in. The lieutenant, who had been looking enviously out of the window at the cool mountains above the schoolhouse, hearing for a moment only the plash of falling water and the tinkle of goat-bells, the rustle and stamp of the mules tethered in the basement under the schoolroom, the click of glasses and dice, the hens and the dogs and the babies, the ploughman on the hillside blaspheming at his ox, all the music of the mountains, was compelled to turn sharply back with a dutiful sigh. He noted on his pad that the new witness was for the defence: the fellow-traveller, he was called in the village. The lieutenant was on the brink of abandoning his C.O.'s policy for the adjutant's.

'What shall I tell you?' said the fellow-traveller, meditating aloud, as if offering a choice between fairy-tales.

'Tell him how you hanged our beloved *pappouli*!' screamed a woman through the window. 'Tell him how you hanged him and shot him and skinned him and cut his throat, may an evil time be yours!'

The priest's surviving brother sagely nodded agreement. The fellow-traveller smiled thoughtfully and said: 'We're a hot-blooded race, after all. . . .'

'Well?' asked the lieutenant. 'What happened? Were you there when the priest was killed?'

'When the priest was killed?' repeated the fellow-traveller in a tone of real surprise. 'It is not to be excluded. . . . It is not to be excluded. . . . With the difference that *I* was not there. . . .'

His whole testimony persisted on the same note of philosophic doubt with gestures and facial expressions to match. But there were admissions which stirred flutters of excitement and waves of muttered exclamation through the crowd. That the day on which he had last seen the priest alive, and the day on which the priest was alleged to have been murdered, were one and the same day, was a possibility that was not to be excluded. That the priest had been heard to invoke his blessed little Virgin in agitated tones at the time, was also not to be excluded; with the difference that this was in no way unusual, since the priest was a religious man, after all, and well known to be in the habit of communicating aloud with the Mother of God. It was not even to be excluded that the priest was bound hand and foot at the time, which might have contributed to his agitation, with the difference that the witness was not among those present, after all. There was no shaking his evidence, or want of it; but the lieutenant was establishing himself in the respect of both parties to the case by the persistence and fairness of his questions. For the first time there was a genuine doubt in the minds of the audience about the outcome of the enquiry, and their interest mounted in proportion.

Witness followed witness in regular rotation, one from each side in turn, as nearly as the lieutenant could arrange it; that was the C.O.'s policy, but the pressure he put on to hasten them was all the adjutant's. In some cases there was doubt which side a witness would take before being called, and in some there was still doubt after the witness had been dismissed. There were some, too, to whom the whole process of giving evidence was obscure, and even the point of it, when everyone knew what had happened, after all, and all that mattered was revenge. The old woman who had screamed through the window at the fellow-traveller, for instance, was called to amplify and elucidate her remarks, but it was only with the greatest reluctance that she could be brought into the schoolroom at all, under the quietly cynical gaze of the schoolmaster and his allies.

'Me?' she muttered as she crept through the doorway. '*Po-po-po....!* What should they want with me, poor wretch? Do *I* know? As if *I* knew people and things....'

'You were talking just now through the window,' the lieutenant prompted her gently. 'About what happened to the priest...'

'As if all the little world didn't know....'

'Did you see what happened, yourself?' he asked; and when there was no answer: 'Did you hear anything?'

'My son was there....'

'Is he here now?'

'How should he be here now? He's gone to America.... He left last week towards Athens, the stubborn block! I told him it was the wrong direction, that America was the other way, but he always was a stubborn block....'

She was escorted out of the room again, muttering to herself: '*Po-po-po....!* What should they want with me?' But on the threshold she stopped and turned suddenly, and cried shrilly: 'It's the truth, once for all—my son heard him. "*Och, my blessed little Virgin, what shall I do?*" he cried as they cut his throat, as he always would, howsoever. It's the truth, I tell you responsibly....'

It was the one point on which almost every witness agreed, whichever side they appeared for, that the priest had been heard, in the last few hours of which there was any certainty in his life, calling or muttering or crying or whispering that one single phrase which he had made his own. The lieutenant heard it endlessly echoing through his head as witness after witness passed before him, whether or not they had themselves heard those last bewildered, despairing words. Only one scornfully denied having heard any such expression from the priest; and he was the man whom the priest's family accused of being the murderer himself. He was a large, rough, unshaven man in the remains of a military uniform, referred to by everyone in tones of admiring awe as 'the gangster'. Even his accusers were proud to have a gangster in the village, and smacked their lips over the foreign word uncomprehendingly for the pleasure of the sound of it. The lieutenant saw from his first entrance that the gangster was aware of being the hero of the drama, but his evidence was summed up in advance by the interpreter, who leaned across and whispered hoarsely: 'Dis guy, he don't say nuttun' . . .' The lieutenant flinched from the garlic on his breath, but he knew the interpretation was right.

'Where is our *pappouli*?' shouted the women in the crowd at the gangster, who halted in mid-stride at the cry, with one leg thrust dramatically forward and a little exaggeratedly to the side. Spreading out his hands in a well-contrived gesture of amazement, he darted quick glances round the room in all directions as if looking for the priest in the crowd. '*Where* is he?' he asked theatrically. '*Where* is he? I ask you myself. . . .'

'*He* knows . . . He must know . . . How should he not know?' exclaimed a series of shrill voices, and others confirmed them conclusively: 'Impossible! Impossible!'

'Silence in court!' shouted the lieutenant, and blushed, hoping that his imperious words had not been understood; they had not, even by his interpreter, but silence fell at once. The gangster remained arrested in his pose, like a statue of penury begging alms.

Before either he or the lieutenant could find a way of setting the tableau in motion again, a new stir of excitement ran through the crowd, starting at the doorway and rippling inwards towards the centre of the enquiry. The chief actors were released from their tension and even from the interest of the audience, while whispers rustled round the room and the schoolmaster sat quietly watching with an indifferent smile.

After waiting for a pause in the excitement, he stood up and announced that he intended to call a new witness for the defence; but the lieutenant asserted the dignity of his status and refused to allow the gangster to be interrupted.

'It is of the greatest importance,' said the schoolmaster without emphasis.

'We must not interfere with the regular procedure,' said the lieutenant firmly, but trying to sound conciliatory.

'Then after this witness...?'

'No: the next witness is for the other side. After him, perhaps.'

The schoolmaster gave way with a shrug and sat down again. But although the crowd was now silent, the excitement had not died away, and throughout the next two testimonies the lieutenant was conscious of a polite impatience on both sides of the room. He closed the gangster's evidence quickly, almost abruptly, aware that no admission would be drawn from him; and the gangster retired disgruntled with the lieutenant and the schoolmaster alike, for spoiling his performance and diminishing his dignity.

But it was difficult to do the same with the next witness, a leisurely, simple-hearted old man who kept the village store and had no inhibitions against wasting time. The schoolmaster tried to dispense with calling him altogether, and sighed thinly with tolerant superiority when the lieutenant again insisted on following the regular procedure. There was no doubt, in any case, that the old man had plenty of information to give: not only was he the priest's most intimate friend, but by his own account he had been an eye-witness of the murder. He had no hesitation in positively identifying the gangster, the fellow-traveller, and the schoolmaster himself among the participants in the murder. His voice broke as he repeated the priest's last agonized exclamation: '*Och, my blessed little Virgin, what am I to do....?*'

'How many others were there?' the lieutenant asked sympathetically.

The old man paused thoughtfully; his head nodded and his lips moved as if he were counting. Then suddenly his right hand churned the air in loose, rapid circles from the wrist, and he let out a low, long whistle.

'He means a great number, very great,' explained the interpreter's hot breath in the lieutenant's ear. 'A number that is not to be counted,' he added, and the old man nodded approval.

'Is all this really necessary?' asked the schoolmaster pityingly.

'Yes,' retorted the lieutenant, making a mental note to postpone the schoolmaster's witness still further down the list.

'But my witness will have an important new light to shed....'

'All in good time,' said the lieutenant brusquely, and turned to ask the old man: 'Then had the priest so many enemies?'

'He was a good man,' said the witness, protesting. 'How should he have enemies? The world loved him.' There were murmurs of agreement from the crowd, and again a voice shouted something through the window, but it could not be made out. The old man saw that the lieutenant was looking puzzled at his answer, and went on to make it clear: 'He was a good and, you understand, with the difference that he had tendencies, so to speak....'

'Tendencies?' asked the lieutenant uncomfortably, with pictures of nameless horrors rising before his mind's eye.

'He was a good man, but he sympathized too much with the Communists, you understand.... He wished to help them when they were in trouble, which was "rivers upstream" in a manner of speaking,' the old man explained, without acknowledgement to Euripides. 'For how should a man help Communists, come what may, seeing that they are not like ourselves...? Men that hold nothing sacred or holy, after all...? It was a fault, it must be admitted... yet he was a good man....'

'Then why should they want to kill him?'

The old man thoughtfully contemplated the deep, dark recesses of the unceilinged roof for a few minutes before replying gently: '*É*, there is God. . . .'

'Shall we not leave this nonsense?' said the schoolmaster patronizingly. 'Mine is a *serious* witness. . . .'

'Don't let dis red guy laugh at you!' warned the interpreter odorously in the lieutenant's ear.

The old man pursued his evidence untroubled by the interruption, untroubled even by the need to wait for questions to be put. 'When our people caught the Communists in the civil war,' he went on, 'we would want to cut their heads off at once, which was only natural, seeing that they were Communists. . . . But he would stop us. "*Och, my blessed little Virgin!*" he would say, "*are they not human like the rest of us?*" And we would spare them to please him, though it was to be doubted, after all . . .'

'My witness is at the door,' said the schoolmaster sharply, standing on tip-toe to peer over the heads of the crowd. Wearily the lieutenant gave way at last, in response to a new agitation on both sides of the doorway, and signalled to the old man to stand aside.

'We will hear any more you have to say in a few minutes,' he told him kindly.

The schoolmaster's smile became almost warm behind the chill barrier of his spectacles as he signalled over the heads of his supporters towards the open door. The lieutenant had never expected him to be capable of showing so much energy or interest, and the crowd parted in response with something like alacrity to admit the new witness.

'Next witness!' called the interpreter officiously.

'Och, my blessed little Virgin!' exclaimed the black-bearded, black-robed figure as he stumbled momentarily at the threshold.

THE CAPTURE OF THE GENERAL

By W. Stanley Moss

APRIL 27.
Well, we've done it.
It's a lovely morning; and the General, Manoli, and I are sitting beside a mountain stream about one mile from the village of Anoyia. The General, looking a trifle pained because of a bump on the leg which he got last night, is sitting on a rock at the water's edge, his trousers rolled up to his knees, washing his feet. Contrary to his behaviour of yesterday evening, he is quite subdued and no longer very talkative. His chief worry appears to be that at some stage of last night's journey he lost his Knight's Cross of the Iron Cross—a decoration which he would normally wear round his neck. I told him that it would be easy enough to have a replica made as soon as we reached Cairo. But no, he replied, that would not be the same thing—he would have to be content to wear the medal in his heart. To this he added that he considered I was being pretty optimistic in thinking we should ever reach Cairo; and then, with a shrug of the shoulders, he clambered down to the rock on which he is now sitting.

Among ourselves we call him 'Theophilus', so that he shall not know when we are talking about him, but at present he is taking very little interest in the world around him. He is brooding, and I think also he is feeling tired after his long march. It seems that he is doing a lot of speculating as he sits there, shoulders hunched, drying his feet, and from time to time rubbing the sore place on his leg. I see that he has a lesser variety of the Iron Cross pinned low upon his breast. Perhaps this will in some way compensate for the loss of his prized medal.

I find it impossible to go to sleep because of the benzedrine which I took last night, so I shall try to put on paper all that I can remember of the events of the past twelve hours.

It was eight o'clock when we reached the T-junction. We had met a few pedestrians on the way, none of whom seemed perturbed at seeing our German uniforms, and we had exchanged greetings with them with appropriately Teutonic gruffness. When we reached the road we went straight to our respective posts and took cover. It was now just a question of lying low until we saw the warning torch-flash from Mitso, the buzzer-man. We were distressed to notice that the incline in the road was much steeper than we had been led to believe, for this meant that if the chauffeur used the foot-brake instead of the hand-brake when we stopped him there would be a chance of the car's running over the edge of the embankment as soon as he had been disposed of. However, it was too late at this stage to make any changes in our plan, so we just waited and hoped for the best.

There were five false alarms during the first hour of our watch. Two *Volkswagen*, two lorries, and one motor-cycle combination trundled past at various times, and in each of them, seated primly upright like tailors' dummies, the steel-helmeted figures of German soldiers were silhouetted against the night sky. It was a strange feeling to be crouching so close to them—almost within arm's reach of them—while they drove past with no idea that nine pairs of eyes were so fixedly watching them. It felt rather like going on patrol in action, when you find yourself very close to the enemy trenches, and can hear the sentries talking or quietly whistling, and can see them lighting cigarettes in their cupped hands.

It was already one hour past the General's routine time for making his return journey when we began to wonder if he could possibly have gone home in one of the vehicles which had already passed by. It was cold, and the canvas of our German garb did not serve to keep out the wind.

I remember Paddy's asking me the time. I looked at my watch and saw that the hands were pointing close to half-past nine. And at that moment Mitso's torch blinked.

'Here we go.'

We scrambled out of the ditch on to the road. Paddy switched on his red lamp and I held up a traffic signal, and together we stood in the centre of the junction.

In a moment—far sooner than we had expected—the powerful headlamps of the General's car swept round the bend and we found ourselves floodlit. The chauffeur, on approaching the corner, slowed down.

Paddy shouted, 'Halt!'

The car stopped. We walked forward rather slowly, and as we passed the beams of the headlamps we drew our ready-cocked pistols from behind our backs and let fall the life-preservers from our wrists.

As we came level with the doors of the car Paddy asked, '*Ist dies das General's Wagen?*'

There came a muffled '*Ja, ja*' from inside.

Then everything happened very quickly. There was a rush from all sides. We tore open our respective doors, and our torches illuminated the interior of the car—the bewildered face of the General, the chauffeur's terrified eyes, the rear seats empty. With his right hand the chauffeur was reaching for his automatic, so I hit him across the head with my cosh. He fell forward, and George, who had come up behind me, heaved him out of the driving-seat and dumped him on the road. I jumped in behind the steering-wheel, and at the same moment saw Paddy and Manoli dragging the General out of the opposite door. The old man was struggling furiously lashing out with his arms and legs. He obviously thought that he was going to be killed, and started shouting every curse under the sun at the top of his voice.

The engine of the car was still ticking over, the hand-brake was on, everything was perfect. To one side, in a pool of torch-light in the centre of the road, Paddy and Manoli were trying to quieten the General, who was still cursing and struggling. On the other side George and Andoni were trying to pull the chauffeur to his feet, but the man's head was pouring with blood, and I think he must have been unconscious, because every time they lifted him up he simply collapsed to the ground again.

This was the critical moment, for if any other traffic had come along the road we should have been caught sadly unawares. But now Paddy, Manoli, Nikko, and Stratis were carrying the General towards the car and bundling him into the back seat. After him clambered George, Manoli and Stratis —one of the three holding a knife to the General's throat to stop him shouting, the other two with their Marlin guns poking out of either window. It must have been quite a squash.

Paddy jumped into the front seat beside me.

The General kept imploring, 'Where is my hat? Where is my hat?' The hat, of course, was on Paddy's head.

We were now ready to move. Suddenly everyone started kissing and congratulating everybody else; and Micky, having first embraced Paddy and me, started screaming at the General with all the pent-up hatred he holds for the Germans. We had to push him away and tell him to shut up. Andoni, Grigori, Nikko, and Wallace Beery were standing at the roadside, propping up the chauffeur between them, and now they waved us good-bye and turned away and started off on their long trek to the rendezvous on Mount Ida.

We started.

The car was a beauty, a brand-new Opel, and we were

delighted to see that the petrol-gauge showed the tanks to be full.

We had been travelling for less than a minute when we saw a succession of lights coming along the road towards us; and a moment later we found ourselves driving past a motor convoy, and thanked our stars that it had not come this way a couple of minutes sooner. Most of the lorries were troop transports, all filled with soldiery, and this sight had the immediate effect of quietening George, Manoli, and Stratis, who had hitherto been shouting at one another and taking no notice of our attempts to keep them quiet.

When the convoy had passed Paddy told the General that the two of us were British officers and that we would treat him as an honourable prisoner of war. He seemed mightily relieved to hear this and immediately started to ask a series of questions, often not even waiting for a reply. But for some reason his chief concern still appeared to be the whereabouts of his hat— first it was the hat, then his medal. Paddy told him that he would soon be given it back, and to this the General said, '*Danke, danke.*'

It was not long before we saw a red lamp flashing in the road before us, and we realized that we were approaching the first of the traffic-control posts through which we should have to pass. We were, of course, prepared for this eventuality, and our plan had contained alternative actions which we had hoped would suit any situation, because we knew that our route led us through the centre of Heraklion, and that in the course of our journey we should probably have to pass through about twenty control posts.

Until now everything had happened so quickly that we had felt no emotion other than elation at the primary success of our venture; but as we drew nearer and nearer to the swinging red lamp we experienced our first tense moment.

A German sentry was standing in the middle of the road. As we approached him, slowing down the while, he moved to one side, presumably thinking that we were going to stop.

However, as soon as we drew level with him—still going very slowly, so as to give him an opportunity of seeing the General's pennants on the wings of the car—I began to accelerate again, and on we went. For several seconds after we had passed the sentry we were all apprehension, fully expecting to hear a rifle-shot in our wake; but a moment later we had rounded a bend in the road and knew that the danger was temporarily past. Our chief concern now was whether or not the guard at the post behind us would telephone ahead to the next one, and it was with our fingers crossed that we approached the red lamp of the second control post a few minutes later. But we need not have had any fears, for the sentry behaved in exactly the same manner as the first had done, and we drove on feeling rather pleased with ourselves.

In point of fact, during the course of our evening's drive we passed twenty-two control posts. In most cases the above-mentioned formula sufficed to get us through, but on five occasions we came to road-blocks—raisable one-bar barriers—which brought us to a standstill. Each time, however, the General's pennants did the trick like magic, and the sentries would either give a smart salute or present arms as the gate was lifted and we passed through. Only once did we find ourselves in what might have developed into a nasty situation—but of that I shall write in a moment.

Paddy, sitting on my right and smoking a cigarette, looked quite imposing in the General's hat. The General asked him how long he would have to remain in his present undignified position, and in reply Paddy told him that if he were willing to give his parole that he would neither shout nor try to escape we should treat him, not as a prisoner, but, until we left the island, as one of ourselves. The General gave his parole immediately. We were rather surprised at this, because it seemed to us that anyone in his position might still entertain reasonable hopes of escape—a shout for help at any of the control posts might have saved him.

According to our plan, I should soon be having to spend twenty-four hours alone with Manoli and the General, so I thought it best to find out if we had any languages in common (for hitherto we had been speaking a sort of anglicized German). Paddy asked him if he spoke any English.

'*Nein*,' said the General.

'Russian?' I asked. 'Or Greek?'

'*Nein.*'

In unison, '*Parlez-vous français?*'

'*Un petit peu.*'

To which we could not resist the Cowardesque reply, 'I never think that's quite enough.'

But it was in French that we spoke, and continue to do so. The quality is scarcely commendable.

Presently we found ourselves approaching the Villa Ariadne. The sentries, having recognized the car from a distance, were already opening the heavily barbed gates in anticipation of our driving inside. I hooted the horn and did not slow down. We drove swiftly past them, and it was with considerable delight that we watched them treating us to hurried salutes.

We were now approaching Heraklion, and coming towards us we saw a large number of lorries. We remembered that Micky had told us that there was to be a garrison cinema-show in the town that evening, so we presumed that these lorries were transporting the audience back to various billets. We did not pass a single vehicle which was travelling in the same direction as ourselves.

Soon we had to slow down to about 25 k.p.h., because the road was chock-full of German soldiers. They were quick to respond to the hooting of our horn, however, and when they saw whose car it was they dispersed to the sides of the road and acknowledged us in passing. It was truly unfortunate that we should have arrived in the town at this moment; but once again luck was with us, and, apart from a near-miss on a cyclist, who swerved out of our way only just in time, we drove down the main street without hindrance. By the time we reached the market square in the centre of the town we had already left the cinema crowd behind us, and we found the large, open space, which by daylight is usually so crowded, now almost completely deserted. At this point we had to take a sharp turning to the left, for our route led us westward through the old West Gate to the Retimo road.

The West Gate is a relic of the days when Heraklion was completely surrounded by a massive wall, and even today it remains a formidable structure. The gate itself, at the best of times not very wide, has been further narrowed by concrete anti-tank blocks; and a German guard is on duty there for twenty-four hours a day.

I remember saying 'Whoops' as I saw the sentry signalling us to stop. I had proposed to slow down, as on the previous occasions and then to accelerate upon drawing level with the sentry; but this time this was impossible, for the man did not move an inch, and in the light of the head-lamps we saw several more Germans standing behind him. I was obliged to take the car forward at a snail's pace. We had previously decided that in the event of our being asked any questions our reply would be simply, '*General's Wagen*,' coupled with our hopes for the best. If any further conversation were called for Paddy was to do the talking.

George, Manoli, and Stratis held their weapons at the ready and kept as low as they could in the back seat. The General was on the floor beneath them. Paddy and I cocked our pistols and held them on our laps.

The sentry approached Paddy's side of the car.

Before he had come too near, Paddy called out that this was the General's car—which, after all, was true enough—and without awaiting the sentry's next word I accelerated and we drove on, calling out '*Gute nacht!*' as we went. Everyone saluted.

We drove fast along the next stretch of road.

The General, coming to the surface, said he felt sorry for all the sentries at the control posts, because they would surely get into terrible trouble on the morrow.

The road was clear of traffic, and it was not long before we had put several kilometres between ourselves and Heraklion. Soon we had passed the last of the control posts, and the road began to rise from the plain and wind gradually uphill. Up and up we went. We had seen the massive mountain forms in front of us as a target, but now we were among them; and high above, like a white baby curled upon a translucent canopy, we saw the crescent of the moon. Suddenly we felt quite distant from everything that had just happened—a terrific elation— and we told one another that three-quarters of the job was now over, and started discussing what sort of celebration we would have when we got back to Cairo. We sang *The Party's Over*; and then I lit a cigarette, which I thought was the best I had ever smoked in my life.

At a quarter past eleven we arrived at the point on the road where Manoli, Stratis, the General, and I were to leave the car. We had been driving for an hour and three-quarters, and during the latter part of the journey the road had spiralled up and up, so that we were now at a considerable altitude, and we felt that until dawn at least we were out of harm's way.

As Paddy and I got out of the car the General called to us, begging us not to leave him alone with the Cretans—so dramatically, in fact, that I'm sure he imagined he would have his throat slit the moment our backs were turned. Paddy assured him that he was not going to be left alone, that I was going to accompany him; and on hearing this the General gave a great sigh of relief. We told him to come out of the car, and he hastily obeyed. Paddy gave him a smart salute, saying that he would meet him, together with the rest of us, on the morrow at Anoyia; and then he clambered into the driving-seat with George next to him.

Paddy had not driven a car for over five years, and it was

with fits of suppressed laughter that we watched him trying to put the hand-brake into gear and pressing the horn instead of the starter. After several starts and stalls, off he went, and we watched the car going up the road, swerving from side to side and grinding along in bottom gear, until the tail-lamp disappeared round a bend. With only two kilometres to go, I hope he made the journey all right.

We set off with the General in a southerly direction. There was no path or track, and we were obliged to scramble up and down cliffs, across streams, and through heavy undergrowth. This was very hard going for the General, and although he was quite co-operative and did not try to hinder us in any way, it was inevitable that we travelled very slowly. Stratis, contrary to his assurances, had little idea of the route which we were trying to follow, and consequently our progress was more or less guided by our reading of the stars. The General said that his leg had been badly hurt when he had been dragged out of his car, and indeed he walked with a pronounced limp. I considered it unnecessary to continue walking behind him with my revolver at his back, so I searched him for concealed arms—he had none—and then walked with him, helping him over obstacles and, with Manoli's assistance, carrying him across streams. We were foolish enough not to drink from these streams, for it was not long before we came to a dry expanse of country, and it was three o'clock in the morning before we reached a spring.

The spring was almost dry, and in order to get any water out of it we had to tie some string round the lid of an emergency-ration tin, which we let down some twenty feet and dragged in the mud until it was full. It took us a long time to quench our thirsts, for we were only able to bring up about a quarter of an inch of water each time. The General said that he was very hungry, for he had eaten nothing since luncheon, so I gave him him a few raisins which were mixed up with the dust in my pockets, and for these he was more than thankful.

We moved on again. The General became talkative and started discussing General Brauer's[1] reactions to hearing of this 'Hussar Act', as he called it. He supposed that Paddy and I must be very happy and pleased with ourselves, but added that the job was not yet over. And then he asked me if we were Regular soldiers. When I replied that we were not he seemed greatly upset, for he had just realized, it appeared, that his career had ceased to exist. He was the thirteenth child, he said, of a family of fifteen; and his father, a poor man, was a pastor, so it was really he himself who was the family's breadwinner. A major-general's pay, he explained, was pretty good in the German Army, and, what was more, he had been expecting his promotion to the rank of lieutenant-general to come through at any moment. (He was, in fact, already wearing the insignia of a lieutenant-general, but I think this was due rather to his local appointment than to eager anticipation.)

[*During the German evacuation of Greece I discovered in Salonika a certain Major von Schenk, who had been an A.D.C. to General Lohr, but had deserted and given himself up. He said that the story of Kreipe's disappearance had at the time been a big joke in Vienna, but the most ironic thing about it had been that his promotion to lieutenant-general had come through on the very day after his abduction.*]

At about five o'clock in the morning we found ourselves within a short distance of Anoyia, but since we were not going to enter the village itself, but wait for Paddy and George in a nearby river-bed, we decided to stay where we were until first light and then set off to find a suitably secluded hiding-place.

The General was feeling very cold, so Stratis gave him his Greek policeman's overcoat. Then we sat down and talked.

The General told me it was a strange thing, but he had

---

[1] General Brauer was Commander of the Fortress of Crete, as opposed to Kreipe, who was the Divisional Commander. Both Brauer and Kreipe's predecessor, General Muller, were sentenced to death at a war-crimes trial in Athens in December 1945.

always felt that if anything were to happen to him in Crete it would be at the very spot where the ambush actually took place—so certain of this had he been, in fact, that he had already given instructions for a guard-post to be mounted on that self-same T-junction. (It is possible that when he saw us there last night he thought that we were the sentries guarding the new post.) Even stranger, he added, was the fact that on the way home he had had a premonition that something was going to happen, and had remarked on it to his chauffeur. Then he went on to ask me about the chauffeur's fate, and I told him—with little conviction, I fear—that the man would be joining us on Mount Ida in a day or two.

As the darkness began to leave the sky, and the first colour of the day, like violet ink rising through the veins of a tulip, fanned out of the east, I was able to have a good look at the General for the first time. He is a thick-set man, and his face possesses most of the regular Teutonic features—thin lips, bull neck, blue eyes, and a fixed expression. His skin is fair, almost delicate; and his hair, cut guardsman-fashion, is slightly grey at the temples. I should say that he is between forty-five and fifty years of age.

As soon as it was light enough to discover our exact whereabouts we moved on again. Stratis said that he knew of a pleasant and sheltered spot not far distant, whereupon he led us to the boulder-strewn stream where we now remain.

I immediately wrote two short letters, which I gave to Stratis, telling him to go to Anoyia and find two trustworthy messengers who would deliver my notes to Sandy Rendel in the Lasithi Mountains, and Tom Dunbabin, who should be on Mount Ida. The note to Sandy was to tell him that our escapade had been successful, that the General was quite a pleasant catch and not the raving Nazi he might well have been, and to ask him to look after Vassily and Ivan as best he could until I returned from Egypt. The note to Tom was to ask him to inform Cairo via his set that we had succeeded with the abduction so far, and to ask headquarters, as previously arranged, to have announcements made over the wireless and pamphlets dropped on the island.[1]

I told Stratis to keep a look-out for Paddy and George and to bring them here if he were to meet them; and I also told him that he should have some food and wine sent to us as soon as possible, because we were all pretty hungry.

The General, tired after the night's march, took off his coat and lay down. It was then that he discovered the loss of his Iron Cross, and this upset him a great deal. Without his medal and his hat he felt decidedly naked. He told me that he had won the award while in command of the push against Leningrad on the Russian Front. Later, he said, he had fought for a long time in the Kuban, and it was with nostalgia in his voice that he recalled his main diet there—caviare. After two years on the Russian Front he had been sent to Crete for a 'rest cure', and it was now only five weeks since his arrival here. He's going to have a nice long rest, I imagine, but not in Crete. The lesser variety of Iron Cross which he wears was won, he told me, at Verdun during the last war; so it certainly seems that he has done a lot of fighting in his time.

It is now three o'clock in the afternoon. At midday a basket of food and wine was brought to us from the village by a jovial little man who tells me that he is an old friend of Paddy's. He fulfilled Stratis's request for provisions, and it was

[1] Our original plan had included an arrangement with headquarters that, as soon as we had caught the General, pamphlets should be dropped all over Crete stating in both Greek and German that the operation had been carried out by a British raiding party. By this method we had further hoped to prevent reprisals being taken on the islanders.

The second arrangement concerned the B.B.C. and other broadcasting stations. When the news of the kidnapping was being broadcast it had been agreed that the announcer should say that General Kreipe was *already on his way to Cairo*, which would not be untrue. In this way we hoped to give the Germans the impression that we had already left the island, thus giving ourselves a fair chance of making our way to the south coast without being chased or hemmed in.

As things turned out, however, the pamphlets were never dropped at all, owing to bad flying conditions; and all the radio broadcasts, including those from the B.B.C., stated that the General *was being taken off the island*. This, needless to say, made matters very much worse for us, and was responsible for the Germans' launching of a full-scale man-hunt.

with real pleasure that we sat ourselves on some rocks in the sunlight and ate and drank our fill. The General tucked into the meal like a schoolboy.

Sleepy now with sun and wine, I feel ready to doze until dusk.

 Patrick Howarth

 Peter Fleming

 C. M. Woodhouse

W. Stanley Moss

Julian Amery

David Walker

CHRISTMAS '40

By David Walker

WEDGES of wild geese were outlined against a sullen yellow-black as we approached Salonika by train. In this normally swampy country south of the port we saw snipe and duck in abundance, looking for food and resting places in the frozen marshland. The tall reeds stood straight as rods, and Olympus was barely visible for snow was still falling in the mountains.

My friend Walter and I had hoped to find a car in Salonika. We had planned to strike west through Florina to Korytsa, which we intended to use as a base. But Salonika was unhelpful. Every car had been requisitioned and Kruger, the Gestapo agent, was running about the town telling all who cared to listen that further resistance was useless. If Greece persisted in fighting the Italians, the Germans would ultimately have no option but to stage an invasion of their own. In the end we left by train for Florina.

According to the time-table the train was due to arrive at Florina at two o'clock that afternoon. (We left Salonika just after eight in the morning.) But by the evening of that day we had made little progress. Walter borrowed some hot water from the engine-driver and we supped off salami and cocoa, with the inevitable brandy. When we awoke next morning the train was again stationary and we were able to wash our faces and hands with snow. At midday we had the good fortune to stop at a village and enjoyed a hurried meal of hot pork and beans, washed down with rough red wine. There was no heating in the train and a strong east wind whipped the cold through the cracks in the coaches. It was twenty degrees below zero, even here on the plain.

Through most of the next night we sang, to keep warm. We had with us a famous Greek singer, a tenor, who was serving in the ranks. He belonged to a regiment that used to sing *God Save the King* after its own regimental song, and it had come to Salonika from Athens the hard way, on foot. The men of this regiment were tough and they provided the best company anyone could wish for on this dreary cross-country ride. We sang every Greek song ever written, and the other coaches would take it up, till the whole train was singing. On the evening of the second day we were still a long way from Florina. We washed again in the snow—the train's lavatories were unapproachable—and tried to settle down once more to sleep. The men were by now sharing their bread ration with the mules. Without the mules the Greek army could never have gone to war.

On the third day supplies began to run seriously low but we saw the great white mountain Kaimaxalan ('cream-topped') to the north, where 30,000 Germans and Bulgars lie buried, and we knew that we were well on the way at last. Ice had now formed all over the train and it looked like one of those ships returning from the North Pole. After three days and two nights we completed a journey scheduled to take six hours. At Greek headquarters in Florina they gave us hot soup and coffee and at dawn next morning we joined a convoy eleven miles long for Korytsa, using a truck loaned to us by General Panagakos.

Korytsa was curiously unscathed by what it had been through. To the north the naked white majesty of Mt. Ivan dominated the town and as we looked at it we wondered how on earth the Greeks had conquered those precipitous bare slopes, which had been honeycombed with Italian machine-guns. To the west, range after range of mountains hid the village of Pogradetz and the road to Elbasan. Lake Ochrid was frozen over but the ice was thin. Nevertheless the Italians played searchlights on it every evening. In the town there seemed to be more Mohammedans than anything else, red-turbaned, with long, white, close-fitting trousers, and the muezzin was still sounded from the mosque. At the Café Munich the people told us that the Italians, even in the haste of their retreat, had taken away all the prostitutes bar one, an Albanian, who could not understand why the Greek soldiers did not find time to visit her.

From Korytsa we made our way into the hills.

Imagine range upon range of mountains, deep in snow, with nothing but mule tracks turned to ice for guidance. There were mean little groups of pine trees and stunted firs but nothing much could grow there. Pogradetz, on the southern shore of Lake Ochrid, was held at this time by twenty Greeks. The Italians were dug in in the hills beyond, and for most of the day a heavy mist hid their positions from view. Sometimes in the stillness you could hear them talking, or the mist would clear and you could clearly see the wisps of smoke from their fires. Up in these mountains, cold was so much the greatest enemy that both sides defied military regulations in their efforts to get warm.

In these mountains that winter a Greek army, ill-equipped and unaccustomed to the conditions (Cretan regiments were there that had never seen snow in their lives before), faced crack Italian Alpini divisions, well-equipped and in their natural element. Behind the Italian front lines were well-built Albanian roads, where the snow soon ceased in the plain towards Elbasan; behind the Greeks there lay nothing but the iced mule-tracks, where even the mules could no longer be trusted to stand. One morning Walter and I helped the men haul up mountain artillery by hand. Everything had to be done by hand.

At night the Greeks slept in holes in the snow, huddled together in groups, fighting off the frostbite that had already begun to decimate them. They had no proper boots and they had been issued with exactly one blanket each.

In those mountains it was easy to get lost. One day Walter and I found a soldier moaning in the snow. We tried to put him on a mule but his hands were useless, and we had to cut off his boots from feet that were already blue and swollen. He kept trying to salute us, murmuring 'God bless England! Victory! Victory!' Another one whom we found dying thought Walter was a British officer and cried out to him: 'Let me salute you, Englishman, then I can die.'

We had a fine Christmas dinner, because it was composed of hot soup. We had two courses—hot bean soup, then hot lentil soup. We washed it down with wine and brandy. But most of the time we ate half-frozen bread, and bits of salami, and olives which the men gave us.

The Cretan regiments in this sector had been there four weeks without being relieved. An almost total lack of ammunition did not appear to worry them in the least: all that they asked for was the chance to get at the Macaronis on a basis of steel, man to man. The tracks of wolves led to the dead, and frostbite increased steadily. As there was no transport, a man with frostbite had to find his own way back to Korytsa, which might take him two to four days, and he was an amputation case when he got there. Yet everywhere we went we found an unconquerable good humour, and everything that the Greek soldier had, he shared with us.

Towards New Year's Eve we went back to Korytsa and spent a day at the hospital, a fine building just outside the town, run by half a dozen doctors and twenty young Greek nurses. The head surgeon came round with us, through wards where small Christmas trees still stood in the corners. He ripped the blankets off a man who had had one of the small red Italian hand-grenades between his legs and what was left of the man winked at us and said: 'Zito o Churchill!' The corridors were full of men lying there in their uniforms, waiting their turn for amputation. All these men had only one complaint: 'Why can't you send us more planes? Our own are lost and our pilots mostly dead. Send us planes, please send us planes, then we can drive the Macaronis into the sea.'

At our billets were a couple of Greek pilots, a tall bearded Captain and a stocky little Lieutenant. Every evening at dusk they used to return together, order coffee, and sit down to poker with friends. At ten every night they went to bed. One evening I asked them whether Walter and I could come out to Korytsa airport, which had been an important Italian base during the earlier stages of the campaign, in order to watch the life of a Greek squadron and observe how it was run.

'If you wish to observe the life of a Greek squadron at the front,' said the Captain with a smile, 'you must first obtain the permission of General Zolakoglu.'

We obtained a reluctant permission the following morning and with Jack, our interpreter, walked out to the airport. There we found our two friends, still playing cards. On the ground lay the remnants of a number of Italian machines, one of them a large transport with American Wright Cyclone engines. The barracks still bore traces of Greek bombardment —a direct hit had killed sixty Italian pilots and air gunners a few weeks before. I asked to see the present mess and be introduced to the squadron. It had been puzzling to notice only two Greek machines on the airfield—both very ancient high-wing monoplanes looking very dilapidated beside even the remnants of the destroyed Savoia's and Fiats and G.52's.

Jack grinned and led us to a small wooden hut, the hut in which we had found our two friends playing cards. It took some seconds before the truth dawned on us: these two, the tall bearded Captain and the stocky Lieutenant, *were* the

Greek squadron holding Korytsa in January 1941 against the Italian air force in the northern sector. The Captain used his aircraft as a bomber; and after loading it with bombs, added old boots, bedroom crockery, anything insulting he could think of to drop on the Italians. The Lieutenant used his machine (I believe it was an old Potez) as a fighter. Since he could not possibly force it high enough to engage enemy bombers, he used to spend his time strafing troops on the ground. For the whole of this part of the northern Greek front, therefore, the Captain constituted Bomber Command and the Lieutenant cheerfully undertook the role of Fighter Command. There was no third machine as a spare.

Even while we were there the field telephone rang and a mechanic (who constituted the ground staff) answered it. 'Important enemy formations' were on the way. Both men smiled happily, like children. 'You are not to disturb the cards,' the Captain told me. Just in case the airport was about to be bombed, it was important to get both machines into the air. This in itself involved a curious ritual: owing to the high wind they were both tied to the ground with rope. We watched them take off and in half a minute they were out of sight in the misty, driving snow.

We waited what seemed a long time before either of them returned. First came the Lieutenant. He had been unable, as usual, to force his aircraft to any height but he had had 'a lovely ten minutes' with a whole column of enemy troops on the Elbasan road. It was nearly half an hour later before the second machine bumped in, with the bearded Captain. They wrote out brief reports, gave some instructions to the mechanic, and settled down to cards again, taking up the game where they had left off.

I think these were the only two men we came across in this sector who did not ask for British planes or British assistance. They appeared to have no complaints. They had carried on day after day, through that dreary, bitter winter, doing their job with the quiet regularity of bank clerks: fighting an enemy for whom they had nothing but a genial and unprintable contempt.

A few days later the Captain was killed, shot down by nine Italian fighter aircraft while he was returning from a bombing mission he had carried through at low level over Albania.

The Lieutenant carried on on his own.

INVITATION TO ALBANIA

By Julian Amery

I RETURNED to Cairo early in February 1944 from a journey in Saudi Arabia to find among my correspondence a small but thick envelope, heavily sealed. After breaking the seals and opening three inner envelopes marked respectively 'Personal', 'Secret', and 'for Amery only', I came to the following text: 'Please call at my office as soon as you are back.'

The signature was that of Philip Leake, the new chief of the Albanian section at headquarters.

I was at some loss to understand why so anodyne a message should have occasioned such expenditure of stationery, but duly repaired to the imposing and somewhat prominent block of buildings where the 'D' Organization was now installed. The perennial reorganization of the Secret Services, rather than any considerations of security, involved frequent changes in the office accommodation of their personnel. As a result, few officers knew where their colleagues were working, while the Cypriot porter who was supposed to guide visitors to their destinations had long given up trying to find out. I now brushed past this worthless individual, as he quietly contemplated the throng of questing staff officers and agents, and made my way to the room which Leake had occupied a few weeks earlier. There I found a conference of Arabists in progress and was obligingly misdirected by one of them to a basement where a group of naval officers were planning a descent on the Dodecanese Islands. At length, after many wanderings, I located the Albanian section in a semi-detached outhouse, or garage, and was eventually admitted into Leake's presence by a blonde and incredulous secretary who kept assuring me that the Persian bureau had moved elsewhere. Leake greeted me rather tensely and, motioning me to a chair, said without further ado:

'Our set-up in North Albania has been badly knocked about by Davies' capture. There are only two chaps now at the Mission Headquarters and one of them has got bad frostbite. The other, between ourselves, seems a bit queer to judge from his telegrams, but that's hardly surprising seeing what they've been through. We wondered if you would care to join them.'

HAPPY LANDING

It was already night when we took off. The aeroplane seemed cold and noisy; and I felt irritated and awkward, trussed in my parachute. I was tired, however, and at some stage must have fallen asleep, for it was past midnight when the despatcher woke me up to say that we were over the target. We each took a gulp of *grappa*—the fiery Italian grape spirit—and formed up by the open door for the jump. Through it I could see the signal fires, set out in the form of a cross at the bottom of a snow-rimmed trough in the mountains. The surrounding ranges made the approach to the target difficult; and we knew that the pilot had overshot his mark when the bulb by the door flashed green—the signal to jump. I went out last, shrinking inwardly from the plunge, and was caught up in the slipstream of the plane and violently shaken. Then the parachute opened; the smell and vibration of the aeroplane ceased; the tension went from me; and I felt suddenly warm. We must have jumped from near three thousand feet, for my arms soon grew tired of straining at the guiding ropes of the parachute to check its oscillation. I could see the mountains rising past me as I drifted down, but the ground was still hidden in the night. For a moment I was aware of something white, then without the slightest jar I found myself sprawling on my face in a deep patch of snow. Luck was with me for I had fallen in a forest and might well have been impaled on a jagged pine. Maclean had come down perhaps a mile away, also unhurt; but Smiley, landing less than a hundred yards from me, bruised his back badly against a tree. Nor was this our only near escape; for, as we saw next morning, Maclean and I had by some accident been issued with cotton parachutes. These were a type designed for dropping stores and, unlike those made of silk for human use, frequently failed to open.

We were about half-way up the side of the mountain trough and presently saw torches moving towards us through the trees below. In the distance wolves were howling; and for a moment I speculated idly on which would reach us first. The torches seemed a long time in coming and we guided them with our own electric flash-lamps. When they drew near, however, we rested these on suitable mounds and retired some twenty yards from them so as not to present a target should the torch-bearers prove unfriendly. The precaution was wise, for such accidents had happened before; but we had fallen among friends; and the torch-bearers turned out to be a Zogist *cheta*, sent to meet us by George Seymour and Alan Hare. There were a dozen of them, still shadowy figures in the night, save for their leader, Bairam, a Tosk with a mighty moustache, who spoke some Italian.

Bairam greeted us courteously, but without emotion, and guided us downhill through the trackless forest for an hour or so until we came to a half-open sheepfold on the mountain-side. There we sat round an open log fire and were presently refreshed with hot tea. Then, seeing it was late, I lay down to sleep, warming one side of my body by the fire while the mountain wind chilled the other. All around the guerrillas sat cross-legged, bristling with bandoliers, pistols, and hand-grenades, their unshaven faces sinister in the firelight.

LIFE AMONG THE CLANS

Abas Kupi[1] and his staff had assembled in the fortress home of Tsen Lezi,[2] set in a cleft in the mountains high above the Mati valley. We joined him there about nightfall and found the Zogist leaders seated round the hearth at the end of a long and narrow hall, lit only by the flames of the fire. The skins of sheep and goats were spread out on the floor as carpets, and the walls and rude cross-beams which supported the roof were black and shiny with soot. So must have been the keep of Dunsinane. Tsen Lezi, the master of the house, was wild and woolly like an aged bear, and grunted as he ambled out to greet us. His eyes were small and bright; his bushy moustache sprouted in all directions; and his clothes were brown and furry, homespun from the shearings of his sheep. He ruled sternly over his family, or clan, for there were more than sixty of them living in the house, and directed every detail of dynastic policy: what land or livestock should be bought or sold, which of the children should be sent to school, what marriages should be made, what blood feuds prosecuted or compounded and, above all, what sides the clan should take in the strife of political factions. Tsen Lezi had long been a supporter of Abas Kupi and he received us well.

It was already May, but in the mountains we had still lived amid the gales and snow of winter. Next morning, however, as we descended from Tsen Lezi's house, we came out of the mists into the sunlight and saw the broad Mati valley spread out below us like a promised land. Fat sheep and cattle grazed in the undulating pastures; whitewashed houses,

[1] The leader of the Royalist guerrilla forces in Albania.
[2] A Mati chieftain.

the tallest in Albania, were scattered over the low, wooded hills; and beyond the sparkling river the ground rose steeply to the wild glens of Mirdita. The guerrillas had not left the mountains since autumn; and now, at the sight of the sunlit valley, the long line of men winding down the hillside broke into a strident song. Presently Abas Kupi called a halt and we sat down to refresh our eyes with the view.

We passed through rolling fields and leafy forests; and each day brought us to some new village where we were feasted by the clans. Their houses varied in size and architecture with the wealth of the owners; but all were essentially built for defence. As a rule, they were so situated as to command a good field of fire over their chief approaches, and were often surrounded by walled courtyards entered through heavy, wooden gates studded with iron. For the most part they were of wood and stone, sometimes whitewashed, and consisted of two stories, joined by a narrow indoor staircase, or by a flight of wooden steps on the outside. The ground floor was the cattle and the women's quarters; above was the guest-room. This guest-room was the centre of the life of the house, and, except for a stout chest in which the valuables of the family were stored, was altogether empty of furniture. At one end of it was the open hearth from which the smoke escaped through chinks in the wall or, in statelier mansions, through a chimney. Narrow windows, usually without panes, served as a means of ventilation or, on occasion, as rifle slits; but so dim was the light which they diffused that it was often difficult to read indoors, even at midday. At night the room would be lit by the glow of the fire, or sometimes by oil lamps or pinewood torches.

On entering a house we would take off our boots and give up our rifles to the host, though retaining our side-arms. As foreigners, we would then be led to the place of honour, which is on the right-hand side of the hearth, next to the wall. Abas Kupi would sit with us, or take the left-hand side, and the rest of the company, including bodyguards and orderlies, assembled in a horseshoe round the fire. The youngest sat at the apex of the horseshoe, and, since there were often a score of us, the evening would begin with much show of 'Friend go up higher'. We sat on carpets or sheepskin rugs, cross-legged or reclining against our saddle-bags. When all were seated, the host rolled cigarettes, which only non-smokers might refuse, and tossed them with unfailing accuracy to each guest. Presently a warm drink would be served, usually coffee, though in the poorer houses sweetened or salted milk was often brought instead. As outlaws we sought to keep our movements secret and our arrival was, as a rule, the first warning of our visit which the host received. Custom demanded that he serve us meat, and, since several hours might pass before the sheep or kid had been killed and made ready, it was often past midnight before we had eaten.

While the meal was cooking we variously slept or talked and let the bodyguards dry damp clothes by the fire or massage our weary limbs. Sometimes, to beguile the time, one of the company would recite from the long epic poems in which the Albanians record the exploits of their heroes. They were weird, monotonous laments, sung in a high-pitched nasal voice to the accompaniment of a one-stringed mandolin. An hour or so before the meal was served flasks of *raki* would be brought, accompanied by *mese* of onions, cheese, and sometimes hard-boiled eggs or lumps of grilled meat. *Raki* is a fiery, colourless spirit, made from the pulp of grapes, or sometimes, like *slivovitz*, from plums. Among the mountaineers it was usually home-brewed, and varied greatly in quality and strength. The principal guests would each receive a small flask, the shape of an old-fashioned burgundy flagon, and holding perhaps half a pint, while the rest of the company fared according to the resources of the host, sharing a flask between two or three. Toasts were drunk to the traditional greeting of '*Tungjatjeta*'—'May your life be prolonged'; and, though the mountaineers habitually drank to excess, they seldom failed to comport themselves with grave, if sometimes mellowed, dignity.

When the cooking was done Maclean, as the chief guest, would be asked if the meal might be served; there was never conversation after meals, and so the greatest compliment which he could pay his host and fellows was to ask for a postponement. As soon, however, as he had given his assent, a circular wooden table some five feet in diameter would be carried in, standing about six inches from the ground. Round this a dozen of us would assemble, sitting cross-legged, but in a crocodile, each sideways on to the table so as to make room for as many as possible. We would then each be given a spoon as our sole piece of cutlery and with this helped ourselves to the more liquid dishes at the centre of the table. There were no plates, so that each spoon plied steadily backwards and forwards between the individual mouth and the communal dish. More solid foods, such as meat or rice, were eaten with the fingers, and, since each dish was communal, those who ate slowly went hungry. The midday and evening meals were both known as *buk*, or bread; for theoretically, and in the poorer houses practically, maize bread was the basic foodstuff, while the other dishes were regarded merely as sauces to make the bread more palatable.

In the course of our journeys we touched life at many angles and experienced extremes of poverty and plenty. Often we were lucky to get even a lump of cheese and maize bread, or a cup of unsweetened milk. At other times, especially in Mati, we were surfeited by a wealthy host on successive dishes of eggs, boiled mutton, roast mutton, *pilaf*, and luscious *halvas* and *baklavas* in the Turkish style. As a general rule, however, Albanian fare was lacking in variety and the average meal might be a soup of beans, a dish of boiled mutton, and a bowl of milk or *yoghourt*. The guest of honour usually received the sheep's head—the brain and eyes were considered the greatest delicacies—or sometimes the kidneys and the tail. Fatness was the quality most admired in sheep, though even with hard exercise all of us except Smiley found the enjoyment of lumps of hot boiled fat an acquired taste. Milk was the usual drink at meals, drunk like soup from a communal bowl and served as a last course. Water was also to be had, but only on request, for there was usually only one glass or mug in the house. Before and after meals the host came round with a basin and ewer, and the guests washed their hands—a most necessary proceeding seeing that these were used for eating. In the richer houses the washing water was warmed and home-made soap was also provided. Each man left the table when he had finished eating without waiting for his fellows; and when the chief guests had done there would be a 'deuxième service' for the rest of the company, or sometimes two tables might be set at once. The guests had the right—and often used it—to criticize any meanness in their entertainment to their host's face; and he would never sit at table or taste food until the last of the guests had eaten.

When all had done, mattresses and eiderdowns would be brought and spread out on the floor for the half-dozen guests of honour, while the others made themselves as comfortable as they might with their overcoats and jackets. It was still considered rather indecent to undress, but before the lights were snuffed out the prudent ones would gather their arms and effects about them against the dangers and confusions of a night attack. In cold weather the fire was kept alight till morning; in summer the room would often become intolerably stuffy from the accumulated animal warmth of a score of snoring sleepers.

The Albanians were not given to early rising, for their evening hours were late, and in the mountains the mornings were cold. They would get up between eight and nine o'clock and, by a generous convention, the younger guests were left sleeping till last. The mountaineers knew not breakfast; but in many houses the host would bring a cup of coffee or hot, sweetened milk when he saw us wake. Ablutions were perfunctory, each man, or the host, pouring cold water from a ewer over his fellow's hands, with which the latter seldom did more than dab his eyes. Moustaches were *de rigueur*, though by exception Abas Kupi was clean-shaven; but only priests or bandits grew beards. Shaving, however, was most often a weekly affair and considered a sufficient occasion to warrant the valedictory greeting of '*Meschnett*'—an equivalent of 'God bless you'—to the shaver. In these matters I conformed to the customs of the country, but Maclean and Smiley insisted on adhering to the standards of cleanliness of their distinguished cavalry regiments. Stripped to the waist and with razors flashing, they washed daily and thoroughly, to the great wonder of the mountaineers who crowded round to watch. Albanian sanitary arrangements were primitive but ingenious. The closet, which adjoined the guest-room, projected, sometimes precariously, from the house over the courtyard below. It consisted of a hole in the floor, often of impracticably narrow circumference; and, underneath it, the thrifty Albanians were wont to keep their poultry, which gobbled up a strange diet with evident relish.

Women among the clans were but the slaves and chattels of their men. In the mountains they went unveiled but almost all were prematurely aged by manual labour and child-bearing. Sometimes we saw one hurrying across a courtyard or peering up at us from the kitchen fire; otherwise they had no part in our lives.

Social distinctions among the guerrillas were subtle and changing; the chieftains and their sons were treated with respect but never with servility; and the bodyguards sometimes as poor relations but always as members of the same family. They ate and slept together, and, in so far as he could, the host provided alike for all. Luxuries in the mountains were inevitably scarce, but, if the choicest morsels went to the

Anthony Quayle

Basil Davidson

Hugh Seton-Watson

Xan Fielding

George Millar

Photo. Mark Gerson
Peter Churchill

Beys and elders, the rest received their portion until the whole was finished. The Ghegs indeed regard hospitality as a sacred duty enjoined upon the host, never as a favour conferred upon the guest. To give of his best was a point of honour, and a tribesman would kill his last ewe lamb, or even his milch goat, rather than fail to set meat before the meanest of his guests.

GUERRILLA WAR

In the evening, we held a council of war and chose for our target a German Battery Headquarters which was commended by its lonely situation and the belief that it contained large supplies of ammunition.

We slept perhaps four hours, and then, with a small bodyguard, set out into the night to reconnoitre the German positions. After an hour's march through the woods our guide turned aside from the path and led us uphill to a rounded summit tufted with a clump of trees. As the night faded out of the sky we saw that we were standing on a range of barren hills, running roughly north and south. Beyond us to the west, and perhaps two thousand yards away, ran another range parallel to our own, but lower and thickly wooded. The fold of ground between lay under a blanket of mist, through which gleamed a single light—the duty office of the enemy's camp. Taking advantage of the obscurity we now crawled some five hundred yards downhill to a projecting knoll, where we crouched in the bracken and waited, chilled and cramped, to watch the Germans awake.

After what seemed an age the sun rose behind us, and, as the mists parted, we saw that a road ran along the bottom between the two ranges. Beside the road, and perhaps four hundred feet below us, stood a wooden hut, where the solitary light still burned. Beyond, in the side of the wooded range opposite, we presently made out three or four barracks or store-houses. As yet no one stirred, but towards six o'clock a German soldier emerged from the lighted hut and stamped up and down on the road, blowing on his hands. Presently he turned into the wood, and a few minutes later a bugle sounded the *réveille*. This was the moment for which we had waited, for we hoped that the movements of the men would reveal the positions of the camp. We therefore searched the wood closely through our glasses, and, as the soldiers woke up and set about their several routines, we became aware of a number of camouflaged tents and dug-outs which had thus far escaped our notice.

At seven o'clock six lorries drove up from the south and were loaded up from what we guessed to be a store-house by a working party of Italians, supervised by a German N.C.O. The drivers manoeuvred clumsily on the narrow road, and once one of them backed his lorry into the ditch. His angry shouts were wafted up to us on the hillside, but, with the help of the Italians, his machine was presently righted; and by eight o'clock the whole convoy had driven away. Each of us drew a rough sketch of all that he saw, and tried, besides, to count the number of the enemy. This proved a harder task, for the soldiers were continually disappearing and reappearing among the trees; but we finally computed the strength of the garrison at some thirty men. Towards nine o'clock the activity of the camp subsided; and, feeling that we had seen enough, we crawled back infinitely slowly to the shelter of the clump of trees on the ridge above. There, with the enemy positions still in full view, we sat down to concert our plan of attack.

We decided to assemble our forces behind the eastern range two hours before dark, and, dividing them into three parts, to develop a pincer movement against the Battery Headquarters. Maclean, with Petrit, Ndue Palli, and a hundred Zogists, would cross the bottom to the right of the German positions and approach them from the north. At the same time

I would take our twenty-eight Tajiks[1] as the other arm of the pincer and carry out a similar manoeuvre, but from the south. Maclean would launch the attack with the Albanians; and, once the Germans were fully engaged, I was to fall on them from behind with the Tajiks. Smiley, meanwhile, would remain on the eastern range with a reserve of some forty Albanians and three machine-guns. With these he would keep the road covered and might complete the discomfiture of the enemy should they try to escape eastwards. Finally, a small group of Albanians were to burn down a wooden bridge on the road, three kilometres from the camp, to prevent the enemy from receiving early reinforcements.

Back at Kurat the day passed slowly, though not without incident. This was the morning when the Tajiks murdered their N.C.O.; a deed which convinced us that, after the excitement of mutiny, their temper urgently required the discipline of battle and the cold douche of danger. Abas Kupi came also to discuss plans; and towards midday we received the first report from the young German officer planted by us in their Corps Headquarters in Tirana. This gave us, among a mass of other information, the identifications of the post we were going to attack. It was the headquarters of the Third Battery of the 297th Artillery Regiment. With so much business, there was no time to rest before the action; and, almost as soon as we had eaten, we set out to join our forces, already concentrating behind the eastern range. We reached the assembly point at five o'clock, and climbed to the crest of the range for a further brief reconnaissance. All was quiet in the German camp; we wished each other good luck, and departed each to his allotted task.

In the morning I had agreed with a light heart to take command of the Tajiks, but, as we marched off to the attack, I

---

[1] These were soldiers from Turkestan captured by the Germans in their invasion of the Soviet Union and regrouped into special units of the German Army. There were several such units in Albania and we persuaded some of them to desert to the guerrillas.

was oppressed by sombre reflections. I knew nothing of their training or their ways, and spoke besides so little of their language that I could not hope to make them understand my orders in the heat of battle. This ignorance might jeopardize the whole operation; but, as I anxiously considered how to impose my will on these wild Asiatics, there suddenly came back to me a fragment from a long-forgotten conversation with a friend who had once commanded an Indian brigade:

'It doesn't matter what you say to native troops,' he had told me, 'because they won't understand you. What matters is what you do. March in front of them and they'll do whatever you do; and, if you don't run away, they'll be as good as the Guards.'

I had been in Cairo at the time, ill from jaundice, and had forgotten his words with the next glass of medicine. Now, by some strange freak of memory, the sick-bed talk was become a counsel of action; and I remembered that Ivan and Mishka at least considered the Tajiks as 'native troops'. I went, therefore, to the head of the column, though not without some apprehension; the danger from the Germans in front might be part of the day's work; but only that morning the Tajiks had murdered their N.C.O., and I had to steel myself not to look back too often over my shoulder.

We crossed the low ground, where a tongue of woodland stretched out from the western range, and, hurrying over the road, climbed on to the crest of the range itself. There we turned northwards, and, devoutly hoping that the Germans were off their guard, moved silently towards them through the trees. Presently we came to a low thorn fence, broken only by a stile, on the far side of which lay a clearing perhaps fifty yards wide. Beyond, the woods sloped steeply down to the enemy positions. I decided that we should cross the clearing and lie up in the fringes of the wood beyond, to wait until Maclean should begin the attack. I led the way, therefore, over the stile, and had gone perhaps ten yards when a machine-gun opened up savagely from a clump of trees some forty yards away. I looked round to see how many of the Tajiks were already across the fence, and, as I turned my head, somehow lost my balance and fell to the ground. I thought at first that I had only slipped, and it was some time before I realized that a bullet had caught me under the chin. The wound indeed was little worse than a deep shaving cut, and caused me neither pain nor serious loss of blood. The Tajiks, however, ran back, seeing me fall; and I lay in the clearing alone. The machine-gun was silent, the gunner taking me perhaps for dead. I waited for a moment, then sprang up and ran for the fence. The German opened up at once, and his bullets hissed round me like furious insects as I vaulted the stile and made for the shelter of the trees. The Tajiks rallied when they saw me safe, and, gathering round me, opened a blind and ragged fire in the direction of the machine-gun.

I checked them as soon as I had recovered my breath and my wits, and, more by instinct than by reasoning, worked my way round the flank of the machine-gun post. When I judged we were well past it I lay down, and, while the Tajiks got into position, tried to decide what to do next. It is sometimes a weakness to see things from the other man's point of view, but, as I imagined myself among the German defenders, I knew that they were beaten. After months of inactivity they had been startled from rest, perhaps from sleep, by our approach. Their machine-gunners had seen a few Turkoman deserters, but, in the darkness of the wood, they could not tell how many were their assailants, or where the attack would come from next. Their nerves must be strained by the uncertainty; and I therefore decided not to wait for Maclean's signal but to go in to the attack.

For a few seconds I vainly racked my brains for orders which the men would understand. Then on a sudden inspiration I stood up, and, hoisting my astrakhan cap on the muzzle of my sub-machine-gun, ran forward shouting 'Hurrah'. The Tajiks did not misunderstand, and, spreading out on either side, charged through the trees, shoulders hunched and eyes glinting. The machine-gunners fled; we dropped over the crest of the ridge, and saw the huts and dug-outs of the enemy less than fifty feet below. I shouted 'Hurrah' again, and the Tajiks bounded down the hill like wolves, letting out blood-curdling yells and pouring a withering fire into the camp. As we carried the first buildings I saw a German standing twenty yards from me, stripped to the waist, with a *Schmeizer* pistol in his hand. For a moment we looked at each other without moving, then he crumpled to the ground, pressing his hands to his naked stomach. I had not heard the shot, but looked round to see Achmet grinning from ear to ear. We pressed forward, and, as I passed the dying German, I noticed that he was still a boy, with straight, fair hair and blue, staring eyes. His hands were clasped over his wound as if in prayer, and the blood was oozing quietly away through his fingers. Looking back a moment later I saw a Turkoman stripping him of his Wellington boots.

The enemy now returned a ragged fire, but we had taken them by surprise and they could not see us clearly for the trees. Several of them were shot down; and, as we came to close quarters, the rest broke and fled towards the road. There they ran into Smiley's machine-guns and were driven back, leaving one of their number dead. We were already masters of their camp; and they, too weak to counter-attack, fell back towards the south, sniping us from the cover of the wood.

Maclean and the Albanians had arrived on the scene just as we had gone in to the assault and had at once advanced to the attack. The first dead German, indeed, had fallen to Petrit Kupi's rifle; but, for some mysterious reason, the main body of the Albanians had failed to follow; and when we took the camp only Maclean, Petrit, and three of their bodyguards were there to join us. The rest of the Zogist forces now surrounded us, and, unaware that the Germans had fled, discharged volley after volley into the camp to our anger and alarm. Nothing could stop them; and the victorious Tajiks were forced to take cover from their Albanian allies in the German slit trenches and dug-outs. Unable to make ourselves heard, Maclean and I sat behind a clump of trees and despondently surveyed the battlefield. A few yards away a Tajik was dying in the arms of one of his comrades. Several dead Germans lay outside the tents and huts; and a group of Italian prisoners huddled behind a heap of rubble under Mishka I's watchful eye. Spent shots whined around us, and it was beginning to grow dark. I felt suddenly tired and intolerably thirsty.

More than half an hour must have passed before Petrit managed to persuade the Zogists to cease fire. Night had already fallen, and it was now too dark to plunder the camp systematically. We told the men, therefore, to carry off such supplies as were easily portable, and, retiring across the road, climbed towards the eastern range. There we found Smiley and Ndue Palli, who produced a most welcome flask of *raki*. We sat down to enjoy it, and were discussing the next move when suddenly a flare burst in the sky above us, casting a lurid, metallic light over the hillside. A moment later two mortar bombs fell quite close, followed by a burst of tracer bullets fired at long range. German reinforcements had arrived; and withdrawing slowly beyond the range, we trekked back to Kurat.

HOME-COMING

At dawn the Balkan coast was lost to sight, and we cruised alone between sea and sky. The autumn night had been cold, but the wind and the spray dropped with the morning; and the M.A.S. made good headway through an oily swell.

Maclean joined me on deck towards eight o'clock; and presently we saw the fortifications of Brindisi rising above the low Apulian shore. We ran our course between the minefields which guarded the harbour approaches, and an hour later were cutting the calm waters in the lee of the granite mole. The roar of the engines sank to a hum, and the M.A.S. nosed gently up against the quayside at the foot of the old castle.

Ashore, a squad of sailors were changing guard, while a few naval and army officers stood talking outside the Harbour Control. Their spotless uniforms and military bearing made a striking contrast to our wild and Balkanized appearance; and Maclean justly observed that we could scarcely be mistaken for officers or gentlemen. Maclean himself was dressed in sandals and torn jodhpurs, a faded green tunic, swathed in bandoliers, and a white Kruya skull-cap on his head. My own headgear was a black sheepskin *shubara*; my field-boots were cracked and coming apart at the heels; and my once smart cord uniform was soiled and stained from seven months' continual wear. I had let my beard grow, too, since the flesh wound under my chin; and it was several months since either of us had had a haircut.

Amid the hardships of an outlaw's life I had sometimes allowed my mind to dwell on those creature comforts which we might hope to find on our return to Bari. The Hotel Imperiale, however, was full to overflowing, and that night and the next we were lodged in the flat which our headquarters had requisitioned. It was entirely unfurnished, save for a single wooden chair, and was equally devoid of hot water or electric light. We were, indeed, accustomed to sleeping on the floor, but in Albania our rest had usually been assured by a mattress or a heap of ferns. No such luxuries obtained in our flat, and the unyielding hardness of the parquet was only mitigated by an army blanket. Nevertheless I slept heavily, for it was forty-eight hours since I had been to bed.

I woke soon after eight next morning and put on my new

battledress, which fitted well enough and only lacked badges of rank. Maclean was still asleep, but I felt hungry, and so made my way to the Hotel Imperiale in search of breakfast and of a barber who might shave off my beard. The dining-room was crowded with worthy officers munching their bacon and eggs, but a scruffy waiter barred the way in. He explained that no breakfasts could be served after nine o'clock and that I was already six minutes late. Baulked by this irksome regulation, I marched off to the hotel snack-bar, and, fighting my way through the crowd, secured a cup of coffee and a sardine sandwich. I had scarcely sat down to this unappetizing repast when I was accosted by an unknown officer and curtly reminded that the wearing of beards was contrary to King's Regulations. At first I thought him drunk, despite the early hour, and offered him a chair, prepared to humour him. My courtesy, however, only aroused his wrath and he went red in the face, spluttering that he was the Provost Marshal. I rose to explain my situation, but, as I did so, his eagle eye observed that I wore no badges or rank. From red he turned purple, and hissed:

'What are you doing here, anyway? Don't you know that this hotel is out of bounds to Other Ranks?'

My explanation drew from him a decent apology, but I was already beginning to regret the freer ways of the mountains.

The rhythm of our lives in Albania had been among the healthiest of our circumstances; for, in the mountains, events could move no faster than a man might walk. Allies, neutrals, or enemies approached alike on foot; and, since no man can run for long uphill, flight or attack proceeded at the same easy pace as the most simple errand. The tempo of the march encouraged meditation; the leisure of the camp afforded ample opportunity for the most detailed discussion. The conduct of negotiations was likewise seldom hurried, for a march of hours, or even days, would often precede a meeting. The business might be trivial, but the needs of the flesh and the customs of hospitality obliged the traveller to spend the night, or at least to take a meal, with those he had come to see. Each word might thus be weighed at leisure; and, since the necessary interludes for food or rest automatically divided each meeting into two or more sessions, there was always time to review conclusions or prepare new arguments. Nor was this even tenor of our work distracted by a multiplicity of routines or interviews. Our way of life tended inevitably to eliminate all that was superfluous, and the dangers of travel spared us from importunate visitors. Above all, we were masters of our own time, for we lived in a world where it was not unusual to be as much as a day late for an appointment. Each of our problems was thus revolved in frequent meditation and prolonged debate; and we had the rare satisfaction of knowing that our decisions or reports were the soundest of which we were capable.

In Bari this wholesome rhythm of life was rudely shattered by the bustle of a mechanized world. Cars rushed us from one office to another; harassed officials plied us with superficial questions; and memoranda on the most intricate problems were required at half an hour's notice. Interviews were continually disturbed by the ring of the telephone; and conversations were brought to an end, not by the exhaustion of the subject, but by the approach of the next appointment. At first I was bewildered; then repelled; and within a week the three of us had agreed to return to the mountains as soon as we could.

PARTISAN LIFE IN ALBANIA

By Anthony Quayle

IN the late evening of the last day in 1943, the hundred-foot *Sea Maid* bucketed her way eastwards across the Adriatic.

The sea was rough.

Down in the hold I lay jammed between a tub of grease and a sackful of boots. With every roll of the ship I slid across the floor with the tub, the boots, and all the other confused tackle with which the tiny space was crammed. I was too weak and sick to resist; I simply lay and sweated.

Water was cascading all round the deck; a lot of it was finding its way down into the hold. From the galley above my head came a terrible din; the ship's puppy had been locked in to prevent him being washed overboard, and now every pot, pan and ladle had come loose and were crashing all around him. He was yelling his head off, but no one paid attention; he was safer in the galley than in the scuppers.

Gradually the sea seemed to grow calmer, and I judged we must be in the lee of the mountains. Soon there was no mistake about it; we were rolling much less and the pandemonium of breaking crockery had ceased. Even the dog was silent; perhaps a mug had hit him on the head. My nausea ebbed away and desire to live returned.

We must be getting near, I thought; perhaps the mountains

were visible. I crawled over the piles of tumbled gear till I reached the foot of the companion ladder, then I climbed up on deck.

A living wind smote me in the face, and from the tarry confinement of the hold my mind spun out into the star-filled, immeasurable distance. I steadied myself against the halyards. The *Sea Maid* was breaking through a rolling swell, whirls and glints of phosphorus slipping away beneath us. The moon had not yet risen, and despite the frosty stars it was very dark. Motionless and silent the crew stood about the deck, stretching their senses into the night to detect an enemy patrol. They spoke in whispers as though their caution could compensate for the din of our Diesel engine or for the showers of sparks which flew from our smoke-stack and trailed away into the night. I hoped no E-boat was about; it could hardly fail to see us.

I made out the captain's form standing on the hatch in front of the wheel-house, and went and joined him.

'What's that?' I said suddenly. I had seen a light on the starboard bow.

'Just a village.' Rawlinson kept his voice low. 'South of our pin-point. You'll see it better soon.'

Ten minutes passed, and the light had become a cluster.

'That's it—Vuno,' said Rawlinson. 'Keep a good look-out for their signal; we should be seeing it any time now. They'll be flashing K.'

He stamped on the thin hatch, our only form of engine-room telegraph, and we dropped to half-speed. It was a relief, for the firework display ceased and the motor ran so quietly that I could hear the swish and ripple of the bow-wave. By contrast men were emboldened to speak louder.

Close to me the doctor said: 'Do you think they'll have Keith down on the beach?'

'I don't know,' I replied.

There was a pause, then he asked: 'How much longer now?'

'I've no idea,' I answered.

Rawlinson gave a quiet order through the open window of the wheel-house, and the steering-cable rattled slightly as the helmsman, eyes fixed on his red-glowing compass, altered course a point or two.

Minutes went by, then the doctor said excitedly: 'There it is!'

Sure enough a light was twinkling ahead of us, but Rawlinson dismissed it. 'Too high up,' he said. 'They signal from nearer sea-level. Besides, that's not Morse. Probably a shepherd's fire.'

Suddenly I became aware that the darkness ahead had taken on a different hue, and almost at the same moment I could hear a noise like a giant hoarsely letting out his breath. It was the sound of breakers. A cold excitement took hold of me. Each instant the land mass ahead became more certain, the skyline, high above our heads, more clearly defined.

'Is this the place?' I asked Rawlinson.

'This is it. Can't think why they don't flash. It's past eight.'

He stamped on the engine-room roof, and the screw stopped turning, the motor idling free. Now the breathing sound came clearer, and I fancied I could see the froth of waves.

'We'll lie here for a bit,' said Rawlinson, 'and wait for them to start flashing. Perhaps they've got the time wrong.'

We lay, strained and silent, for half an hour.

The moon had been behind the mountains, throwing them into silhouette; now she rose in the heavens, and as she poured a pale flood of light on the coast before us, I had my first view of Albania. Cold and grey, mammoth-ribbed, the mountain rose up out of the fret of white water round its base. So bare the hillside looked, so utterly devoid of life, that it might itself have been one of the mountains of the moon.

The doctor said in my ear: 'Is this the place?'

'I gather so,' I said.

'Then why don't they flash?'

'I don't know.'

'Perhaps they're captured. . . . Perhaps they're killed.'

'Perhaps,' I said.

'But if we don't get Keith out tonight he may die.'

'I know that.'

'Then . . .'

'Listen, doctor,' I said, 'I'm just as nervous as you are, and I don't know anything. So it's no good asking me. Just keep quiet and wait.'

I walked away from him; I had to.

Rawlinson was uneasy. 'I know this is the place,' he said when I stood by him. 'I know it well even in the dark, but with this moonlight . . .' He made a sound of exasperation, then gave a stamp on the engine-room roof.

'We'll take a turn down the coast,' he said. 'I suppose I *might* have made a mistake.'

At half-speed we turned south and crept along not three hundred yards from the coast. Once a shepherd's fire glowed high on the hillside, and twice I could have sworn I saw a flash—but it was only the phosphorus in the breaking waves. After half an hour we turned about and steered northwards till we were back at our starting-point.

Rawlinson stamped, and once again we lay rolling in the swell. 'Dammit!' he said, 'I'm not going to patrol the enemy's coast for him when I *know* this is the place.'

A breeze struck us from the south. If the wind shifted to that quarter we would lose the protection of the hills and it might be hard to make a landing.

'I'm going to risk signalling,' said the captain. 'D'you mind?'

'No,' I answered. 'Go ahead. W is our letter for the night, isn't it?'

With a flashlight Rawlinson sent 'W' towards the coast. Though he screened the beam with his hand he could not prevent the light from spilling on to the bulwarks, the rigging, the still figures on the deck.

There was no reply.

He steadied himself against the wheel-house, ready to signal again, when suddenly an answering flash leapt out of the hillside.

'There it is!' we all cried.

'Long-short-long. That's them all right!'

Again it came, stabbing out across the water, unfaltering, linking us upon the dark sea to our countrymen ashore in a hostile land. There were tears of excitement in my eyes as the *Sea Maid* moved slowly forward and I plunged down into the hold to collect my scattered gear.

When I regained the deck the *Sea Maid* was close in under the cliffs, and the weight of the mountain above seemed to be crushing down on us. Rawlinson was at the wheel himself, heading us straight for the narrow entrance to a bay; he had judged it carefully, swinging his clumsy boat in a wide arc to get the right angle of approach. Nearer we came—nearer; now I could hear the slap and boom of each separate wave as it hit the rocks and burst into spray above our heads. Tensely we stood as the *Sea Maid* slipped through the entrance without a dozen yards to spare on either side.

Orders were given; quickly the engine went into reverse, and our makeshift anchor of weights was dropped over the stern. From the side of the ship came the sound of splashing and a confused shouting in foreign tongues. Torchlights were turned towards the noise; for a moment the beams wavered across empty, tossing water, then fastened on a small canvas boat in which crouched half a dozen men, paddling furiously and all shouting unintelligible directions.

Suddenly, there rang out a voice—unmistakably, blessedly, authoritatively English—a voice with an edge of exasperation in it:

'For God's sake catch that rope and make it fast!'

*   *   *

'Major, we are now in the hills of Trajas, and Trajas is

Partisan.' Chela spoke apologetically. 'It is not safe for me to go any farther with you. Zechir will guide you now. The Partisans will not hurt him; he is only a poor one.'

'Thank you for your help, Chela.' I handed back to him the civilian greatcoat which he had given me to wear over my uniform as we crossed over the road inland. 'I hope the Partisans will not be too hard to find.'

'I will wait for you at my house till you come back. Goodbye, Major. Remember at Trajas to ask for Doctor Georgie; he will surely be able to help you.'

Two hours brought us to Trajas. It was the first Albanian village I had entered, and it was a desolate sight. Out of some six hundred little houses, not more than fifty were inhabited. Walls gaped, roofs had fallen in, stones cascaded into the narrow paths that served for streets. At a spring, some women were washing clothes, but without soap. A few men sat about. There was no sign of food; neither crops, vegetables, fruits, fowls—just nothing.

Zechir left me at a corner while he went to find the man who, Chela had said, would know where I could find the leaders of the Partisan Brigade. Four or five people gathered round, staring at me.

'Inglese?' asked one.

'*Si*,' I replied.

Some words were spoken in Albanian, and a boy who was there went running off. The others continued to stare, neither with gaiety nor yet with hostility.

The boy returned, leading a scarecrow of a man in tattered, Western clothes. He was pushed in front of me, and stood there looking me up and down. All the faces in the group were turned to him unexpectantly.

'English?'

His voice was like a rusty hinge.

'My name Hassan. Speak good English. This goddam country she no good.'

He held out a filthy claw.

The combination of American accent and unexpected vehemence took me by surprise.

'You've been in America?' I asked.

'Me . . . janitor . . . Detroit . . . Twelve years.'

I could see the words come painfully into his head. His face was set with concentration. Then he blurted: 'This country son-of-a-bitch. All finished.' He pointed to the ruined houses. 'Italians . . . Germans . . . Balli.'

With the last word his gummy eyes lit up and the little crowd murmured. For how much of this desolation, I wondered, were my Balli friends of last night responsible, together with the Italians and Germans?

'Where will I find the Partisans?' I asked.

The prophet's face remained blank, so I repeated the question slowly; but he couldn't understand. His English was at an end, and so was his strength.

As the boy led him off I could see an expression of doubt on the faces of the little crowd. Had their champion acquitted himself well? I felt that I could not fail him.

'*Parla benissimo Inglese*,' I said. '*Benissimo.*'

They seemed reassured.

Of Zechir, or of this Doctor Georgie whom I should meet, there was no sign, so I sat on the wall in the sun watching some children playing in the distance. Children make the same noise in any language, and the sound of those squeaking voices was the only thing that linked the stricken village with any normal form of life.

A whole hour had gone by before Zechir returned, bringing with him the elusive doctor. The latter came up smiling all over his face.

'My name is Doctor Georgie. I sure am pretty pleased to see you.' The newcomer's accent was more strongly American than that of my first interlocutor.

He was a little man, quite young, with a pleasant, sensitive face. His clothes hung about him, as though he had shrunk inside them, and he wore a curious tweed cap with ear-flaps that tied together on the top of his head.

'And mine's Overton. I'm a British officer just arrived in this area. I'm told you can help me get in touch with the local Partisan leaders. Is that true?'

'Sure. I'll do all I can to help.' He was nearly stammering with eagerness. 'Two days ago the Commissar was in Gjormi; I think maybe we still find him there.'

'And where is Gjormi?'

'It's on the other side of the mountain. Farther inland.'

I looked up at the monster that hung above our heads.

'Well, I'm very anxious to meet them.'

'Gee! They'll be anxious to meet you too, Major.' He looked like an earnest and intelligent guinea-pig.

'How long will it take to cross?'

'Five hours, I guess. We could make Gumenitza tonight and go on to Gjormi in the morning.'

'Will you come with me?'

I liked the little fellow, and it was a relief to find someone who spoke English.

'Sure. I guess I'd better. And we'll take three good boys as guards.' He gave a deprecatory laugh. 'I don't know the way so good.'

He spoke to the men who stood round us, then turned back to me. 'Well, let's go.'

'But haven't you anything to collect before you leave?' I asked.

He laughed.

'No, I got nothing. Nor have they.' And he indicated the men who were to guide us. 'Let's go. We've not got too much daylight left.'

Four hours' steady climbing brought us to the top of the mountain, and by then night was falling.

Of our three guards, one had been a schoolmaster and the

other two were father and son. The boy had a thick, black scab all round his mouth—caused by fever, I was told. We were too busy climbing to speak much, but when we reached the plateau on the top the boy started to sing quietly. He had a pleasant voice, and he sang one after another of the Partisan songs. They were in a minor key and sad, like Russian tunes.

The moon came up, and it was evident that we had lost our way. I was feeling rather weak, as I had had nothing to eat since breakfast. I made a note to carry my own food with me on these walks in future.

We were going along in single file, the old man leading and I next, when he slipped on a rock and fell. The rifle he carried went off in my face, but luckily the bullet missed me. The others thought it was an ambush and flung themselves on their faces. When they realized what had happened, they thought it was a very funny joke.

Once, as we floundered along through the dark, we heard a shrill whooping, and the next moment stones started to fall among us. We halted and the old man called aloud. Out of the darkness emerged a small boy; though very sturdy, he could not have been more than eight years old. They spoke together and something he said made the men laugh.

'He's telling us that he's up here alone guarding the goats,' the doctor explained. 'When he heard us coming he thought we must be either wolves or robbers, so he threw stones at us to scare us away.'

I looked at the little creature pattering along bare-foot beside us.

'And he is left up here in the mountain all alone?' I asked.

Georgie nodded.

'Yes, all alone.'

An hour later, thanks to the directions of our diminutive guide, we were coming into Gumenitza. As far as I could tell in the darkness, it was much like Trajas. It was quite silent till, suddenly, every dog in the place began to bark; one huge beast ran at us and had to be driven off with a rifle-shot.

The ex-schoolmaster had been sent on ahead to announce our coming, and when we arrived a room was already prepared for us in the house of the village commissar. It was a high, white-washed room, and although empty of furniture save for two great chests which stood one on each side of the door, it did not look bare; it was filled with the glow of a crackling wood fire, and with the warmth of the brightly coloured rugs and cushions that were strewn about the floor.

The leaders of the Fifth Brigade, it seemed, were still in Gjormi—the next village on—and already a messenger had been sent through the night to warn them of my coming. I felt rather pleased; it was the first time my presence had aroused any enthusiasm since I had arrived in Albania.

A bottle of *raki* was brought in—a clear, colourless spirit that would have tasted disgusting if I had not been in such need of a drink. It was very strong.

My clothes were sodden with sweat and the doctor's were the same, so we dried our vests and shirts in rotation, wearing one for warmth while the steam rose from the other. The boy with the scabby mouth took off his top coat and revealed his only upper garment as an Italian sailor's white blouse, complete with big, blue collar. I wonder how he had come by it, but decided not to enquire. The boy was ready enough to go into gory details without being prompted.

Food came, a mush of sodden bread and entrails; we gobbled it down, scrabbling in the bowl with our fingers, and when it was all gone I leaned back against the wall, my belly like a drum and my head buzzing with the *raki*, staring bemusedly at the fire.

'Say, Major.'

'Yes, Georgie?'

'These boys you'll meet tomorrow—I'd like to tell you something about them.'

He started off, a long story about Partisans and Balli and Albania, and the Allies, but I couldn't concentrate, and I didn't hear the end of it; I had fallen asleep.

I heard about the leaders of the Fifth Brigade, though, as we walked towards Gjormi next morning in the cold, clear sunlight.

'Petchi, the Commander, used to be an officer in the Albanian Army.'

'And the Commissar?'

'He's called Besnik.'

Georgie pronounced the name with a kind of awe.

'You'll like him, Major. He's tough, but he's a pretty swell boy.'

The doctor was not a good walker. There was something pathetic about him as he flopped along in his loose clothes. His Alpine boots were so worn and battered that the nails round the edge, instead of pointing down, stuck out sideways like a ragged moustache.

'I take it they're both communists?'

At once the doctor was on the defensive.

'Maybe they are; they fight well against the Huns.'

I hadn't heard the word 'Hun' since I arrived in Albania.

'Where did you learn your English?' I asked.

'I spent three years in America. I took a degree in bacteriology at Collingwood University. That's why these folks call me "doctor". I'm not a doctor really; I just do what I can.'

His face lit up when he spoke of America, and he prattled on about its wonders till we arrived at Gjormi.

The place was nothing but a heap of ruins, but it swarmed with Partisans waiting for my arrival. They came clustering round me, shaking hands, giving the communist salute with the clenched fist. They were young men for the most part, with hard, thin faces, most of them wearing a red star in their caps.

Besnik and Petchi were expected any moment, I was told.

While I waited they bombarded me with questions. How was the war going? When would it end? How were the armies doing in Italy? Would the Russians break through in the spring? I answered their questions as best I could, with an appropriate mixture of tact and enthusiasm, but it was a slight ordeal and I was glad to be rescued from it by the arrival of a messenger.

'Death to Fascism!' he shouted.

The men round me vied with each other in the ferocity of their tone as they replied: 'The Freedom of the People!'

'They are coming!' said the messenger, and stamped off.

Another seven or eight minutes went by before another courier came walking quickly towards us.

'They are coming!' he said, and disappeared after the first.

'They are coming!' said the Partisans around me, and they began to lead me away.

'... To the meeting-place,' Doctor Georgie informed me as we approached one of the three hovels that were still standing.

In the yard a large goat was being done to death, its blood running over the stones. So, I thought, the talk was to be followed by a lunch-party. Three wretched-looking women eyed us as we trooped into the little house.

The room inside was better than I had expected—clean, white-washed walls, the fire burning, and on the floor a few rugs and cushions of bright red.

'What's the matter, Georgie?' I asked.

The little man was a picture of dejection as he pulled his boots off.

'They're going to use me as interpreter.' He sighed and gave a frightened smile. 'It makes me kind of nervous.'

The entrance, when at last it came, justified the build-up; there was no denying it was good. There was a noise of voices in the yard and the crash of heavy boots in the corridor outside, then the door flung open and: 'Death to Fascism!' ...

'Death to Fascism!' rang out simultaneously from the Commander and the Commissar of the Fifth Partisan Brigade.

I came to attention and gave my best 'King's Regulations' salute; I had purposely kept on my beret so that I could do so.

They were hung about with all the implements of war—automatic rifles, revolvers, field-glasses, map-cases, and, in the commissar's belt, a hand-grenade. I was glad to see him discard it, for it looked very precarious. Quickly the accoutrements were shed, boots removed, and in a very short time we were sitting on the floor round the fire, ready for business.

I had expected that this was going to be a tough interview, and as I looked at the two men opposite me I knew that I had been right. Two purposeful faces looked back at me. I braced myself.

'Ask them if they will speak first, or if they want me to.'

Georgie translated.

'They say will you please begin.'

Again I glanced at the two Partisans. Fair words would butter no parsnips here.

'First of all, I wish to state clearly the purpose of my mission here in Albania.'

I spoke slowly, picking my words with care.

'I have been sent here to give assistance to all who are fighting the common enemy. I am, therefore, here to help you. How that help is to be brought, and in what quantity, is for us to discuss today.'

That, I thought, should set the ball rolling.

'Will you give me your comments so far.'

When Georgie had translated my words, the two leaders spoke together for a minute, and I had time to study them. Petchi was a short man of perhaps forty. Curly black hair topped an animal face, deeply seamed in the cheeks, with a full, aggressive, lower lip. Besnik was ten years younger, I judged, and considerably the taller of the two. He had fair, straight hair and a pointed face that might have been over-subtle had it not been so weathered and toughened by his life. Both were clean-shaven.

Though I could not understand a word they spoke, I guessed that Besnik was asking in effect: 'Shall I give him the works?' and that Petchi agreed. At any rate, he proceeded to do so. For a long time he spoke quietly in Albanian while the doctor, with a worried face, made notes. When he had ceased speaking, Georgie turned to me.

'These guys are pretty sore. They've suffered pretty bad and . . .'

'Come on,' I cut in. 'I want to know exactly what he said—exactly.'

'This is what he says,' began Georgie miserably. 'The words "to give assistance" are very welcome, especially as after many fair promises we have received absolutely nothing.'

The little man looked at me with frightened eyes.

'Don't get me wrong, Major. I'm only translating what he said.'

I nodded. 'Go on.'

'Major Keith dropped by parachute into our area and we took care of him. He made us many promises of help, but instead of fulfilling them he left us and moved his base into Balli territory. He gave to Dukat the help that he had promised to us. Major Keith was not for the war. And so, though we are glad to hear the word "help", we do not believe you, for we have been too often betrayed. That's what Besnik says,' the doctor finished lamely.

The attack on Tom was both absurd and irritating.

'Major Keith was a regular officer for ten years before ever this war began,' I replied. 'His profession was to fight for his country. To say, therefore, that he was not "*for*" the war is ridiculous. The reason for his moving to Balli territory is simple; he was ordered to. He was ordered to open a base on the coast, and he obeyed his orders. It was a geographical accident that the perfect place for a sea base was in Balli hands. As to help, you do not tell the truth; to my knowledge you received four plane-loads of material while the major was with you, while Dukat has been given only some clothing—as payment for the protection of the base. To conclude, I do not wish to discuss what Major Keith did, or did not do. I am here now; and I do not care to have my word doubted.'

Georgie could not have softened my words much, for Petchi flushed deeply. The Partisans, he said, loudly and with great vehemence, had begun their war against the fascist invaders without any help from the Allies, and though he would not deny that help was badly wanted yet, if need be, the Albanian Partisans would continue to the end without it.

The Brigade Commander had put himself into such a passion of rage that I did not find it difficult to remain calm, and I pointed out to him that however the Partisans began their fight, they had not lacked for support since the arrival, some months back, of British missions. Large quantities of material, as well as considerable sums of gold, had been given to the Central Partisan Council, quite apart from the assistance given to individual groups and brigades.

Petchi merely shrugged and said that he didn't care what had been given to others—the Fifth Brigade had gone without help.

Now Besnik interrupted, using a boyish and extremely genuine smile. He apologized for the outburst of the Commander, an emotional man, he said—so much so that he had earned the nickname of 'The Thunderer'—and he hoped I would not be offended by the bluntness of Petchi's speech.

'Of course,' he went on, 'of course we need your help, and badly. We should be grateful to hear your suggestions on that score.'

Now for it! If I could only get them to accept the Dukat proposal and so get the two parties thoroughly interdependent, I might be in a fair way to stopping the civil war in my area, thus leaving both sides free to concentrate on the common enemy.

I explained that for my stores I was dependent on the sea, and that this fact, therefore, limited me in the location of my base. The only possible place for a sea base that I could see was behind Dukat mountain.

'However,' I continued, 'I think there is a solution which I hope will be acceptable to you.... I will retain my base in Balli territory, where it is unlikely to be suspect by the Germans, and the material I bring ashore can be secretly transported to you across Dukat valley by night.'

I made Georgie translate so far. A look of amused incredulity came over the faces of the two men.

'And Dukat?' asked Besnik.

'The men of Dukat are agreeable if you, in return, will give them an assurance that you will not attack them.'

At the translation of my last words, the two Partisans smiled broadly at each other.

'Splendid!' said Besnik. 'Dukat evades any dangerous work, and asks us not to attack them!'

Another talk between the two, then Petchi spoke.

'Major, we will have no compromise with the men of Dukat. We will enter into no compact with them. The right to attack them or to refrain from attacking them, we reserve to ourselves; and if the only way we can get arms is through Dukat then we will do without the arms.'

Full stop. So that was that.

'Why do you not drop arms to us by plane?' asked Besnik.

Now this, I knew well, was what I might have to come to one day, but to agree to it now might be to throw away the one means I had to effect a truce between the parties. It would only confirm the Partisans in their intransigence towards Dukat, and render my own position in that area quite impossible. I could hardly expect the men of Dukat to give protection to my base while I supplied to their bitter enemies the very instruments for their destruction. Yet the maintenance of the sea base was part of my allotted task. Besides, in one sea sortie we could bring into the country more stores than in six air sorties, and I was unwilling at the first sign of difficulty to discard the whole organization of sea supply which had been so carefully built up and which I was there to employ. I therefore dodged that one.

'I have been told to depend for supplies on the sea route,' I said. 'We have not enough planes to supply the whole of the Balkans.' And I enlarged on the advantages of sea supply.

'But you can have a sea base in Partisan territory.'

This was new to me, and I was genuinely glad to hear it. I had no idea that the Partisans controlled any suitable part of the coast.

'I can? Where?'

'South of your present base. At Vuno.'

Vuno. That was the village whose lights we had seen from the *Sea Maid* as we were approaching the coast ten days ago—or was it ten years?

'Then by all means let me see the spot,' I said. 'If it is possible I will run the stores in there.'

'Good! Then you can make your base with us and leave the Balli.' Besnik smiled. 'If only for the sake of your own safety you should do that. We would put a company, a battalion even, at your disposal as a guard; but among the Balli you will never be safe. They are fighting *with* the Germans. Any day they might betray you.'

I knew that in this he might well be right, yet still I was unwilling to commit myself at this early stage. Until I saw their proposed sea base with my own eyes I preferred to be sceptical about it, and not run the risk of losing one sure sea link before I had established another. My reply was that I would certainly establish a base with them, but that I would retain Sea View as well for the time being.

'Major,' said Besnik, 'we feel that you are a little over-concerned about the relationship between ourselves and the Balli.' His voice was silky and his smile disarmingly frank, but he could not hide the subtlety of his face. 'Let me remind you of two statements, both of them made by your own government. The Allies have said that they will help all those who fight the common enemy, regardless of their political opinions. I therefore demand help from you; we are fighting the Nazis. The Allies have said that they will not interfere in the internal affairs of other countries. I demand, therefore, that you leave us to settle our domestic quarrels in our own way.'

And now get out of that one, his expression seemed to say.

'In spite of your argument,' I replied, 'my path is not as clear as I could wish it. To give you arms with which to fight the Germans'—I deliberately avoided the use of the word "Nazis"; that would be to concede to these Partisans their own political angle on the fight—'may, in certain circumstances, be equal to interfering very seriously in your country's internal affairs.'

The interpreter had hardly finished before Petchi broke in.

'It is perfectly clear,' he blurted. 'We Partisans are fighting the Nazis. If you want to help us you can; there is nothing to stop you.'

Besnik glanced quickly at his commander. I fancied he would have liked Petchi either to be more tactful or else keep his mouth shut.

'That is an argument into which I do not want to be drawn now,' I answered. 'This is what I will do. In six days from now I shall be at Vuno; I suggest that your representative be there to meet me, and that he is competent to discuss the problems of transport inland as well as the actual reception of the sortie. Six days from now is the earliest that I can be at Vuno, since I must first go back to my own base. Let us for the moment go no farther than that.'

This seemed to content them, and we broke up the conversation to eat lunch. The goat, now carved into lumps and gobbets, was contained in a large dish, and the dish stood on a low stool round which we squatted. Eight or ten other Partisans joined us for the meal, among them a young girl, the first so-to-speak emancipated woman I had seen in Albania. Every other I had seen hitherto had been extremely ugly, dressed in peasant costume, and both segregated from, and subordinated to, the men. But this girl was pretty; she had bobbed hair, and wore a skirt instead of the usual baggy trousers, and she sat eating and talking with the men like an equal. She could hardly have been more than seventeen, but she looked as though she took life very seriously, writing a number of notes and never smiling once. She appeared to be Besnik's secretary, and I wondered if she was also his bed-fellow, but decided that this was unlikely, or she would have looked less solemn.

The head of the goat, as being the greatest delicacy, was courteously placed in my hands by Petchi, but as yet I was too much of a novice to extract from it more than the obvious brains. The meat was very tough, as was to be expected with an animal that had been killed only two hours, but it disappeared in a flash. Fingers were licked. Petchi jumped to his feet, and a moment later, with a final brandishing of clenched fists and a battery of 'Deaths to Fascism!' he and his little staff had gone stamping off.

Besnik remained behind with me to discuss details of the material that was needed by the brigade, and it was only now that I discovered that he spoke good French. This meant that we were able to dispense with the services of Doctor Georgie—which was just as well, for the undercurrent of emotion that had flowed through the meeting, coupled with his dread of offending either side, had reduced the little man to such a state of nerves that he was incapable of further translation.

Besnik's first request was no modest one. 'I want seven hundred rifles.'

'What is the size of your brigade?'

The brigade, apparently, numbered a thousand, all of whom had rifles, though little ammunition. There was also a reserve, a kind of 'Home Guard', of about the same number, but lacking arms of any kind.

The revelation of such numbers came as a surprise to me. It also struck me that their advantage, since there was little to be gained militarily from a half-armed mass, could only be political.

'Please don't think,' I said, 'that I am trying to teach you your own business, but would it not be better to organize your brigade in small raiding parties, highly mobile and well-equipped, rather than in such unwieldy numbers?'

Besnik smiled. 'You do not understand our type of warfare.'

There was a firmness in his voice which decided me not to pursue that point for the time being.

'What priority do you want given to food and clothes?'

Again the smile, this time with a trace of bitterness.

'You have seen for yourself what we look like. We have no coats, and the snow will soon be here; but arms and ammunition are our greatest need. Do not send food and clothing at the expense of ammunition. If we have arms we can still fight—even if we are a little cold and hungry; but we cannot kill Nazis with blankets and tins of meat.'

As he was leaving, he turned in the doorway. 'You must excuse any hot words that have been spoken. Our need is very great.'

He took a step back into the room towards me.

'There is a reason why I do not think that you will fail us,' he said quietly. 'It is because you, too, are young—and the young do not fail each other.'

THE COST

By Basil Davidson

Our journey to the Danube, nearly a hundred miles as we should go, would not be an easy one. In normal times, when we were masters of the countryside at least by night, the journey would involve a day's ride to the Sava and then, still riding, another night and day. But with the enemy so thick on the ground in Semberija, we should have to walk, and hope that horses might be found in the villages of Bosut: otherwise we should walk the whole way. It would be long and tedious. The first part would be touch-and-go; much would depend on reaching and crossing the Sava before dawn.

We were thirteen. There were Kolya and myself and seven couriers, picked lads from Srem of eighteen or nineteen who were tough and proven and could walk long distances. Upon such couriers depended our whole system of intercommunication between units and commands: they had to be intelligent as well as enduring, good horsemen as well as strong walkers, and know the countryside so that whatever happened they could still find a way to get through to their destination; above all, they had to be so reliable that they would keep going in all circumstances, no matter how long they were beyond the reach of supervision. The seven who went with us were old beyond their years, self-confident in their own surroundings as only peasant boys can be, contemptuous of the enemy, calculating in the risks they took. There was no kind of horse they could not ride. They were seldom or never at a loss. The other four members of our party were bound for the Banat; three we took as reinforcements for ourselves, and the fourth, a woman, because she was a nurse and was willing, so she said, to walk as fast and as far as we must walk. Thus we had ten sub-machine-guns (of which seven were Stens) and two rifles: anyone that got in the way would be likely to pay dearly for it. We took no baggage of any kind; only the woman had a little knapsack on her shoulders. The woman walked without shoes, in a thick pair of woollen socks; before dawn, not reckoning on the killing pace that we should set, she was lagging behind and exhausted, her feet blistered and cut, so that we had to leave her on the south bank until she could cross the following night.

We came down from the Mayevitsa in the late afternoon, whilst it was still light. As far as Trnovo we were still with the rest of the staff; and at Trnovo, where Lekitch had one of his main field hospitals, Slobodan arranged for us a farewell sing-song by Zhika's choir. We sat among the pale-faced casualties and listened to our old favourites; and at the end, by Slobodan's command, they sang 'God Sev ze Kin', and Kolya said: 'D'you think we should stand up?' and I said: 'No, not with these casualties . . .' And we went away with the singing still in our ears.

From Trnovo we struck north-eastwards, heading for the Drina; and just short of the plain we stopped until it was twilight. We had three main problems: to cross the main road that ran from Yanya to Bijeljina, to skirt round Bijeljina without raising an alarm, and to get over the Sava in darkness. We should regard everyone we saw as a potential enemy. The reason for this was that enemy-controlled chetniks would not wear uniform, but would look like ordinary peasants; and at the moment there was said to be a nucleus of them in every village. If they raised an alarm we could expect to be pressed hard; the enemy had plenty of troops available and there was no forest cover to be found until we were over the Sava. Speed and silence were therefore essential.

We achieved both. Short of the Bijeljina main road we stopped in a small village where a national liberation Odbor had been established some time before. One of our couriers knew the chief Odbornik's house, a mud and plaster affair with a thatched roof and white-washed walls, and we knocked him up; but recent weeks had shown him another side to the coin and he developed that night a sore ankle which unfortunately prevented him from going with us over the road. He was very sorry.... This was bad because we would not force him to go with us in circumstances like these when he might prefer to betray us; but to cross the road on the main village track was to risk running into an ambush, and an exchange of shots at this point would give us away in the middle of hostile country. The man was shivering with fear.

Kolya was angry, but said nothing. Two dogs barked in the distance. We stood there in the darkness of a hedge and whispered to each other. The night was clear and full of stars. Nothing gave one a sharper sense of loneliness and self-reliance than these long night marches through enemy-held country: it seemed as if one had walked far beyond the reach of friends, to me as if England were a far-off forgotten country where people now were sleeping in another dimension, another world; as if this war of ours were another than the war they knew.

The Odbornik stood shivering in his night-shirt. The white hem flapped around his ankles; the hair stood in shocked unruliness upon his head; he was half-asleep and yet fearfully awake, confused, frightened, uncertain what to do. It would be safer to go without him. And yet without him we would not know the way. Not to know the way might mean disaster.

'Well, come on, what shall we do? Are you coming or not?'

'Look, it's only just down there. You turn to the left beyond the hedge, and then through the trees, and over a little stream...'

He was trying to explain, miserable and shivering. Then we saw another white figure come out of the darkness of his doorway and bob across the mud to where Kolya and the Odbornik were arguing in fierce whispers. This second figure did not stop to speak, but simply pushed the Odbornik towards his cottage and ran on at once down the path.

'It's his wife!' someone whispered. We ran after her.

Down the path, and round the bend and through the trees, and across several streams knee-deep in slime, and through more trees; and then a brief pause to catch our breath, with two couriers creeping ahead of us, and then on again and this time over the road that was paved with starlight and stretched away straight on either side, over the road and then another and longer pause. We crowded round the woman who had shown us the way. She was young, perhaps twenty-three, and quite pretty, in nothing but her night-gown, and barefooted.

'My God,' Kolya said admiringly. 'My God, what can you do with a man who's a coward?'

She smiled at us, pleased and proud, confident of herself. 'Ah, don't think of it, he's an old man.'

'You're young enough, anyway,' George or Marko or Zhika or one of them said. There was a laugh; it was a relief to be across the road.

George opened a gate into a cottage yard and knocked at the door. After a time he came back with a flask of *rakija*. We passed it round, raw spirit that bit into our weariness. As we went on, George kept refilling his flask whenever opportunity offered; altogether I think we drank over a gallon of *rakija* that night.

Once over the road we took to ploughland and went across country for six hours. We skirted east of Bijeljina, hitting the left bank of the Drina and walking due north until we were beyond the town. The ploughland held us back, the earth sticking in gobbets to our boots and weighing us down. By three o'clock we were still plodding northwards, still eight or nine miles from the Sava. And dawn was at five. We began to run.

By five o'clock we had come up with the Sava down-stream from Racha and lay waiting in a clump of saplings a mile or so from the river while two couriers went ahead and found where the boat was hidden. The dawn was breaking and Kolya cursed. Enemy patrols along the south bank were regular from dawn onwards. The woman was played out and crying with exhaustion; she would have to stay behind. We lay in the ash saplings and the sky broke pale blue above our heads. In half an hour it would be full daylight.

In the end it was an anti-climax. We crossed at six o'clock with the sun already shining up-stream from the eastern horizon; a quarter of an hour later the first patrol passed by the saplings in which we had hidden, as we learnt the following day from the woman we had left behind. But by that time we were safely on the north bank, and the north bank was free.

This in itself might seem extraordinary. But the enemy, vainglorious and stupid, had thought the sacking of Racha and the village of Bosut sufficient to end our movement in those woods. *Thirteen S.S.* reported all partisans annihilated and passed over to the south bank. For them it was then a simple problem of preventing partisans from Bosnia from coming back again to the north bank. They filled the plain of Semberija but they left the north bank free. Free and terribly mutilated.

The day following the enemy's evacuation of Racha and the village of Bosut the Odred came back to them from its concealment in the woods. At the beginning of March Lala and the others from Bosnia arrived in Racha, passing the Sava by a narrow margin of disaster. They found a scene of unrelieved frightfulness. The corpses of 220 human beings, of which eighty-three were women and fifty were old men and the remainder children too young to have crossed the Sava in our retreat, were lying about the village, in little heaps in backyards, in the shallowest of graves, hidden under sheaves of maize stalk, or simply abandoned in the road. In the village of Bosut, three miles away, they found the corpses of seventy-five women, forty-five children, and thirty-eight old men; and the story was much the same in Morovitch and two other villages. A later calculation showed that a total of 460 old men, women, and young children had been murdered in these villages, apart from several who could not be accounted for. In most cases we found that they had had their throats cut. Seventy or eighty houses had been burnt.

We dragged ourselves that morning into the village weary beyond words from thirty miles of plough and marsh and farm track, much of it at more than walking speed. If we had felt any pleasure at success Racha would have cut it short and killed it dead. At one of the first houses we found a half-company of the Odred eating their breakfast; they told us what we needed to know. The truth was worse, it seemed, than the wildest rumours we had heard. They were pleased to see us, and thought it fine that we had come across Semberija; but their welcome seemed beside the point.

Lala came, a bundle of nervous energy, angry, undershot a little like a bulldog, very like a bulldog himself, obstinate, forthright, no respecter of persons. He was like an electric field in any situation that was neutral, negative, inactive. He attracted or repelled, and both with violence. He galvanized people, bullied them, bustled about, made order in chaos, chaos sometimes in order. It was unheard-of that Lala should be satisfied. No matter how a thing were done he could always show a better way; and the worst thing about him was that he was usually right. Nothing was beyond him, nothing was too much for him, nothing was not his responsibility. He was impatient, impulsive, blowing hot and cold but never lukewarm. And the men, though a little afraid of him, liked him very well; and that was the acid test.

He rushed in as we sat in our exhaustion and overwhelmed us with his welcome. He was immensely pleased to see Kolya. Until now he had been alone in responsibility, dealing with a situation that was unprecedented in its frightfulness even in Lala's long experience. He was boiling with rage, and he swore loudly as he talked. He gave us a rapid description of what had happened, firing off sentences like the crackle of a sub-machine-gun. He had looked to the food situation. He had completed the burying of the corpses. He had re-established the Odbor. He had set up field kitchens. He had inspected the wells. He was worried about the wells. Too many corpses had been lying for too long in the subsoil for the wells not to be contaminated. He feared an epidemic of typhoid or something similar. We had better not drink any water. He forbade us to drink any water. His anger and enthusiasm were good to see; for nothing could demoralize Lala.

'I would never have believed it,' Lala said. 'Up there at Trnovo they told us some rubbish about murders and burnings in Racha. And I thought, I thought, Ha-ha! some nonsense they're talking: why do they have to come to *us* of all people and tell this kind of thing? Don't we know what Fascists are? *Maiku*, the murderers that they are! You'll see.' His voice was hoarse with anger, rasping. 'There are more than two hundred people in this village dead. Their throats cut . . .'

Later on we walked round the silent village, Kolya and Lala and I, and saw for ourselves. Lala gave me a leaflet the Germans had dropped from an aircraft some days after the village had been sacked. The leaflet was headed: 'Mass Killings in Racha'; and it was signed 'Fighters for True Freedom'. Dr. Goebbels himself might have been proud of it.

'. . . *When the Bosnian Moslem Volunteers*', it read, '*came into the village, they found a gruesome picture of slaughtered people. Only a few Jews who had been in the village had left with the partisans. The horror of this slaughtering is indescribable. At last the true features of the communist war for freedom have revealed themselves!'*

'Down with communism, Freedom for the people!'

'Never forget that the sufferings and misery, sickness and death of innocent victims will continue until the foul communist snake is expelled from our land....'

The burden of it was that the Bolshevist bandits had killed everyone in the village who had 'refused' to go with them into Bosnia. It seemed that cynicism could not reach greater depths. We walked round the village and saw for ourselves. In a large cottage the Germans had apparently used as company headquarters, for their unit signs were painted black upon the walls, we found an old man who had somehow survived and remained now one of the two or three living witnesses of what had been done. He was a little off his head, smiling and gesturing. He pointed to the place in the garden where he had found his wife with a hatchet gash in the back of her skull, lying on her face in the earth, the blood clotted round her. Further on there was a room where a mother and baby had been killed in bed; the mattress was stiff with blood where they had cut her throat and left her to bleed. One little girl, whose name was Slavitsa Tsrnitch, had run away through the woods to Grk with a story that written words simply do not grasp.

At first they had not been able to understand her childish gabbling; little by little they understood. This is what they understood. Slavitsa had been hit on the head with the back of a hatchet, but it seems that the blow was poorly aimed (perhaps the man was drunk) and caught her on the side of the neck; Slavitsa fell on the ground but recovered consciousness in time to know that her mother's body was pressed hard over hers, alive and struggling, and that blood was pouring all over her and over the ground from wounds on her mother that a man was opening with an axe. Slavitsa remembered this perfectly well, so she must have been conscious; but by some incredible sense of self-preservation she made no sound or movement; and she stayed like that all day until the evening, with the blood from her mother's corpse running down over her and seeping into the ground; in the evening she struggled out from under her mother's corpse and ran away into the woods. They said she was gradually coming back to sanity. They added that they feared she might be a little queer in her head for the rest of her life.

In a wrecked front garden we found a heap of ashes: the witnesses said that nine women and three children had been immolated there. Lala stirred the ashes with a careful hand; he had trained for medicine and knew something of anatomy. I remember that he fished out a baby's leather shoe, then the flat disc-part of a very young skull, a few bones that were recognizable. Kolya took pictures and said nothing. It appeared that someone in the village had turned traitor some time before, and had given away to the enemy the houses in which members of the staff and of my mission had been living. The old lady in Slobodan's house was dead; all the houses we had used were burned down; the tale of murders seemed endless.

RESISTANCE IN EASTERN EUROPE

By Hugh Seton-Watson

THE two opposed notions of resistance and collaboration are products of the Second World War. Small-scale banditry and full-scale guerrilla had of course been known before, especially in the three southern peninsulas of Europe—Spain, Italy and the Balkans. But it was usually accepted in European wars of the last century that in territory occupied in war the conquering power established a system of government with recognized rules, which were obeyed by the civilian population. To obey them was not treason to the lawful government, and there was no obligation to undertake sabotage or armed warfare against the occupying forces. The change is due to the 'total' nature of modern war and to the ideological nature of the Nazi German regime. Regarding Slavs and Jews as racially inferior, and both liberal and Marxist ideas as heresies to be extirpated, the Germans behaved in such a manner as to provoke resistance. Moreover, they met with nationalist and revolutionary fanaticism no less implacable than their own. When it is added that both the anti-German Power groups—the Anglo-Saxons and the Soviet Union—deliberately encouraged resistance, and supplied some of the means to make it effective, the general reasons are clear.

Resistance movements varied considerably, but certain basic conditions were required for all. The first was widespread national hatred of a foreign invader as such. This was almost universal among Czechs, Poles, Serbs and Greeks. It was much less strong, particularly in the first years, among Slovaks and Croats, who had received from the Germans a national independence which was not immediately felt to be a sham. It hardly existed at all among Rumanians and Bulgarians, whose states were allied with the Axis and were not subject to occupation. This was also true of Hungary up to March 1944, after which opinion undoubtedly changed. A second condition was a state of intolerable oppression, such as to drive people into action. This existed in Poland and Yugoslavia, and as a result of the famine of 1941-2 it existed also in Greece. Once resistance started, it brought reprisals, and these further increased hatred. In Czechoslovakia, however, these conditions did not exist to the same extent. The Czech peasants and workers enjoyed material prosperity, and thus showed little inclination to revolt. Persecution was concentrated against the intellectuals, who reacted by the means at their disposal but were not able to organize a mass movement. This brings us to the third condition, the nature of the country. In mountainous and forested areas, armed resistance on a large scale was possible, as the rebels were able to take refuge in remote places which it was too troublesome for the enemy, with the time and personnel at his disposal, to explore. Yugoslavia, Greece and Albania abound in such country, and Poland has suitable forests. The Czech lands, however, are thickly populated and low-lying: in the mountainous parts of Bohemia, Germans predominated. Where conditions do not favour armed resistance, sabotage, assassinations, espionage and the rescue of escaped Allied prisoners or baled-out pilots are possible forms of resistance.

Polish resistance had a military and a civilian origin. From the officers and soldiers who escaped through Rumania and Hungary to France, a small Polish army was created on Allied soil. At the same time a new government in exile was set up, led no longer by the politicians of the Pilsudski-Beck regime but by the great soldier General Sikorski and the representatives of the traditional Polish parties who had been opposed to the old regime—National Democrats, Socialists, People's (peasant) Party and Labour (Catholic) Party. After the first period of confusion, communications began to be established between the exiles and patriots inside Poland. Couriers could pass through Slovakia and Hungary without great difficulty, and radio communications were soon restored for shorter messages. Political ideas and organization plans began to be exchanged between Poland and the free world. The successive Polish governments in exile never lost this contact. After the Polish government moved from France to Britain, and the entry of Italy into the war reduced the value of the Slovakia–Hungary route, there was still contact by radio, and courier lines were organized, not only to send special messages but also to evacuate escaped Allied prisoners of war, right through Germany, France and Spain to Gibraltar. The Polish governments in exile were more constantly in touch with opinion at home than any of the others from Eastern Europe.

The official policy of the exiled government and of the leaders of the underground movement which grew up, was non-recognition of the German and Soviet occupations of Poland. The Polish state was considered still existing. The underground movement was to build up a secret government, administration, army, press, and even law courts and schools.

The German invasion of the Soviet Union greatly increased the military value of the Polish Home Army. During the following years the Poles performed valuable services by destroying rail communications in the rear of the German armies. At times they engaged in considerable battles with German troops. Owing to the different nature of the terrain, these were

RESISTANCE IN EASTERN EUROPE 91

never on the scale of the battles of the Balkan resistance movements. One of the most important battles took place near Kielce in March 1944, when a force of some 4,000 S.S. troops were engaged. The Polish underground movement also carried out sabotage in factories, and passed valuable information to the Allies. As Poles were employed in industry throughout the Reich, they were able to inform the Allies also about conditions inside Germany. All these activities of course brought brutal reprisals on the population. Already in May 1940 the Germans were sufficiently alarmed by Polish resistance to carry out a special repressive movement, of arrests and executions, known as the 'A.B. Action'. The Poles decided to fight reprisals with counter-reprisals. When Polish patriots were executed Polish resisters executed prominent German officials. Among those thus executed were Colonel Gassler, head of S.S. in Cracow, and General Kutschera, military commandant of Warsaw (1 February 1944). An attempt on Governor-General Hans Frank on 29 January 1944 was unsuccessful.

Special mention should be made of the resistance of the Jewish ghetto in Warsaw from 19 to 28 April 1943, which was independent of the Home Army's actions. Of the 400,000 Jews who had inhabited this ghetto at the end of 1940, some 300,000 had been deported to extermination camps. The remnant were being slowly starved. When the Germans decided to finish them off, they resisted desperately, with no weapons. Of 56,000 persons accounted for in the official German report, 7,000 were killed fighting, while an unknown additional number perished in the sewers or in burning buildings. German losses were fifteen dead. The German commander saw fit to congratulate his men on their heroism.

The climax of the Polish resistance was the battle for Warsaw. Just as Paris rose before the arrival of the American and British forces and freed itself from the Germans, so Warsaw rose as the Red Army approached. But there the resemblance ended. The Red Army did not help the Poles, and after sixty-three days of heroic resistance, Warsaw surrendered to the Germans on 3 October. The reasons for this horrible tragedy have never been made fully clear. Perhaps the Red Army failed to cross the Vistula because it could not, because German resistance was too strong. But this the Soviet leaders, and their native and foreign propagandists, cannot admit: to them the invincibility of the Red Army is a dogma. Or it is possible that the front in Poland was temporarily depleted in order to send troops round through the gap in the German defences left by Rumania's defection of 23 August, which opened all Central Europe to the Soviet forces. This would have been a perfectly defensible military manoeuvre, and was also recommended by political considerations, as it gave Soviet troops a chance to get into the Balkan peninsula before their Western allies and rivals. But this again has not been given as the reason by Soviet propaganda. This propaganda instead has denounced General Komarowski ('Bór'), the Polish commander-in-chief, for plunging into an adventure without co-ordinating his action with the Soviet command. It does not explain how the general could have done this, in the absence of diplomatic relations between his government and the Soviet government, except by asking his government in exile, with which he had wireless contact, to communicate through the British government, and by attempting to make local contact with Marshal Rokossovsky's forces. Both these means General Bór used. A Captain Kalugin of Rokossovsky's army reached Warsaw, and sent a message to Stalin, through the London radio link, explaining the situation in Warsaw and the needs of the defenders. It, and the repeated representations by the British authorities, remained unanswered. Yet up till the outbreak of the rising the Polish broadcasts of the 'Kościuszko station', directed by the Union of Polish Patriots in the U.S.S.R., were urging Warsaw to rise against the Germans.

The rising started on 1 August. It was ordered by the Polish government in exile, with the agreement of the Delegate in

Poland, the Home Council of Ministers under him, the Council of National Unity, and the Commander of the Home Army.[1] The regular units of the Home Army were three 'divisions' forming the 'Warsaw army corps' numbering 35,000 troops.[2] About one-third of their arms had been dropped by parachute from British and Polish aircraft based on the British Isles, one-third produced by underground arms plants organized by the resistance, and the rest mainly captured from the Germans in previous engagements. Apart from these regular units, most of the civil population, both male and female, joined in the rising, arranging hospitals, supplies, improvised fortifications and other essential services. The Germans used against them five divisions, including the S.S. 'Death's Head' and 'Viking' divisions. After a week they had succeeded in splitting up the Polish forces into four sections.

In response to Polish requests for help, the Allied governments asked the Soviet government to allow their aircraft to use Soviet aerodromes in order to operate a 'shuttle service' to help the insurgents. Whether from considerations of prestige[3] or other reasons, the Soviet government refused until 18 September. Meanwhile, Polish, British and South African pilots based on Italy made several journeys in unusually risky conditions and with extremely high casualties. This help was, of course, on far too small a scale to influence the battle. In mid-September the Red Army captured Praga, the suburb immediately opposite Warsaw across the Vistula. Contact was for a time established, Soviet artillery fire was co-ordinated with Polish fighting, and a few supplies were dropped by Soviet planes, most of which were broken because

[1] According to General Anders, *Army in Exile*, both he himself and General Sosnkowski were opposed to the rising.

[2] Zaremba, *Powstanie sierpniowe*, a pamphlet describing the rising, written by a prominent exiled socialist and based on the exiles' sources of information.

[3] The sensitiveness of the Red Army authorities in matters of prestige, and unwillingness to allow their allies to see the primitive conditions in which their troops lived, amounted almost to mania. It is not inconceivable that fear that American airmen might see the primitive airfields used for support operations near the front may have been an important factor in the refusal.

no parachutes were attached. At the end of the month the Soviet forces ceased their frontal attack, and decided to by-pass Warsaw in their advance. The Polish soldiers were reduced to two isolated groups, both cut off from the river.

When all resistance became hopeless, General Bór surrendered, in the hope of protecting the surviving civil population. The Germans had decided to recognize the Home Army as combatants, entitled to prisoner-of-war treatment. Eleven thousand soldiers, 942 officers and six generals were taken prisoner.

The first effect of defeat on the Yugoslavs, and especially on the Serbs, was depression and bewilderment. The Serbian Army, with its glorious traditions, had crumpled up in a few days. The state machine, which had seemed so powerful, and had been so heavy a burden on the citizen and peasant, was smashed to pieces. The political parties disintegrated. Families were divided by new frontiers. There was general disillusionment with the old political, military and bureaucratic chiefs, with the ruling class as a whole. There was disappointment with Britain, which all had admired, but which had given no help, and which now seemed threatened by great dangers of its own.

The earliest active resistance was in Bosnia, where Serbs began to defend themselves with arms against the Ustash bands of Pavelić. The leaders were in some cases regular army or Chetnik officers, in others simply local men of initiative and and courage. The groups included people of all social classes and most political opinions. Their motive was protection of themselves and their families. In so far as they had a common political idea, it was nationalism and hostility to the Croats as such.

The whole situation was transformed by the German invasion of Russia. Throughout Yugoslavia, and particularly in the Serbian provinces, sympathy for Russia was deep-rooted and traditional. The Serbs not only loved Russia, but greatly over-estimated her strength. The mood of the Serbian people now suddenly changed from bewildered despair to extravagant optimism. Now at last the Serbs had a great ally on land, who would destroy the Germans and liberate Yugoslavia within a few weeks. Meanwhile it was their duty to do what they could by resistance to help their 'big brother'. The new mood was fully exploited by the Yugoslav Communist Party, which for some time had been building up an underground military organization. The attack on Russia was the signal for action.

In July fighting began in Serbia. It was due partly to communist planning and partly to the spontaneous reaction of the peasants, who, carried away by patriotic fervour and the optimism of the moment, joined any bands in their neighbourhood—communist, Chetnik, regular army remnants, or any other—which seemed likely to fight the Germans. The enemy was taken by surprise, and his forces in Serbia were soon confined to the neighbourhood of Belgrade and the Morava valley.

The communist forces took the name of partisans.[1] They were directed by a 'Supreme Staff' which took all political and military decisions. The leader of the whole movement was Joseph Broz, the Secretary-General of the party, soon known by his *nom de guerre* of Tito. In accordance with the official Comintern policy of a People's Front of all patriotic forces against the invaders, the communist leaders approached the nationalist resistance groups with suggestions for common action. Tito had several conversations with Colonel Mihailović between September and November. Mihailović was against large-scale armed resistance, on the grounds that the Yugoslavs could not stand up to the Germans with inadequate equipment, and that the invaders would carry out merciless reprisals on the civil population. He believed that they should husband their resources, and await a more suitable moment when a general revolt could be launched. But when, despite

[1] The origin of the word 'partisan' is uncertain. It was used in the Russo-French campaign of 1812 to describe the guerrilla forces of Denis Davidov (see, *inter alia*, Tolstoy's *War and Peace*). It was also used in the American Civil War.

his wishes, fighting broke out on a large scale, he was forced to join in, and for a time his forces co-operated with the partisans.

This did not last long. There were many minor causes of conflict between the partisans and Mihailović, but the essential cause was the incompatibility of their political outlook. By the middle of November they were irreconcilable enemies. First the partisans beat Mihailović. Then during November the Germans, who had brought up considerable reinforcements, attacked on a serious scale, using armour and aircraft. By the end of the month the partisans were driven from their base at Užice, and fled in confusion to the south. Mihailović's forces also disintegrated, and many of his men joined the troops of General Nedić.

The defeat in Serbia taught the partisans that they could not face the Germans in open country, and that it was unwise to operate in areas where they could not protect the civil population. From now onwards they abandoned the plainlands, and withdrew to the central mountain massif of Bosnia, Hercegovina and Montenegro.

Three separate sections of Yugoslavia were of strategic interest to the enemy—the Slavonian plain, the Morava and Vardar valleys, and the Adriatic coast. The first affected communications between Austria and the Black Sea, and the second communications with Greece and Turkey, while the third was regarded as a possible objective for an Allied landing. Between these three sections lay the mountain stronghold of the partisans. Within this area the partisans were a constant menace to the invaders, and from the end of 1943 onwards they extended their activities outside it, into the strategic areas. Within the mountain area, movements of enemy troops and supplies always needed strong guards. The few railways and roads which cross the mountain barrier, and link the Danubian plain with the coast, were constantly cut. Attacks were also made, from the north Bosnian ranges and from the outlying base in the Slavonian hills, on the main Zagreb-

Belgrade railway, the most important single line in southeastern Europe. Factories and mines were raided and put out of action for weeks at a time. Smaller enemy units were surrounded and destroyed, and arms and ammunition stores captured. Considerable numbers of enemy troops, dearly needed on other fronts, were permanently tied down.[1]

The partisans, as far as possible, avoided engaging strong enemy forces. But from time to time the Axis Command undertook major 'cleaning-up' operations. The partisans then had to defend themselves, break up into smaller formations and scatter into the least accessible fastnesses. These enemy 'offensives' caused the partisans heavy losses, and on one occasion at least their main force narrowly escaped annihilation.[2] But each time they survived, and the cost to the enemy was also severe.

As the National Liberation Movement developed, and considerable territories were liberated, the practical tasks of civil administration became urgent. To deal with these, National Liberation Committees were created, for villages, districts and regions. In theory they were elected by the population: in practice the electors and candidates were inevitably limited to

[1] It is, of course, impossible to say what proportion of the enemy troops in Yugoslavia were tied down by partisan activities, what proportion by the fear of future Mihailović activities, and what proportion to ensure against possible future allied landings in the Balkans. Tito's propagandists exaggerate their number, and claim every enemy soldier serving in Yugoslavia as the result of their prowess. Writers determined to depict Tito and his men as pitch-black villains, e.g. F. A. Voigt, *Pax Britannica*, deny them any merit at all in holding down the enemy. The truth is obviously, in general terms, that the enemy was bound in any case to keep some troops there, but that their number was notably increased as a result of partisan action. It is also, of course, true that if Tito and Mihailović had not fought each other the enemy would have had to send still more troops. The blame for this cannot be exclusively placed on either side, but in my opinion more blame should attach to Mihailović than to Tito.

[2] The partisans themselves speak of seven main enemy 'offensives'. The first was in Serbia in 1941, the second in Bosnia in early 1942, the third in Montenegro in June 1942, the fourth in Hercegovina and the Dalmatian and Montenegrin hinterlands in January–April 1943, the fifth in Montenegro in June–July 1943. The sixth and seventh were in 1944, on a considerable scale but in less clearly defined areas. The fourth and fifth were the most severe. British officers were with the partisan forces during the first and the fifth. For enemy evidence on the fourth offensive see the Mussolini–Hitler correspondence, pp. 132–5, 142–3, 156–9.

supporters of the partisans, who in some liberated areas formed a majority, and in others only a small minority. The tasks of the committees were to direct agriculture, primitive industrial enterprises, and recruitment and supplies for the army. They also organized anti-illiteracy campaigns and political propaganda. Several newspapers were regularly published.

National Liberation Committees were also created in enemy-occupied areas by the underground Communist Party. Their functions included raising of funds and recruits for the partisan forces in the mountains, smuggling of food and medical supplies into liberated territory, and provision of information on enemy intentions and movements. They also undertook sabotage in some industrial centres and on some sectors of enemy-controlled railways. Throughout most of the war, the main partisan force was operating in the so-called 'passive regions' of Bosnia, Hercegovina, Dalmatia and Montenegro, regions which in normal times do not produce enough food to support their population. Thus a part of the partisans' supplies had to be smuggled, at great risk, by the peasants from the fertile plains of the Sava into the mountains. This is in itself an interesting indication of the degree of support which the partisans at this time enjoyed from the peasants.

In the summer of 1943 Mihailović left Montenegro, and with a much reduced force, now accompanied once more by the British mission, set up his headquarters in south-west Serbia. Here he made firmer contact with those Chetnik commanders who had remained at large in Serbia since the disaster of autumn 1941. These men had fought occasional skirmishes with German or Bulgarian troops, but avoided battle whenever possible. They had seldom fought partisans, because there had been few partisans in Serbia. From the spring of 1943 British missions had been attached to several of their headquarters. When Italy surrendered the Chetnik leaders who remained in Dalmatia, Hercegovina and Montenegro believed for a few weeks that British and American troops would land in Yugoslavia. But when it became clear that this would not happen, and that meanwhile the partisans had greatly strengthened themselves by acquiring Italian war material, they decided to co-operate with the Germans, who with the Ustash now overran the former Italian zone. Mihailović was pressed by the Allied Command to undertake some operations against Axis communications in Serbia. The only result achieved was the destruction of an important bridge over the Lim east of Višegrad, which was carried out by Mihailović's men in the presence of the British mission officers in the first week of October 1943.[1] But requests for attack on the more vital railways running through Serbia were evaded or refused.

Eventually a breach between the Allies and Mihailović became inevitable. No material support had been given to him since the summer of 1943. After a number of delays due to technical difficulties, in May 1944 the British mission was withdrawn from Mihailović. A small American mission stayed some months longer. During the summer the penetration of the partisans into Serbia caused even the independent Serbian Chetniks to collaborate with the German and Bulgarian occupation troops. When the Red Army entered Serbia, some Chetnik units at the last moment turned their arms against the Germans and went over to the Russians. Others retreated westwards with the Germans. When finally in April 1945 the Germans abandoned Yugoslav territory, some Chetniks re-

[1] The Višegrad exploit was attributed in error to the partisans by a B.B.C. broadcast. This mistake caused great rage among supporters of Mihailović. They are perhaps not aware that in 1941-2 B.B.C. broadcasts attributed to Mihailović's forces many exploits of Tito. The B.B.C. was also used by the Yugoslav government in exile to announce decorations of Chetnik officers who were fighting with the partisans against the enemy. Thus the B.B.C. broadcasts won the hatred of both sides in the Yugoslav civil war. Personally, I consider that the B.B.C. deserves little blame for this. It was obliged to accept the information given to it by those more familiar with Yugoslav affairs. These in turn had to rely on irregular and imperfect sources of information. In my opinion the services of the B.B.C. in maintaining the morale of occupied Europe far outweigh its mistakes, and those British who accept with enthusiasm the criticisms of foreign sectional interests against the British radio only expose their own lack of judgment.

treated with them, and surrendered to the British or Americans in Italy or Austria. Others, including Mihailović himself, remained in Bosnia.

It would be wrong to conclude from these facts that Mihailović, and the Chetniks who recognized his leadership, were 'pro-German'. He hated the Germans, and was a friend of Britain, which he believed would win the war. He believed, however, that the government in exile, and its British hosts, wished him to fight the communists. He simply refused to believe that the Western Powers considered the Soviet Union as an ally, or wished in Yugoslavia a united front of all patriots against the Axis. When he was assured of this officially, he brushed it away as a piece of diplomatic cunning by the British to 'keep the Soviets sweet'. Up to the end, he gave concrete proof of his sympathy for the Western Allies, of which the most important was the rescue of a large number of Allied pilots who had baled out over Yugoslavia on flights to Central Europe. These men were treated with great hospitality, and delivered to the Allied authorities even after the Allied governments had broken relations with him.[1]

After the defeat of April 1941, Greece was occupied by troops of three Powers. The greater part of the country was ruled by the Italians. The Germans held Crete and some of the other islands and the province of Evros on the Turkish frontier. They also had garrisons in Salonica and Athens. The Bulgarians had eastern Macedonia and Thrace.

In the first year of occupation the Greeks suffered more from economic than from military causes. Greece could never feed its population. The occupiers made little provision to feed the conquered, and blamed the results on the Allied blockade. In the winter of 1941–2 there was starvation in Athens. At the pressing request of the Greek government in exile, the Western

---

[1] With Mihailović's ready co-operation, American aircraft evacuated airmen from landing-strips in his territory as late as the summer of 1944.

Allies agreed to make an exception. Grain was supplied from Canada and the United States, and distributed with German permission by the International Red Cross.

The defeat of the Greek army had also been the defeat of the Metaxas royalist dictatorship, which had had many enemies. The Axis Powers were able for a time to exploit this to their advantage. They showed some tolerance to republicans. Though the latter sympathized strongly with the Western Powers, the fact that they were not maltreated by the occupiers at least removed an incentive to active resistance. It was the starvation of the first winter which created bitter hatred of the Axis, especially in the towns. The organization best fitted for active resistance was the Communist Party. Like its sister party in Yugoslavia, it had opposed 'imperialist warmongers' of either side until June 1941, but in the last months it had been somewhat more anti-Axis than anti-British. Both the obvious facts and the mood of the people showed that those who most gravely threatened the Greek people were the Axis. When Hitler attacked Russia the communists' doubts were removed. They began to organize a Popular Front to oppose the Axis. In September 1941 was formally founded the National Liberation Front (E.A.M.). It included the Communist Party (K.K.E.), three communist-controlled puppet parties, and two small but genuine parties.[1] It put forward the usual Popular Front programme of national independence, democratic liberties and resistance to the enemy. It was to organize civil and armed resistance—strikes, non-co-operation and guerrilla bands.

Guerrilla was an old Greek tradition. The Greek mountains have probably never been entirely free of bandits. When the Greek army surrendered, a good many arms were hidden. During 1942 armed bands came into being in central Greece. In April 1942 E.A.M. announced the formation of a People's

[1] The most important was the socialist group led by Professor Svolos and Mr. Tsirimokos.

Liberation Army (E.L.A.S.) but this did not really take shape until the following year. In the autumn of 1942 the most important bands were led by a communist, Velouchiotis, who bore as a pseudonym the name of the old Greek war-god Ares, and by Colonel Napoleon Zervas. Ares's band was the nucleus from which developed E.L.A.S., the Communist Party's private army. Zervas's forces owed a somewhat uncertain allegiance to a political organization called E.D.E.S. (National Democratic Greek Union). The nominal head of E.D.E.S. was General Plastiras, the republican officer who had made the *coup d'état* of 1922, and was living in exile in Vichy France. E.D.E.S. stood for a republican, democratic, non-socialist regime. The course of the resistance war, and the growing power of the communists, made it more anti-communist than anything else. There was always a certain difference between E.D.E.S. leaders in Athens and Zervas's command in the mountains. This difference became wider as time went on.

In the autumn of 1942 a party of British parachutists was dropped in Greece, and made contact with both Ares and Zervas. On 24 November the combined bands attacked the important railway bridge over the Gorgopotamos river, and British sappers blew it up. In the following months British parties were dropped to a series of bands in Greece. As in Yugoslavia, wireless contact with Middle East headquarters made possible the supply of arms, explosives and other supplies by air. By the summer of 1943 there were two large resistance forces in the country.

E.L.A.S. had perhaps 20,000 men. It was well organized in the Pindus, western Thessaly and central Macedonia, and had some forces in the Peloponnese. It had a central headquarters, to which was attached a British mission, with authority over the British missions attached to various regional E.L.A.S. commands.[1] The commander of the British mission for the

[1] The most authoritative work in English on the Greek resistance and Greek politics immediately after the war is C. M. Woodhouse, *Apple of Discord*. A useful shorter account is MacNeill, *The Greek Dilemma*.

first year was Brigadier E. Myers, and for the second year Colonel C. M. Woodhouse. E.L.A.S. commands at regional and national level were organized on a tripartite basis. There was a military commander, a political representative, and a 'kapetanios'. The kapetanios was responsible for supplies and morale, the military commander for the conduct of operations, while the political representative was thè real chief of the whole force.

The forces of Zervas were less numerous, less well organized, and had no such complicated hierarchy. Their stronghold was Epirus. There were also some minor resistance organizations in other areas.

The immediate concern of the British Command in the Middle East was to increase the commitments of the Axis troops all over the Mediterranean area. Piraeus was used by Axis ships supplying the army in Libya. Greek organizations were encouraged to sabotage this shipping. The Axis by 1943 suffered from an all-round shortage of manpower. Every additional unit tied down in Greece relaxed pressure on the Allies in North Africa and in Russia. Moreover the Axis had to reckon not only with Greek resistance but also with the possibility of an Allied landing on the Greek coast. In the summer of 1943 the British Command ordered a special effort of guerrilla warfare and sabotage of communications, in order to attract a maximum of Axis troops into Greece. The defeat of the Axis in Tunisia was clearly to be followed by a landing somewhere in the Mediterranean. The guerrilla operations in Greece were to be a 'cover plan' to make the Axis expect action in Greece while action was in fact being prepared for Sicily. Maximum guerrilla effort required maximum unity between the bands. The British mission therefore pressed the Greeks to make a 'National Bands Agreement' for common action against the enemy, despite political disagreements. E.L.A.S. at first consented, but then refused to sign. Individual bands, however, including local E.L.A.S. bands, with the advice and in some cases leadership of British officers, did substantially harry the enemy and so help Allied military plans.

As the tide of war turned, it became more important for E.L.A.S. to eliminate their rivals than to combat the enemy, who was clearly not going to win. Ultimate political power in Greece required also that E.L.A.S. should minimize its casualties. From this time onwards, E.L.A.S. showed growing reluctance to carry out the operations proposed by the British mission. Zervas on the other hand was co-operative. With 5,000 men to 20,000 of E.L.A.S., and concentrated in a strategically unimportant part of Greece, he could not hope to win postwar power unaided. British help was essential to him, so he must gain British gratitude.

Behind these military reasons for friction between the British and E.L.A.S., and British support to Zervas, lay deeper political reasons. All communists hated Britain as the greatest Imperial Power, and Greek communists were no exception. British soldiers might get on well with individual communists, but the British government could not favour the establishment of a communist, Russian-influenced government in the Eastern Mediterranean.

Perhaps more important even than this was the fact that Britain had obligations to King George II of Greece. The King had decided to continue the war at Britain's side after the Germans had decided to support Italy, though the prospects were dark, and many conservative Greeks would have preferred surrender. The British government in general, and Mr. Churchill in particular, felt bound to see that the King returned to Greece. What the Greeks should then decide was their affair, but Britain must not let down a gallant Allied monarch.

When the Italian army surrendered in September 1943, some of the Italian units in Greece decided to go over to the guerrillas. It was E.L.A.S. which got their arms. Being now very much stronger, E.L.A.S. was less dependent on British supplies of arms, and therefore less bound to please the British. Now was the time to deal with its rivals. In October E.L.A.S. attacked Zervas. No more British supplies of arms were sent to E.L.A.S., though British missions remained, and food and clothing were still dropped to E.L.A.S. units. British supplies to Zervas were increased. It was only this which saved his forces from annihilation. The civil war came to an end in February 1944, when British pressure persuaded E.L.A.S. to sign the Plaka agreement, delimiting the respective territorial zones of E.L.A.S. and E.D.E.S.[1] This only stopped the shooting. The two sides remained implacably opposed.

Albania between the wars differed from the general social and political pattern of Eastern Europe. If the other Balkan countries were in many respects backward, Albania had hardly changed since the fifteenth century. There were important differences between the north and south. The northerners (Ghegs) spoke a somewhat different dialect from the southerners (Tosks). More important was the difference of social and political organization. The Ghegs formed a tribal society, comparable to that of the Scottish clansmen before the 'Forty-five. Most were Moslem, but one important tribe, the Miridites, led by the Markagjoni family, were Catholics. The land of the tribes was mountainous, poor and relatively overpopulated. The Tosks were led by big landowners, or beys. The land was more fertile in their territory, especially the coastal plain with its substantial towns Tirana, Durazzo and Valona. The system of land tenure was a Moslem type of feudalism. The majority of the Tosk population owned little or no land. Industry was very backward, but such as it was, it was in the Tosk region.

When the Italians occupied Albania, they made Premier a bey named Shevket Vrlaci, who had once been a supporter of

[1] The texts of the National Bands Agreement and the Plaka agreement are contained in Woodhouse, op. cit.

Zog. In the Italo-Greek war some Albanian forces fought under Italian command. The victorious Axis annexed to Albania the whole Kosovo area and the western fringe of Macedonia. In both areas the population was mostly Albanian. But these gains did not really popularize the Italians. The Albanian mountaineers resented any sort of central authority, and if it was foreign the resentment was greater. Moreover a generation of relative independence had shown them that the main enemy of their country was Italy. Thus the Albanians were in the right mood for resistance: they only needed an organizer.

This was provided by the small group of communist intellectuals, educated in France, Italy, Yugoslavia or Russia, and having contact with the more powerful communist organizations of Yugoslavia and Greece. In accordance with the over-all Comintern directive to form Popular Fronts, the communists summoned a meeting of Albanian patriots at Peza in September 1942. At this meeting was founded the National Liberation Movement (L.N.C.). It had the usual programme of armed resistance to the invaders and political and social democracy after victory.

Soon after the Peza meeting and foundation of L.N.C., the conservative Albanian opposition to the Italians organized itself in a National Front (Balli Kombetar). This was led by prominent persons who before the Italian invasion had opposed King Zog. The movement was republican and mildly liberal. It was also strongly nationalist, and wished to keep for Albania the provinces annexed to it by the Axis in 1941.

As news of the Albanian resistance trickled through to Allied territory, the British military authorities in the Middle East began to take an interest. The official attitude of the British government to Albanian independence had been stated by Mr. Eden. But as Yugoslavia and Greece, Britain's allies, had lost territory to Albania, and some of their leaders hoped to annex Albanian territory even beyond the frontiers of April 1941, Albania's situation after ultimate Allied victory remained obscure. The British Command therefore decided to establish contact with Albanian resisters and help them to make themselves a nuisance to the Axis, but to avoid political commitments. Two British officers, Major Maclean and Captain Smiley, were parachuted to northern Greece, and thence made their way into Albania. They first met supporters of the Balli Kombetar, and then reached L.N.C. territory. They attended a L.N.C. conference at Labinot near Elbasan in July 1943. By this time communist control of L.N.C. was already very strong. There were also close links with the Yugoslav partisans. L.N.C. were becoming more preoccupied with the struggle against their internal Balli rivals than with the fight against the Italians, who were obviously losing the war. The British mission was concerned to attack the enemy, and for this purpose did not mind whether Balli or L.N.C. forces did the fighting. But Hoxha and his friends viewed with suspicion any British help to Balli forces, believing that this was directed not against the Italians but against themselves. The British mission wished to unite Balli and L.N.C. in common resistance to the enemy. This also commended itself to Abbas Kupi, still a member of the L.N.C. central committee. At Kupi's suggestion a conference of delegates from both movements met at Mukai near Tirana in July 1943. The news of the overthrow of Mussolini roused them all to a patriotic enthusiasm in which mutual suspicions were for a time swept away. They agreed to fight together against the Italians and to form a directing committee with an equal number of members from each side.

The collapse of Italy brought a national revolt. Recruits poured in to the guerrilla forces. A large part of the country, including such lesser towns as Korcha, Elbasan and Berat, was liberated. Two Italian divisions went over to the guerrillas, who took their arms. Only the ports and Tirana and Scutari were still in enemy hands. At this point the Germans intervened. They could not leave the Adriatic coast open to an

Allied landing: they must therefore take over the occupation of Albania. At the end of September German troops entered the country by air and from Macedonia. Soon the guerrillas were driven out of the towns and back into the hills.

During the winter, the number of guerrillas fell. The enlarged British mission, under Brigadier Davies, was ambushed in January 1944 by Albanian quislings and most of its members were captured. Kupi dissolved his forces and remained at large with only a small group. The L.N.C. forces were mostly concentrated in the south. This had always been their most promising region, as wide social differences and the penetration of some European political ideas made the people accessible to their propaganda. In the north, personal loyalty to the chieftain remained the main force.

In the spring L.N.C. renewed its efforts, and fought against Germans as well as rival Albanians. In May there was a battle against a mixed German-Balli force numbering some 2,000. At this time it was estimated that L.N.C. had some 13,000 troops in regular units and several thousand more in scattered groups. L.N.C. forces were becoming something like an army, on the model of the Yugoslav partisans. They now took the title National Liberation Army, adopted by Tito's partisans more than a year earlier. In May they also set up an Anti-Fascist Council of National Liberation—modelled on the Yugoslav A.V.N.O.J.—and a committee which formed a provisional government. Enver Hoxha became the head of this government. Like the Yugoslavs at Jajce in November 1943, the Albanian Council in their May meeting, held at Permet, denounced the exiled king and forbade him to return until the people had freely decided whether it wanted a monarchy or a republic. Zog was denounced as having been a dictator and a helper of fascist Italy. It was quite clear which way Enver Hoxha intended 'the people' to decide.

The main resistance effort in Czechoslovakia was performed

by the Slovaks in 1944. The north and centre of Slovakia, being mountainous, sparsely populated and poor in communications, provided good terrain. As the Red Army approached the Slovak frontiers, enthusiasm for the 'Slav brothers' grew. It was fostered by the underground communists and by Russian parachutists. Partisan bands began to appear. Some were led by Red Army officers, and one was stiffened by a number of escaped French prisoners of war, who specially distinguished themselves. In the cities the communist organization became more active in propaganda and in recruitment of partisans.

The communists were not the only force in Slovakia opposed to the Axis. An important minority of the Slovak middle class and peasantry had before 1938 supported the Agrarian Party. The Slovak agrarians had wished to preserve the Czechoslovak republic, though with greater autonomy for Slovakia within it. When their rivals, the fascist People's Party, obtained power with Hitler's help, and the 'independent state' of Mgr. Tiso was set up, they did not change their view. They had most support among the Protestant minority in central Slovakia, especially in Turiec country, the birthplace of nineteenth-century Slovak nationalism. Some of their leaders communicated from time to time by secret channels with the Czechoslovak government in exile. As the Germans retreated on all fronts, and increased their demands from Slovakia, even the leaders of the Slovak fascist regime grew restive. Mach, the Minister of the Interior and once the most fanatical of the Slovak fascists, deliberately overlooked the activities of the underground communists and the middle-class pro-Czech politicians. The commander-in-chief of the Slovak army, General Catlos, toyed with the idea of taking his forces over to the Russians. Three colonels—Golian, Vesel and Ferenčik —planned a rising of the army against the Germans.

During the winter of 1943-4, whether at the Tehran conference or after, it seems to have been decided that the Red

Army should have the responsibility for liberating Czechoslovakia. The Western Powers had other commitments. A few aircraft flew from Italy to a Slovak airfield, and British and American missions were sent to keep the Allied Command informed of events. But material help from the West was negligible.

The Russians on the other hand had the opportunity and the obligation to help. Their efforts were disappointing. Attempts had been made in mid-August to co-ordinate the action of the Slovak forces with that of the Red Army, through the Czechoslovak government. The Russians had been evasive. When the rising had begun, they sent the airborne brigade of Colonel Přikryl, part of the Czechoslovak forces in the Soviet Union. Přikryl's men fought bravely, but they were too few. The Soviet attitude to the Slovak rising was less brutally cynical than to the Warsaw rising which was going on at the same time, but in practice it amounted to the same thing. The Slovak patriots, like those of Warsaw, were left to their fate.

Free Slovakia had at first one advantage, that its frontier in the south was safe. The Hungarians, at this time engaged in preparing their surrender, did not act against Slovakia, and no German troops passed through Hungarian territory to attack. During October, however, the Germans made a serious attack on Free Slovak territory, and after the Szálasi *coup d'état* of 15 October they could use Hungarian territory as well. On 27 October Banska Bystrica, the 'capital' of Free Slovakia, was taken. After this only guerrilla resistance was possible. The regular army units which had joined the rising were demoralized and melted away. The advancing Germans wreaked savage reprisals, massacring civilians and burning villages. The Slovak partisans and the remnant of Přikryl's forces took to the mountains. During the winter they suffered terrible privations, but some survived until the Red Army advanced in March. Among those who perished were the officers and men of the British and American liaison missions, led by Major Sehmer and Lieutenant Green. They were captured by the Germans in uniform, but shot, contrary to the rules of war. The Germans also captured and executed both Golian and General Viest, whom the exiled government had sent to command the rising.

In the Czech Protectorate conditions did not favour armed resistance. There was an underground organization, in fairly regular contact with the exiled government. Information was passed to the Allies which may have been of value. It is also possible that passive resistance and 'go-slow' tactics by the Czech workers harmed the enemy. This cannot be proved. The industrial workers were relatively privileged under the Nazi regime. Many seem to have carried on their jobs without bothering about politics, waiting for the Great Powers to liberate their country for them. The communists were against resistance until Russia was attacked. Then they were for sabotage of the German war effort. But not very much sabotage seems to have been done. The peasants too, while remaining Czech patriots at heart, submitted to the occupation, and materially did quite well out of it. Those who resisted most, and suffered most, were the intellectual and the civil servants and army officers of the old republic. Many were arrested, tortured, sent to concentration camps or executed. The 38,000 executions of Czechs during the six years of Nazi rule came mostly from the middle class. If it seems that the Czech resistance effort was less heroic than that of Poles or South Slavs, and even that many Czechs prospered in the land furthest removed from all the fronts, it must not be thought that life was easy for them. Physical and mental wounds of the Czech people will take a long time yet to heal.

The most sensational act of resistance was the assassination of Heydrich in May 1942. Carried out by parachutists sent from England, it was a brilliant stroke, but it cost the Czech people dear in reprisals. In the summer of 1944 partisan bands began to appear in the Moravian hills. They were mostly organized by communists. Among them were Red Army parachutists and even some escaped British prisoners of war. Their struggle was hard and brave, but the total effect of their actions was small. The climax was the rising in Prague in May 1945.

It soon became obvious that the mass resistance movements were fighting not only against the Germans, but for aims of their own. These can be not unfairly simplified into two alternatives—restoration of the pre-invasion regime or a social and political new deal. When the Germans invaded Russia, a further division appeared, between those who looked for liberation to the Anglo-Saxon Powers or to the Soviet Union. The two divisions were not identical. All who looked to the Soviet Union desired a new deal, but not all who desired a new deal looked to the Soviet Union. All who wished to restore the old regime preferred the Anglo-Saxons to the Soviets, but not all who sympathized with the Anglo-Saxons wished to restore the old regime.

These differences are especially important in the case of Poland. A united resistance movement was formed at a time when the Soviet Union still had friendly relations with Germany, and within the resistance the 'new deal' elements, represented by the peasant movement and the socialists, were stronger than the supporters of the old order. Moreover, the Polish government in exile was not led by representatives of the Pilsudski-Beck regime.

By contrast, in Yugoslavia resistance was in a very primitive stage, and in Greece it had not begun, when Russia was invaded. Russia had always been regarded by the people of Yugoslavia, especially by the Serbs, as their natural protector, and the Greeks had often benefited from Russian friendship in the past, whereas to the Poles Russia was a traditional enemy. Thus a political party looking to Russia was likely to win strong support in Yugoslavia and considerable support in Greece, but had little prospect in Poland. For these various reasons then the communists were able in the Balkans to put themselves at the head of the 'new-dealers', but were unable to in Poland.

When the communists began their resistance, they had the same aim as always in the past—political power. This was to be obtained by two means—by strengthening the defence of the U.S.S.R., 'the territorial base of the world revolution', through diversion of German troops from the front to crush rebellion in their rear, and by turning the war of liberation against the occupying forces into a civil war against their own ruling class. In liberated areas they set up their own administration, which not only organized supplies for the fighting men but prepared itself to take over political power in the country when the Germans were defeated. At first they had to fight, in addition to the invaders, only the quisling forces of the first four categories described above. But as the communists' political organization became a serious rival to the pre-invasion order, so the loyal supporters of the exiled governments grew to regard the communists as a more dangerous enemy than the Germans. Another cause of bitterness was enemy reprisals. These fell most severely on those who had property to lose. Destruction of property did not worry the communists much, because most of their supporters had little, and any weakening of their future rivals was of advantage to them. But the wealthy peasants feared reprisals, and tried to prevent actions which would incur them.[1] From this it was not difficult to take the further step of armed collaboration with the occupying forces against the communists.

[1] For some interesting reflections on the subject of resistance movements, see article by Julian Amery in *The Nineteenth Century and After*, March 1949.

ARREST IN FRANCE

By Xan Fielding

EARLY next morning, leaving Lizzy still asleep, I went off to contact Roger and Christine in the village of Seyne a mile further down the valley. I found them both in the 'safe house' which had been described to me during my briefing in Algiers as belonging to the local grocer, Monsieur Turre. Since his name was in fact Turrel, I was glad I had with me a member of the maquis band who was known to him; for without this personal introduction I should never have been admitted into that valiant but cautious household, even though headquarters had obligingly given me at least the correct password.

The Turrels were typical of the hundreds of thousands of 'small' people all over France, whose role in the resistance was unspectacular but beyond measure valuable. Without any of the vainglorious conceit that characterized some of the self-styled *chefs*, and with no thought of ultimate reward or glory, they had placed their home at our disposal since the beginning of the occupation, thereby endangering their lives far more than any member of an armed maquis band. Yet neither their expression nor manner betrayed the slightest sign of the precarious existence they were leading. Monsieur Turrel, fat and jovial in a waistcoat three sizes too small for him, looked as carefree and contented as an actor in a documentary film.

He offered me a glass of wine while his wife, with peasant impassivity, went upstairs to wake up Roger and Christine.

Headquarters had given me no description of Roger, so I was not prepared for his great height and apparent youth. I had pictured him as a swarthy middle-aged man, sufficiently nondescript to be able to pass unnoticed in a crowd; instead I was faced with a smiling young giant whose coltish appearance was exaggerated by sloping shoulders and an easy resilient poise. These features, to begin with, obscured the contradictory qualities of leadership and modesty with which he subsequently impressed me. It was only later I realized that for him resistance was tantamount to a new religion, which he had been preaching and practising with remarkable success for over three years.

Christine was similarly dedicated, and appeared to be more obviously so only, perhaps, because I already knew something of her exploits in the past. Ever since the military collapse of her own country, Poland, she had been employed on the most hazardous missions in other parts of occupied Europe; and this reputation of hers had led me to expect in her the heroic attributes which I fancied I immediately divined beneath her nervous gestures and breathless manner of speech. Not that she in any way resembled the classical conception of a female spy, even though she had the glamorous figure that is conventionally associated with one; but this she preferred to camouflage in an austere blouse and skirt which, with her short, carelessly-combed dark hair and the complete absence of make-up on her delicately-featured face, gave her the appearance of an athletic art student.

She and Roger were an imposing pair; and since I was still in uniform, which in the circumstances I despised as lay clothing, I felt rather like a novice in the presence of a prior and prioress as we climbed up to the dropping-zone together after breakfast.

I felt not only strange to the job but also strange to the

country; for I had been out of Europe for six years, and the overnight transition from Asiatic and African landscapes to Alpine scenery left me momentarily stunned with delight. These mountains, though higher, were tamer than the crags of Crete; motor roads ran through them; and instead of the gaunt stony slopes over which I had grown accustomed to stumble, which barely offered pasture for goats, we walked now through meadows which in peace-time must have been rich grazing ground for cows—animals which for so long I had not even visualized that to me the species almost seemed to have become extinct.

Our conditions of work, too, were so manifestly different that I could scarcely believe I was on a clandestine mission. The only occupied territory that I had so far known was a dangerous and uncomfortable Tom Tiddler's Ground, where we led a hole-in-corner existence, surrounded by an ever-present and ubiquitous enemy. But here, where whole areas the size of counties were to all intents and purposes free, we could sleep secure indoors and walk, and even drive, for miles with no fear of an ambush round the corner.

Collecting the material that had been dropped with us during the night therefore presented no problem. We took the whole leisurely day over it, while Roger told me something about the development and present state of the resistance movement in Région Deux. His clear, concise summary confirmed what I had already begun to suspect: that the arrival of Lizzy and myself at this late stage of the war was an embarrassment rather than a help—there was no specific task for either of us. As far as Lizzy was concerned, this was just as well; for a doctor had examined him, diagnosed two cracked vertebrae and arranged for him to be admitted into the nearest Maquis hospital. But I could not be so conveniently disposed of. Rather than abandon me to boredom and inactivity, however, Roger generously suggested that I accompany him next day on a tour of his area.

'At least it'll give you some idea of what's going on,' he concluded.

And so, while Christine was despatched to the Italian frontier where she was organizing the mass defection of a Polish unit that had been pressed into Wehrmacht service, Roger and I drove off to his wireless station which was installed in a house a few kilometres outside the village. There, after an excellent dinner with the two French operators, we spent a comfortable night before setting out next morning in a private car with a driver and another colleague, a French major, who was introduced to me as 'Chasuble'.

The car, I believe, was ostensibly a Red Cross vehicle and the driver had a special licence, so that there was little danger of our being stopped or questioned in any of the enemy garrisons on our route. And even if we were checked, we only had to show our identity cards and other personal documents. While I was examining mine so as to make sure they were all there, I counted out the money I had brought in with me. Such a large sum might have looked suspicious if discovered in the pockets of one man, so Roger and Chasuble between them relieved me of over half of it; and as an additional precaution we agreed that, if stopped, we would disclaim any knowledge of each other and say that we were hitch-hikers who had been individually given a lift.

It was full of confidence, then, that I started out on my first journey through enemy-occupied France, my only worry being the baggy Charlie Chaplin trousers I was wearing without braces—for since the container with my clothes and personal equipment had not been found, I had had to borrow a suit from one of the operators. In these flapping garments, I felt almost a freak beside Roger and the dapper Chasuble, a suave, silent man with greying hair, neat dark features and a tired, urbane manner.

Our drive was so uneventful and enjoyable that I had to

keep reminding myself that I was not on holiday but on active service—a fact which escaped me at each of the delightful villages where, while Roger conferred with the local leaders, I drank a glass of wine outside the café under the plane trees. It was only on the way back, as we were approaching the large garrison town of Digne, about noon the following day, that the wail of an air-raid siren put me in mind once more of the war.

Since the enemy were in the habit of manning additional road blocks during a raid, we got out of the car and asked the driver to pick us up again at the opposite end of the town; meanwhile we took cover with the rest of the civilian population. As soon as the All Clear sounded we mingled with the crowds emerging from the shelters, made our way along the busy streets, and found the car waiting where we had arranged to meet it. We got in and started off on the last lap of our journey back to Seyne.

We had not gone more than a few hundred yards, however, when we noticed straight ahead of us a barricade across the road, and beside it some figures in Feldgrau uniform with a machine-gun trained on the bridge over the river which we were due to cross. 'I wonder what they're up to,' muttered our driver. None of us, in fact, had accounted for this unexpected obstacle; but since our car must have already been observed, we could not turn back. We therefore drove on without altering our speed, until we were brought to a halt by one of the enemy section standing in the middle of the road with his rifle at the port.

Our feigned expressions of innocent surprise were wasted on the soldiers who immediately surrounded us and motioned us out of the car. Nor could we make ourselves understood to them since they spoke no French, no German, no European language at all. For they were Caucasian troops whom the enemy, short of man-power, were now employing on garrison duties. Their sub-human Mongolian features remained inscrutable while they searched our vehicle and prodded us to see if we were armed; and their expressions did not alter when we showed them one by one our identity cards, labour permits and ration coupons. They clearly could not make head or tail of these documents; but impressed, no doubt, by their number and the official stamps on them, they indicated with non-committal grunts that we would be allowed to continue on our way.

We were on the point of driving off, when a second car drew up behind us and I heard Roger mutter out of the corner of his mouth. It was not his tone of voice that set me tingling with alarm—for he had purposely kept it under control—but his single word of warning:

'Gestapo!'

The newcomers had apparently turned up with orders for the road block section to withdraw now that the air-raid was over; but seeing our car halted there as well, they at once turned their attention to us, and the young civilian who was evidently in charge started questioning us—to my secret horror, in perfect French.

Though that language had once been my mother tongue, after so many years' absence from France I could no longer converse in it with practised ease. My vocabulary and accent were still sufficiently convincing for me to be taken for a native by any German I might have accidentally met, and even, in a short conversation, by a Frenchman; but I was not confident of my ability to delude for any length of time a trained local interrogator, which this young *milicien* clearly was. It was therefore with considerable trepidation—which manifested itself physically, I regret to say, by an uncontrollable tremor in my right leg—that I answered the questions he started firing at me:

'Where do you come from?'
'Forcalquier.'
'Where are you going?'

'To Gap.'

'What for?'

In spite of the care I had devoted to my 'cover story' in Algiers, I had never imagined I would really have to use it, and so had not prepared myself in advance for the contingency I now had to meet. I hesitated for the fraction of a second before giving the first reply that came into my head:

'To see about a house for my parents. They're old and sick, and want to get away from the bombing at home.'

'Where's your home?'

'Nîmes.'

'What's your job?'

'I'm clerk in the Electricity Works.'

'Let's have a look at your papers.'

I handed over my wallet, which contained all my money as well, and as he examined the documents he asked:

'What about these two fellows with you? Who are they?'

'I don't know,' I answered—readily enough this time, for I had expected the question—'they were already in the car when I stopped it and asked for a lift.'

Still with his eyes on my papers, he murmured:

'So you're a clerk in the Electricity Works at Nîmes, are you?'

'That's right.'

'Then can you explain why this'—and he waved one of the papers in my face—'is out of date? There's no stamp on it for this month.'

Naturally, I had no explanation to give.

'I'll deal with you later,' he said, pocketing my wallet; 'go on, get in.' And as he motioned one of the soldiers to escort me to the Gestapo car, he switched his attention to Roger and Chasuble.

I was bundled into the empty back seat; and as I sat down, the soldier next to the civilian driver in front turned round and—rather unnecessarily, for I was far too bewildered to move—covered me with his machine-pistol.

I suppose I should have forthwith cudgelled my brains for some plausible excuse for being in possession of papers which, thanks to an oversight on the part of our Algiers staff, were invalid; but my mind was a blank, and I found myself instinctively trying to divert my attention from the man with the gun by staring with involuntary intensity at the back of the driver's neck—or rather at the place where his neck should have been, for he appeared to be one of those monstrous men described by Othello, 'whose heads do grow beneath their shoulders'. He sat there motionless, his ears barely visible above the black hump of his back, so that I was unable to tell what he looked like until, glancing accidentally at the driving-mirror, I saw reflected there a single eye of hideous malevolence which gazed without blinking straight into mine.

I knew it was only half his face I saw, but this optical illusion which had transformed him into an apparent Cyclops unnerved me so much that the tremor in my leg, which had stopped as soon as I sat down, immediately started again. Fear took the form of a sense of abject loneliness, and I realized to my shame that I was almost consciously longing for my two companions to be arrested with me so that I should not have to face whatever was to come entirely by myself.

There seemed little likelihood of my cowardly prayer being answered, however. Both Roger and Chasuble appeared utterly unconcerned as they showed their documents and emptied their pockets, the former with an expression of surprised amusement on his face, the latter with a look of contempt. As I watched them with admiration, I could not help wondering if they were genuinely less frightened than I was, and if not, how they were able to conceal their feelings with such a brilliant display of self-assurance. But just as I was beginning to derive a little courage from their example, I sensed—not from their attitude, which remained unchanged, but from a sudden sparkle of triumph in the eyes of their interrogator—that something had gone wrong. Exactly what,

I could not say—until, unexpectedly, I was myself summoned from the car to be questioned again.

'You say you don't know these two men?'

'No, I don't,' I answered; 'I've never seen them before in my life.'

The next question was addressed to all three of us:

'Then can you explain how these bank notes, which each of you was carrying individually, happen to be all in the same series—no, don't answer; I won't have any more lies. Into the car, the whole lot of you.'

I was horrified by this abrupt development, partly because I felt I was actively to blame for my companions' arrest, but mostly because I had consciously wished for it and the wish had come true; nevertheless I could not help deriving a certain comfort from their presence as we were driven off together to the central prison.

Here, as soon as we arrived, we were made to stand for several minutes facing a wall of the courtyard with our hands held above our heads. If this was a psychological move intended to intimidate us, it had on me the opposite effect; for it served only to increase my sense of apathy and irresponsibility now that I realized that not one of my actions depended any longer on my own free will. It was therefore with a feeling of complete indifference that I followed the armed guard who finally pushed all three of us into a basement cell.

Even here I remained unaffected by the surroundings and devoted no more than a cursory glance to the four dirty bunks in two tiers ranged along one of the bare stone walls, to the small barred window above the level of my head, and to the half-filled bucket of excrement and urine standing in the corner underneath. In this squalid isolation we could have destroyed any incriminating object we might have been carrying, for surprisingly no attempt had been made to search us thoroughly; but no doubt we should then have been reported by the cell's fourth occupant, a stranger who might or might not have been a *mouchard*, or stool-pigeon. Working on the assumption that he was, I discouraged his attempts to draw me into conversation, for fear that my accent might betray me as a foreigner; and leaving my two companions to answer his questions, I lay down on one of the bunks and pretended to go to sleep.

Little pretence was needed. I was soon actually sleeping, regaining consciousness from time to time only when I felt the recurrent and alternate need for a cigarette and some food. But there was nothing to smoke, and we were given nothing to eat. After twenty-four hours in this comatose condition I was woken by the clatter of the door being unlocked. I was hoping this heralded the arrival of our first meal; instead it was a summons for us to move. We were herded out of the prison and into a waiting car, and after a short drive were deposited outside a house called the Villa Rose, which I knew was the local Gestapo headquarters.

Here we were locked up in a room on the first floor which, like our previous cell, already contained another occupant. I followed what was now becoming my normal practice and lay down at once on one of the four bare mattresses—the only furniture I could see—and, closing my eyes, listened to the conversation that followed. Our new room-mate seemed to be a more obvious 'plant' than the one we had suspected in prison; for after a few minutes I heard him demonstrating how to undo the handcuffs which fastened together the shutters of the two windows.

'That's all that separates us from freedom,' he explained; 'unfortunately it's a seven-metre drop, and they've got trained police-dogs outside.'

I went to sleep with surprising ease, considering I had already spent almost a whole day and night sleeping, and did not wake up till the late afternoon, when the door was opened with, I suppose, intentional violence to reveal a young man standing on the threshold in a theatrically menacing attitude.

He was a perfect young Nazi—blue eyes, fair hair, fresh skin, breeches and jackboots: not a single essential feature was missing from this typical example of the Stormtrooper—and he waited in purposeful but senseless silence, darting glances at each of us in turn, before he finally fixed his eyes on Roger and barked out:

'Du! Komm!'

So we were to be interrogated at last, one by one.

Roger came back within half an hour, when the young Nazi again enacted the same comedy before picking on Chasuble. Then it was my turn. I was encouraged by the length of time each of my friends had been absent, and also by the fact that in that short period neither of them apparently had been maltreated. Even so I could not help thinking of what I had heard about Gestapo methods of extracting information, as I was marched off along the corridor, down the stairs and into a room leading off the hall.

The first person I saw there was the *milicien* who had arrested us at the road block; then I noticed, silhouetted against the window, the figure of another man seated at a desk, in front of which I was brought to an abrupt halt by the Nazi jerking my collar from behind. Coming straight from the shuttered room upstairs, I was dazzled at first by the sunlight in my eyes, so that the features of my interrogator shifted into focus only gradually; but as soon as my vision was adjusted I found to my amazement that his appearance was, if anything, reassuring. With his grey hair, dark suit and almost benign expression, he looked rather like a provincial bank-manager. But I detected in his voice the cold precise tones of the professional over-draft-refuser, as he put his first question:

'What exactly were you doing, where were you making for, at the time of your arrest?'

It was no use pretending I was legally employed. A man with an out-of-date permit like mine could only be engaged on one of two sorts of criminal activity: either as a *réfractaire*, in other words an outlaw; or as a black-marketeer. I chose to associate myself with what I thought to be the lesser offence and, since I had been caught with hundreds of cigarettes on me, confessed that I was selling smuggled tobacco.

This statement provoked no comment from my questioner, who at once changed the subject by asking me to give him a short account of my previous career. I knew that my 'cover story' was pitifully transparent; to explode it completely all he needed to do—and had probably already done—was to ring up the Electric Company at Nîmes, where he would at once learn that Armand Pont-Levé was a myth. Yet I had to say something. In despair, then, I embarked on my palpably false autobiography, expecting at the end of each unplausible chapter to be interrupted by an angry refutation. Instead, I was listened to in silence, prompted only at each hesitation by a thump in the kidneys and once by a blow in the face delivered by the man standing behind me.

I came to the end of my story, and still the interrogator said nothing. He gave no indication that he disbelieved me, no sign that he suspected me of anything at all; and I found this silence more unnerving than any threat, as I was quietly dismissed and escorted back to the room upstairs. Yet as soon as I lay down again I fell into a deep untroubled sleep, from which I woke only when the door was flung open in the early morning to reveal once more the young Nazi of the evening before. I thought we were in for another interrogation; but this time, instead of one of us, it was our suspected stool-pigeon who was summoned—no doubt to report to his superiors on our demeanour during the night.

His short absence from the room gave the three of us an opportunity—the first we had had since our arrest—of discussing the situation together. A comparison of our individual interrogations, all of which seemed to have followed an identical pattern, made it quite clear that the enemy suspected us of clandestine activity and that the only way of saving our lives was to attempt a mass escape. We therefore hurriedly drew up a plan of action and agreed that as soon as night fell we would throttle our room-mate, break open the shutters and jump out of the house; even with the sentries outside and the police-dogs prowling round the garden, there was a reasonable chance of at least one of us getting away safely.

But we had no chance of putting this plan to the test. For early that morning we were taken back to the central prison, not to our old cell but a larger one in a different part of the building; and we knew without being told that it was the death cell.

We knew, too, that since our arrest the Allied landing had taken place on the Riviera and that Digne, being so near the coast, might be liberated within the next few days. I was therefore frightened that in the heat of the moment we might be shot out of hand; but that fate, on further reflecion, seemed preferable to the torture, both physical and mental, that might be inflicted in the process of a 'legal' trial and official execution. I kept thinking of the poison tablet sewn into the lapel of the suit I should have been wearing, and wondering at what stage of the proceedings I would have nerved myself to swallow it. The problem was purely academic, but it had the practical result of diverting my mind from thoughts even more unpleasant.

Now that there was apparently no possibility of escape, the idea of the firing-squad held no terror—provided there was no pain beforehand. Incongruously, what I resented most was the prospect of dying under a false identity—for presumably my true one would never be established—and I envied the three American prisoners whom I could see across the courtyard in a cell directly opposite ours. Members of the crew of a damaged bomber, they had baled out over France, and after being picked up by a local maquis band, had fought in its ranks and been captured in a recent engagement with the enemy. They had subsequently been brought here for interrogation, and though their own position was scarcely less lamentable than ours—for they, too, were likely to be shot—I should have given a great deal to be in their shoes; for at least they could converse together without pretence in their own language, and each of them wore, strung round his neck, a little piece of stamped plastic or embossed metal which, though worth nothing, I now prized as highly as an amulet—a solider's identity disk.

I gradually worked myself up into such a morbid frame of mind that when, about midday, the first meal we had been given since our imprisonment was brought in—an ominously good meal of vegetable soup and brown bread—I could not help regarding it as the last we were ever likely to have. And when, later that afternoon, the *milicien* who had arrested us called to summon us outside, I felt sure it was for execution, especially since he now wore, over his civilian trousers, a Wehrmacht tunic which invested him with the same air of formality and ceremonial gravity as the black cap on the head of a judge delivering the death sentence.

But once outside the prison gates, instead of turning left towards the football ground which the firing-squad normally used, he led us in the opposite direction, walking with Roger by his side while Chasuble and I followed a few paces behind.

A thin drizzle was falling, and the darkening sky seemed to have caused the sun to set earlier than usual. Soon it would be night. Now, if ever, was our chance to escape. Escorted by a single semi-civilian whom we did not even know to be armed, we could have made a sudden dash up one of the cobbled sidestreets and dispersed through the town in the dark with every prospect of being safely away in the hills by the morning. But my mind, at least, had become so dull after three days of apathy and irresponsibility that I lacked the necessary resolution.

In any case the situation was beyond my personal control.

Even the events of which I knew myself to be an integral part —like walking down this street in this rain—seemed to be happening outside myself, as though I was a disinterested spectator; so that when, after a few hundred yards, we drew level with a waiting car, I reacted without hesitation and without surprise to the *milicien's* order:

'Quick! Get in, all three of you!'

Slamming the door on us, he got in himself beside the driver, and at once we were skidding round the nearest corner and heading straight for a road block on the outskirts of the town. The sentries there, seeing an official car approaching at high speed with a uniformed man leaning out of the window, automatically drew back; and we flashed past them into the open country—only to stop a moment later at an isolated building round the first bend in the road. A solitary figure was standing there, outlined against the white wall, and I recognized—with bewilderment, but still without surprise—Christine.

After so much had already occurred that I could not explain, her presence there did not seem altogether incomprehensible. From her harassed expression as she squeezed into the front seat I simply assumed that she, too, had been caught; for, as the car started off once more, she seemed determined not to risk betraying by the slightest word or gesture the fact that she knew us, but stared straight ahead, like ourselves, in silence.

Presently, on the edge of a steep embankment, the car stopped again. The *milicien* jumped out and, since I was the one nearest the door on his side, he motioned me to follow him down the bank to the river-bed beyond. Incapable by now of keeping pace with this dream-like sequence of events, I slithered through the mud behind him and incuriously watched him as he took off his uniform jacket.

'Here, help me with this,' he said, as he began to scoop a hole among the pebbles and boulders at the water's edge.

Indifferently, I helped him to bury his discarded garment;

then together we climbed back and got into the car again. As we drove off in the direction of the mountains, Christine for the first time turned round and smiled.

It was only then that I realized we were free.

Characteristically, Christine never told us exactly what methods she had used to secure our release. But from what I heard on the spot immediately afterwards, together with the little I learnt from her years later, I managed eventually to form a rough idea of the events leading up to our unexpected reunion at the isolated roadside house.

The news of our capture reached her on the Italian border. She had acted at once with outstanding speed and self-sacrifice. Within twenty-four hours she had established contact, through a series of intermediaries, with the prison authorities and the Gestapo; and by the end of the following day she had come down to Digne in person for a meeting with the *milicien* who had arrested us. In other words, she had voluntarily risked her life in the hope of saving ours.

Fortunately, her courage was matched by her wits. The Allied landing which had taken place that very day was a happy coincidence, and she was quick to exploit it. To the *milicien* she openly confessed who she was and who Roger and I were—exaggerating, however, our importance and stressing the fate in store for our captors if we were to be found dead when the liberating armies entered the town.

She pointed out that he, the *milicien*, being not only the man who was primarily responsible for our imprisonment but being also a Frenchman, would be the first to suffer; there was no escape for him even though he was for the time being under enemy protection. The German garrison, as he had no doubt seen for himself, was unable to withdraw in the face of the Allied advance since every line of retreat was blocked by the local resistance forces; it would therefore have to surrender. For the Wehrmacht troops this would not be catastrophic;

they would simply be sent to a prisoner-of-war camp, and since the war was now nearly over they would soon be free again. For him, however, the liberation of Digne would have more serious consequences. As a civilian, he would be handed over as a traitor to the maquis authorities—who had a peculiar way of dealing with those found guilty of treachery.

On the other hand, if he engineered our release he would be guaranteed a safe conduct to our nearest G.H.Q. outside France.

Sensibly, he had agreed.

The plan he subsequently made for our joint escape had worked so perfectly that in retrospect the whole operation seemed absurdly simple; and indeed for the three of us under sentence of death it was simple, since it involved no effort of will or action on our part. But for Christine, who had of her own volition risked the death penalty, the responsibility must have been almost beyond endurance. For apart from the considerations of personal courage, she had also had to decide whether from the S.O.E. point of view her action was ethically permissible. As an individual, she would not have hesitated to barter her own life for the lives of three others. As an agent, however, she was obliged to assess the value of those lives against hers; and if hers proved to be worth more, it was her duty to keep it.

In the assessment she made it was Roger's life that weighed the scales in favour of the decision she took; for in comparison Chasuble's and mine were of small account. Had Roger not been arrested with us, Christine would have been perfectly justified in taking no action if action meant jeopardizing herself. Indirectly, then, I owe my life to him as much as I do, directly, to her.

DESCENT TO THE MAQUIS

By George Millar

GOING down. I waited a moment to make sure it was really true. Yes, the big umbrella was open all right, and I was gently swinging from the lovely nylon ropes that gleamed like silk wigs in the moonlight. So I waggled my bottom out of the strap that held it, swung up both arms in the rather affected arc they had taught me, grabbed the lines in each hand and took up the crouched, looking-down landing position. Now I could see the ground below.

All I saw was wheat, wheat blowing in a wind, sometimes showing partings like a woman's long hair in a wind. I had no time to be obsessed with the beauty of the wheat. Before I could be obsessed with anything I had made a reasonable landing, quite a fast one with a bump and a roll. Then I found myself being towed through the wheat. That wind really was strong. I sluiced round on one side, spilling the air from the big bag. The heads of the wheat lashed me about the face and eyes.

The parachute lay, a mighty, untidy, dark splash of deadness on the living wheat. I got it into a straight line and rolled it, then twisted the lines into that in-and-out pattern they liked at the training school, climbed out of my parachuting clothes and rolled them into the parachute.

Now I had earned a drink. So I drank from the little

flask they had given me. Rum it was, and good. British Army rum from the West India Docks. Not a soul was to be seen. That did not worry me because I knew they had dropped me late, and I had certainly over-shot the reception ground.

Here came my aeroplane on its final circuit. Beautiful in its queer heavy way, and powerful with its roaring, it crossed right over me, but a long time before it reached me eight white puffs magically appeared under its belly, as though it were were spawning. The eight packages floated down, landing out of sight, lower down than my wheat-field.

'Hey,' I told myself. 'My two suitcases are among all those.' The Liberator was flying off, waggling its wings in farewell. I left in the opposite direction.

But three figures, in line, appeared ahead of me, like figures in a wheat-field in a Russian film. I sank slowly to my knees, then lower until I was completely hidden from the men who approached. They came on without caution, shouting to each other. This worried me a little. They were too far away for me to distinguish their shouting. I had been taught to believe that only Germans shouted, and that the Resistance worked slyly, silently.

So I took my pistol from my pocket and crouched there. Until I heard them say:

'I'd swear a container fell near here. It dropped after the the others.'

'Better go on a little farther. How in the name of God will we get it back? Can't bring a cart through this field because of leaving traces.'

On hearing such reassuring talk in definitely non-German French, I rose from the wheat feeling like a rather washed-out Aphrodite, and gave them a hearty 'Good evening' which, on second thought, I changed to a 'Good morning.'

Instead of replying the three Frenchmen vanished. They had flung themselves face down in the wheat. The following sound was unpleasant; it was the click of a Sten gun being changed from 'safe' to the 'fire' position. The wind tore across the wheat-field, swaying the grain like silver-blonde hair.

'Who are you?' asked one of the Frenchmen.

'Who are you?' I answered, without raising my head.

'Come out of there and give yourself up!'

'Is Albert there?' I asked.

'Never heard of him. Who are you?'

Another Frenchman who lay slightly farther away now fortunately intervened.

'Perhaps he's a parachutist,' he said. 'I thought the last tube was a man. Not a tube,' he added, to ram his point home.

'Yes, I am a parachutist.' A long pause followed, then the first Frenchman said triumphantly:

'If he were a parachutist he would have a parachute.'

'Yes, let him produce his parachute,' chorused the other two.

I came forward holding my absurd bundle in front of me, and when they had inspected it they led me away, one holding me by the arm, the other two behind me with Stens at the ready. They were rough-looking men in caps and ordinary clothing.

We arrived at a wide space, lightly strewn with boulders. In the middle of it I saw a bunch of figures.

They were all making so much noise that they paid no immediate attention to our party. I just stood there while my guides or captors tried to shout louder than the others. At length one figure, stocky and powerful-looking, detached itself from the crowd and came towards me, followed by two or three others. This man was the chief. In that light I could only see that he had one arm in a sling, and wore a soft hat pulled forward over his eyes.

'They say you are a Boche spy, pretending to be an Englishman,' he began. 'You must prove to me quickly that you are English. We have much work to do here.'

'Is Albert not here? I thought he knew I was coming.'
'You know Albert?'
'Yes.'
'Then what is the password for this parachutage?'
'I don't know. London gave me no password.'
'He is a spy,' said the first man who had spoken in the wheat-field. 'We were all told that the password was "Cambronne".'

This appeared to influence the chief in my favour.

'Shut it, loafer,' he boomed at the last speaker. 'This man is an Englishman, he speaks like Henri, and Henri was English, wasn't he. Excuse my left hand, Englishman, my right was wounded by a Schleuh in Dijon yesterday. My name is Jacques, do they know of me in London?'

'Yes,' I lied, for I had never heard of him. 'I call myself Emile.'

'And you are a British officer?'
'Yes. But don't shout it around.'

'Good. Very good. There is much work to be done.' A chorus of approval went up from the uncouth men who crowded round us. I saw in the moonlight that some wore ordinary civilian clothes, while others were dressed in the odd scraps of rags, old uniforms, and leather coats that I had learned to expect in the Maquis. When everyone had shaken hands with me they returned to their work, arranging the twelve containers in one pile. They worked much faster than we had done in practice operations at the schools. They were strong. But they made a terrible noise.

A little goblin-like man came dancing up to me. He wore few clothes, and was so thin that I expected to see him carried away by the wind like the skeleton of a dried leaf.

'Petit-Henri,' he said.

'Enchanted. Emile,' I replied. 'Are you the Petit-Henri who worked with Gut? Then I have heard much of you in London.'

'Really heard of me in London? How wonderful. How wonderful. All that distance away. And you come in the big aeroplane and tell me.'

He was nearly weeping with pleasure. I saw that this Petit-Henri, *the Petit-Henri*, was only a boy.

'Tell me, Emile,' he asked. 'I was flashing the letter, the "K". Was it well done?'

'Yes. Well done. I saw it from the air.'

'You saw it from the air, and now you are here with us. Fantastic. They told me "Dah-de-dah" was "K" so I flashed it, but I was relieved when the aeroplane came over and dropped the things. Well, I must go to my post now for the second aeroplane, and tomorrow, when you are rested we will have a long talk.'

'Yes, indeed. Try to make your "K" very regular if the other aeroplane comes. Count to yourself like this, "one, two, three, *cut*; one, *cut*; one, two, three, *cut*". But I do not think the aeroplane will come now.'

'Why not, Emile?'

'Perhaps it failed to find us. They do not use wireless to plot their courses, because the Boche has many radio-locating stations. So the navigation is difficult. Also now there are many Boche night fighters, and the flak is bad for the aeroplanes.'

'Poor things, what dreadful risks they run. Still, we must wait on in our positions for them, must we not?'

'Yes, you must wait on for two hours. If they do not come then, something has happened.'

The squat leader, Jacques, came up to me with a young boy, who led me away to the side of the field. The men were loading the containers now on two of the long French farm carts which they call 'platforms'. One cart had two horses in it, the other had a horse and a mule, sign of the occupation.

I walked easily and springily in the dark woods. My body felt good again, relieved of the bulky parachute clothes. Only my neck was a little stiff. I must have failed to relax it properly when I rolled out the landing shock.

Occasionally the boy asked me odd questions about England: were there still cinemas? were there still farms? was it true that most of the cows were milked by machines, and that the fields were fertilized not with dung, but with scented products manufactured in the cities? And, of course, the eternal question then: was there going to be a second front?

'Yes,' I answered to this.

'Why do you say yes?'

'Because I have seen the armies massing in England, and where you find armies massing you will always find war. France is the nearest country to England.'

'But my father says that the only way to have peace after this war is for us to have a great and powerful army and air force. Surely that will not mean war?'

'Surely not,' I said in a tone that ended conversation, for I suddenly felt tired and depressed and lonely in the bleak moonlight. The farm lay ahead. In the kitchen he lit an acetylene lamp, gave me a glass of Marc and a slice of the bread they make with honey, then led me up to the best bedroom. The double feather-bed looked good. I told myself it was risky to sleep in bed so near the parachutage, but I told myself too late. Before I had time to consider the problem and agree that it *was* dangerous, I was in bed and asleep.

That is how people get killed.

A warmer sun than I was accustomed to was pouring into the room. I got quickly out of the feather-bed, and looked out of the window. There were fields and some big woods. I eyed the woods carefully, but saw no smoke, or other sign of the Maquis. There were three men in greyish shirts and faded blue trousers working in different parts of the field. I tried to attribute sinister, underworld motives to these industrious figures. But it was difficult to explain away their hoes, and bent, toiling backs.

My first reaction was to see either the dark hand of the Resistance or the dark hand of the enemy in everything I saw in France. This reaction lasted for about two weeks as far as the Resistance was concerned, and for about a month as far as the Germans were concerned, decreasing after then, but coming back strongly every time that they gave me a fright. These feelings were normal. Other people who did the same work always told me that they felt exactly the same way about things. Our organization believed that it took a normal man about ten days to get settled in and begin working seriously. It took me longer, but I am of a naturally timorous disposition.

Down in the farm kitchen I washed myself. There was an old woman there, who seemed pleased to see me. She gave me a bowl of imitation coffee and milk and a huge round loaf of dark bread and about six months' British butter ration on a dirty plate. Lastly she put down a cardboard box of French sugar in long lumps. Not a bad breakfast.

Jacques came in to watch me eat. He had brought my two suitcases, and was very impressed with them, even the imitation leather one. He set them down as though they contained diamonds or eggs, and asked the crone to get a duster and wipe them over.

'The second aeroplane didn't arrive,' he told me, when he had accepted a packet of my cigarettes from England. 'But we have a lot of wonderful things, Emile. Some things we don't understand. We are uneducated men here, Emile. We have the spirit, but we need a man like you, someone educated.'

'I am uneducated.'

'Oh, then you don't know how to use the "Arbalette"?'

'What's that?'

'The American anti-tank rocket thrower.'

'Oh, the "Bazooka". Yes, I know how to use that, and I will show you and your men.'

'And the English anti-tank mine, and to take the Bren gun

into all its pieces, also the big "Casse-pot", the big American Colt.'

'Yes, I know how to do those things.'

'And you say that you are uneducated.' His wolfish face broke into a charming smile. 'Emile, you *must* stay with us. Your arrival puts heart into the whole band. The winter has been long. My hand hurts me, and now I think I will always have to fire with my left. But if you can stay here we will not only kill the boche, we will *murder* him. Can you stay with us?'

'I don't know. Albert will say. I take orders from him.'

'Albert will want you to go with him,' he said moodily. He was a big, exaggerated child, now sulky, now friendly. His voice was like the deep booming voice of a huge Spanish priest I had met in an inn at Burgos. He was dark-haired and he had a white skin despite the gipsy life, a skin that shone with health where it was not covered with black hairs. There was a spot of blood forming at the bottom of his sling. I asked him how he had hurt his hand.

'Fired on, stupidly, in the street. After such a success,' he answered sadly. 'Such a success in the night. It was the nephew of the chief of the Gestapo in Dijon. He and his mistress. They thought they had laid a trap for us in their pretty bungalow. But Bobby (you will meet Bobby, he's good fun), Bobby and I decided to bait the trap ourselves. So we watched the bungalow and we arrived there, entering by a back window, two hours before our appointment. There was nobody there, but we already knew that. We settled down to wait, happily. For we had another pal with us, a "silencieux" [silent pistol]. They arrived, the pair of them. They did not turn on the light. But our silent pal does not mind that, he has luminous sights. Bobby took the first shot. The man fell. He handed me the "silencieux". I shot the woman. She fell across her Boche. We left by the window. The bungalow was quiet. A real love-nest. Then I had to go and get myself shot in a street brawl.'

Our relations were strained when I had seen the containers that had dropped to Jacques' group with me. They had taken them into a thicket, only about two hundred yards from the farm where I slept. No attempt had been made to hide the tracks made by the carts. Nor to conceal the trail of broken branches and bruised grasses that led to the spoils of the parachutage.

'No danger in that. Ça ne risque rien,' said Jacques, when I politely pointed out the lack of precuation. As the months passed with the Resistance I was to come to know this phrase: 'Ça ne risque rien.' 'Ça ne risque rien,' always the excuse of a lazy or a bad soldier, killed many a man in the end. Jacques did me a favour. He introduced me to the phrase when I had just begun work, when I was fresh from the principles and energy of London.

I went through the bushes, along the too-well-marked path to the containers. They had been strewn about in a small clearing. A lot of the contents were lying about on the trampled mud.

'What happens if it rains?' I asked.

Jacques looked for a second at the clouds crossing the sky:

'I don't think it will rain,' he said. 'But as you say, we had better take our precautions.' Within five minutes he had ten men stowing the material properly in container cells and tidying these up. He got his men moving by strong-arm methods when he bothered to put them to work.

In one corner I saw a great pile of parachutes. On the top lay my own (a parachutist's parachute, different from the others) still with the jumping-suit wrapped up in it. I gathered these things in my arms and went off to burn them.

'Hey,' said Jacques as I stuffed all this then priceless nylon into the farm incinerator among the burned-out refuse of cabbage husks and the only parts of sheep that peasants find inedible. 'Hey, Emile. You gone crazy? That stuff is beautiful. You can't buy it here, you know.'

'Supposing the Gestapo pay a visit here, what will they find?' I asked him.

'Everything,' he answered immediately. 'Mais ça ne risque rien.'

'But in ten minutes, when all this stuff has turned into tar, there will be nothing to tell them if they come that, along with the containers, there arrived last night a British officer.'

'Huh,' answered Jacques, and I could see that he thought I was over-scared. When the parachute had burned, in the sunny farmyard I began to wonder how I would get back to Britain, if ever. I thought the answer then was 'never'. But there was plenty to do.

And I wondered how to do it.

Despite the protests of Jacques and his men, who could not understand why I wished to discard comfort for discomfort, I had Petit-Henri help me move my things to the shack in the woods where they lived. The shack's lineaments resembled those of a wigwam built in rectangular, instead of circular, form. It was long and narrow and pointed in section, being made of birch branches leaned together at the top to form a ridge. The interstices were blocked with lovely bright moss from the forest, and in places with none too clean-looking sacking. The floor, which fulfilled also the function of communal bed, was covered with fresh-cut hay.

Installing my things in this home, and unrolling a sleeping bag alongside the space reserved for the chief, I committed what I think was my worst mistake in all my life in the Maquis. I locked my suitcase. True, it had a million francs in it. But I locked it.

That evening, when the carbide light was turned low, and sixteen of us began, with difficulty in the narrow hut, to compose ourselves for sleep, I suddenly realized my crime. Being of Scottish parentage and origin, I believe in second sight, and I believe in speech that is unspoken. But I was not thinking of that as, bending beside my sleeping-bag, I unlocked my suitcase.

Nobody said anything, of course. They were terribly polite to me. Nobody even looked at me. I was thankful that the suitcase was of the one lock and two straps variety. The one lock, being strong and stiff, of best British brass, made a horrible hard click as it yielded to my gentle key. The click seemed to me to echo and linger in the strange hut like the quartz chuckles of Shylock.

I never locked anything again, in all my stay in France. No, never. If I had anything secret or terribly valuable I buried it under a bush or hid it in a hollow tree. Like that I only insulted myself.

SEMNOZ

By Peter Churchill

AT 7.30 one evening in mid-April 1943 two saboteurs were listening in to the B.B.C. for a personal message which, if given, would indicate that the third member of their team would be dropping by parachute on to a snow-capped mountain ridge some 300 yards long by 80 yards in width at a height of some 6,000 feet. They had chosen this spot themselves for reasons of security and the wood for a bonfire to guide the plane in had already been gathered. The war names of the two listeners were Arnaud, a radio operator, and Lise, a courier. They were waiting for Michel, the organizer of this small team. The real names of these three were the late Captain Alec Rabinowitch, Croix de Guerre, Mrs. Odette Churchill, G.C., M.B.E., Légion d'Honneur, and Captain Peter Churchill, D.S.O., Croix de Guerre. The last-named had been told by the navigator of the Halifax bomber bringing him out that if he jumped on the green light he, the navigator, would drop him on a sixpenny bit.

Despite the German jamming of the wave-length Lise somehow managed to hear the B.B.C. message indicating Michel's arrival and by 8.20 p.m. it was a tired Lise and Arnaud who were ready to set off for their second climb of the Semnoz within twenty-four hours of having reconnoitred the mountain.

With them came Jean and Simone Cottet, the proprietors of the Hotel de la Poste, St. Jorioz, Haute Savoie, who belonged to the same Resistance group.

In order to hasten over the eleven kilometres of road before reaching the mountain paths, Jean was driving them to the pass in his charcoal-burning V8 Ford. Rather than go straight up from the Hotel he decided on the easier gradient of Road 512. Consequently they started off in the direction of Annecy with a view to picking it up at le Crêt—four kms. away.

They reached this first objective not without mechanical misgivings and turned off to the left. A few hundred yards of the slight gradient of road 512 were enough for the engine. It petered out and no amount of coaxing would bring it back to life.

By the time they had given up hope of doing the twelve kms. in comfort it was getting on for 9 p.m.

These night operations were all scheduled to take place between the hours of 10 p.m. and 2 a.m. and past experience had shown that planes could arrive at any and all hours between these limits. With twelve kms. to go before their 2500 feet climb up the steep wooded path the four friends wasted no strength in idle conversation. Had they walked up the steeper road, leading straight up from the Hotel, they would have reached the pass by 9.45. The realization of this fact only added to Lise's determination to maintain a speed dictated by her mind and far beyond her normal physical capacity, already strained by the previous day's exertions.

On leaving the road for the stony path, more time was wasted in the sleeping village of Leschaux looking for the gap in the houses where the track began. It was Jean Cottet who finally led them to it and the steep climb began.

Owing to the blackness of the night—the moon was rising on the far side of the mountain—they could not even see the tracks they had previously left in the snow. Torches were of no avail and it meant retracing their steps.

A near panic seized the anxious climbers. Should they go back? Should they go on?

Pointing up to the left Arnaud said, with his customary assurance,

'I swear there's a short cut to the top if we climb up that way.'

Looking in that direction Lise, depending on instinct rather than on her somewhat hazy bump of direction, said,

'Never! That's simply miles off our line!'

'What do you say, Jean?' asked Arnaud, turning to their friend who had lived his entire life in the district.

'I confess I don't know,' said he.

'Look!' said Lise, pointing to a telegraph pole. 'I remember those poles go straight up the side of the mountain and end up on the top. Why, there's even one by the very spot we chose for him to land on. Don't you remember, Arnaud?'

'I seem to remember the one at the top, but frankly I don't connect the rest with it. . . .'

As this statement was one of the closest things to an admission that Arnaud had ever made, it was now mere child's play for Lise to persuade her friends that by following these poles they would reach their goal by the surest and swiftest route.

Leading them on, sometimes from boulder to boulder, Lise was now tackling an approach to the top that averaged one in two.

At midnight they stopped for a few seconds to catch their breath and listen for the possible sounds of a distant bomber. With their bodies soaked in sweat they could hear nothing but the pounding of their hearts.

At 12.30 and again at 1 a.m. they repeated this process with identical results.

By now the pace was too hot for Simone and, after assuring her husband that she would find the way following the telegraph poles, she fell behind.

Arnaud was the next to lose heart. Turning to Lise in the snow, he gasped, 'This is hopeless! We're not getting anywhere. Just look at the time! Are you sure you heard that message, Lise?'

'Of course I did,' she replied.

'We'll never get to the top in time.... When they see no lights they'll turn back and he'll be fast asleep in England before we get to the top.'

'Come on, Arnaud! Don't waste your breath! We'll get there all right.... You'll see.... Besides, we've got G.M.T. on our side.'

On they climbed, their ears pounding with the strain and altitude.

It was nearly half past one when Arnaud heard Lise's triumphant voice just ahead of him crying out: 'Look, Arnaud! Look!'

Coming up he saw that the long forest belt was over and in front, rising steeply before them, lay the snow-clad hog's back —a mere 900 yards away. The rising moon lit the silvery crest, casting its rays on to the tops of the pines under which they now stood.

The three friends scrambled up the last slippery stretch with only one aim in view; to get those branches out of the chalet in double quick time.

As the red specks of strain burned her sore eyes, Lise prayed,

'Oh, God, let me get there before the plane!'

The last 900 yards can be a very long way especially when you already have so many miles weighing down your weary legs, but buoyed up by the vision of their goal, they accomplished the final spurt and mounted the rise abreast.

And now the exhausted climbers dashed for the hut and snatched up armfuls of branches, staggering out and piling them up on a foundation of straw in the centre of their little pitch that looked so much smaller by moonlight.

L

Back and forth they ran, Arnaud doing double the work of Lise to make up for his moment of weakness and to save her from complete collapse. The giant bonfire was no sooner ready than Lise flopped down panting beside it in the snow.

Pulling out a match which he held at one end of the striking board, with the open bottle of petrol stuck into the snow between his feet, Arnaud glanced at his companion's fragile form, lying half-conscious beside him. Never had he admired her so profoundly.

What was that sound in the distance? He peered into the northern sky and listened hard. Were his wishful ears playing him another trick? Jean was now kneeling beside Lise, holding up her head and making her drink some brandy from his flask. In the deathly stillness their black shapes stood out vividly against the moonlit snow.

Yes! It was an aircraft all right. An involuntary thrill of excitement ran through him. Michel had said he would come back and here he was, inside that very plane. Soon he would come tumbling out towards them.

'Here it comes!' he cried, pouring the petrol over the branches. Seeing that it was not pouring out fast enough he smashed the top of the bottle against his foot and dropped the lot on to the heap. Striking his match he threw it in while the sulphur still sizzled. With a small explosion the mighty fire caught light.

Whilst Jean moved away slightly, looking for Simone whom he hoped would not miss the show, Lise and Arnaud stood side by side watching the 30-ton bomber come in towards them. Every now and then he squeezed her affectionately with the arm he had placed around her shoulder. It was then that he decided that he would stand back and let her receive Michel first as he sailed earthward.

And here it came, cutting across the hog's back diagonally. Now it was almost straight above them.

With mouths wide open they anticipated the great moment; nothing dropped from the aircraft's belly as it flashed over their heads. The Halifax flew off on a slow turn to port.

'Oh, God!' said Lise. 'I can't bear it... After all this sweat, they're taking him home again....'

'Don't be a chump!' said Arnaud, 'You can see this fire for one hundred miles except in the valley.... They're only turning round to come in along the length of the hog's back. Don't forget, they've got six 'chutes to drop on a mere three hundred yards....'

Lying on his stomach in the glass nose of the four-engined bomber, Colonel Philippe Livry-Level, the French navigator, suddenly spotted the fire.

Holding the 'inter-comm' close to his mouth, he announced 'Bonfire ahead.... Action stations!'

The despatcher pulled away the two semi-circular boards covering the dropping hole, over which he switched on a maroon bulb. Groping his way carefully past the hole in the dim-lit fuselage, he tapped Michel on the shoulder and led him to the hole.

Michel sat down on the ledge, with his back to the engines. The despatcher then pulled out the loose thong of his parachute and clipped it to the static line, pulling on it hard to show Michel that it was well and truly fixed.

The red warning light came on and Michel glanced rapidly down to see the snow-clad mountain side rising until they were a mere three hundred feet above the trees. A hand on his arm drew his attention away and the despatcher shouted into his ear,

'We're going round once so as to make a better approach.'

The warning lamp was swtiched off as the aircraft went into a slow turn. Looking down once again Michel saw the green murky waters of Lake Annecy, now some 5,000 feet below them. As he looked away he wondered if his reflection of that colour was visible to the despatcher.

And now the circle was being closed and as the snow-covered trees flashed by, the red light came on again.

The usual panic swept down from his mind and gripped his entrails in a vice. He felt the flaps go down and the variable-pitch propellers reducing their speed to something like 175 m.p.h.

Here it was again! He knew it all.... When the light turned green, the hand that would simultaneously flash down beside his face would be the hand of destiny and the voice that shouted 'Scram!' the voice of doom. If he did not go out at that precise second, he knew very well that he would land on the wrong Alp.

Gritting his teeth, he waited for it....

As the red light gave way to green he was half-way down the chute before the despatcher's shout died down.

Closing his eyes and putting up his hands beside his face to keep the wind from snatching off his glasses, he was thrown back horizontally by the slip-stream. A violent jerk in his groin and below his armpits told him that the 'chute was safely open.

He had swung round 180 degrees and was now facing the departing aircraft. It was only two hundred feet away and just above him, the full roar of its motors deafening his ears. Almost at once the sound dwindled to nothing, but his eyes remained glued to it, fascinated by the tongues of flame shooting out of the eight exhaust pipes of the four engines.

Now, one by one, the five other parachutes flapped open and hung, staggered, within a short space above his head.

From his right came the full brilliance of a five-eighths moon shining out of a peerless sky and all around him lay the majestic scenery of the Alps cloaked in silvery snow.

It was a sight he would never forget. But knowing that the drop would only take some fourteen seconds, he grudgingly looked away to see what lay below. It was at this moment that he remembered the navigator's words: 'I'll drop you on a sixpenny bit...' and fully understood them.... He was falling straight into the fire.

A swift pull on the forward set of nylon cords billowed out some air and made him move backwards. Lucky thing that this exercise was included in the parachute training....

Now below him he saw two figures standing beside the fire. The larger of the two then began running towards the second 'chute, probably thinking it was he.

Michel was glad of this move for it meant he would be dropping very close to the smaller form which was peering anxiously into the sky, as though wondering which could be his 'chute.

As he came closer he saw that he was coming down straight on to her head. At the same time the air currents rising from the flanks of the hog's back caught and filled his 'chute so that his normal descent at twenty m.p.h. was reduced to something nearer six.

It seemed, as he got lower, that he was no longer moving at all. But as he hovered over Lise's head, reaching down with his feet, as though this might speed things up, he refrained from saying anything to the upturned face that still did not see him.

Only at the very last moment did he speak.

'Hallo, Lise!' he said quite softly. 'If you'll take a step backwards, I shan't land on your head.'

With an ecstatic cry, Lise caught sight of him and moving back out of the way she reached out her arms as though to catch him.

Michel glided down, landing on his feet in the soft snow before her. He did not even have to bend his knees to take the shock.

As they embraced each other at this crowning moment of their lives, the silk canopy fell lifeless on to the snow and, in the crackling of the fire, he heard her sweet voice repeating his name, 'Pierre, Pierre,' in tones that told him everything a man could ever wish to hear.

A huge form now came running up into the firelight, calling out, 'Sacré Michel!' and, as he tore off his rubber helmet, Arnaud hugged him in a bear's grip, burying his face in his neck.

With an arm round his two companions, Michel smiled speechlessly from one to the other of these two beloved faces.

WOMEN OF THE FRENCH RESISTANCE

By Christopher Sykes

T HE core of strength in this French life which refused to accept defeat lay chiefly in the women—those powerful middle-aged women of France. I know now what Joan of Arc would have looked like in later years if fate had been kinder to her in youth. I remember that in England before the invasion some doubts had arisen as to the reliability in battle of a certain French unit with which I was connected. It was reported that not only was the unit mutinous and corrupted by political dissension, but that the men themselves had said that once arrived in France they would go the quickest way home. One of their officers said to me: 'Don't worry, when they see French women they'll fight.' I thought at the time that the remark was facetious, but now I know why he made it. These women, above all, showed that deep boredom with the Germans which came from contempt born of a profound sense of moral superiority, a certitude that on the French side was a great right and on the other only a great wrong, and which was at the centre of the feeling which made the Resistance the powerful force it was. They didn't give a damn for the Germans. Helpless as they were, by the sheer force of personality they kept the invaders at bay and recklessly cheered on any who bore arms on the right side. They were not people before whom it would have been easy to show panic. They unnerved the Germans, however. They were queens of truculence and back-chat, and when they did services for the Germans, as sometimes they had to, they did so in a manner which did not allay the enemy's disquiet. But as a rule the Germans kept their distance—that is to say, they either turned these women out of their houses and lived there by themselves, or else they left them and their houses alone. That their truculence could be positively overwhelming I know well enough from having been mistaken once in the dark for a German. We used to call them 'our Madames'.

Their persistent boredom with the Germans meant that they had little sense of that odious necessity of war, 'security', to maintain which they had a few over-simple rules. Not a word except a highly misleading one was ever spoken to the Germans about our military dispositions, but our place in everyday life, that stressed everyday life which they loved as never before, led to many mad risks. They liked to entertain us to enormous celebration lunches and dinners; it was often necessary to sit through meals the size of banquets while the Germans were in the town, and visible through the windows. Perhaps my most dramatic memory of the war is of passing the open door of a house, on a rainy night when the North, South, and Eastern horizons were intermittently bright with gun-flashes, through which issued the strains of the 'Marseillaise' from a rusted gramophone, and a loud female voice taking up a line 'A bas les Doryphores!' (the potato-bug, a nickname for the Germans).

Madame Rossi, who lived in a tall, shuttered house on the road, about half a mile from our town, was an archetype of our protectresses. Her physical appearance suggested ponderous immobility, while her loud laughing voice, which filled the room like the sound of a coaching horn blown indoors, gave but a slight indication of her indomitable vitality. She was as persistently merry in the face of danger as though she actually relished it: my memory of her is always first of loud hearty peasant laughter. She was exposed to far more danger than most, she had had far more distressful experiences, and this because she was not the type made for subterfuge; the Germans knew well enough that this large, full-bosomed, fair-haired mirthful woman was their bitter enemy. Her house was on a little subsidiary road which left the town for an adjoining valley running, as they all did, between immense pine-clad mountains, and its situation was near one of the few mountain paths which led to the darkness of the forest and to our hiding place. Visits by Gestapo agents were frequent, and her house had once been searched while she had six of our men hidden. It is not difficult to imagine how such experiences can rack the toughest nerves. But Madame Rossi never gave a sign of a twinge. She never suggested that her house should not be used as a refuge and a rendezvous. 'Oh la! les Boches!' she would cry as she leaned against her kitchen table with red arms crossed and her blue eyes rolling. 'Boh! Those filthy creatures! They're brutes, that's what they are.' Then she would laugh; not ironically, just at the whole crazy business. I think it is not extravagant to say that her sense of humour was not, as with most people, an affair of jokes and comic surprises, but went deep down in her nature. She was terrifically sane.

The first time I met her happened as follows. As I approached the house one night with my colonel, we were held up by two melodramtic figures with pistols. Recognitions were whispered and arms lowered. There was an agent abroad, we were told. The house was surrounded by sentries. When we knocked we heard a hushed pandemonium within, and the daughter, a hillock compared to the mountainous mother, but of great proportion and trumpet-tongued as she was, looked out, and, recognizing us, beckoned us in. We found Madame leaning against the table, as I was so often to see her after, and the pandemonium recommenced, as it were in reverse order, doors opening and shutting all round as in an old-fashioned

French farce, while the local commander of the Maquis emerged with other hidden beings. The agent was described in detail by the daughter: how he had come into the house, looked round with a hideous snarl, spoken with a heavy German accent, and how he wore a black cap. The cap gave me an idea and I drew a pencil sketch of a Maquisard lately arrived in the district—yes, it was the man. There was a general gasp of relief, and the sentries were called in for a drink. And when they were sitting down drinking Mirabelle out of little glasses, Madame spared a moment from her cooking to scold them for their false alarm. 'Frightening honest women like that—Mon Dieu! Because a man's face frightens you?' and heaping abuse on them, she ended up by falling forward on the table and laughing till both she and the table quivered together. 'Tu es un imbécile!' she gasped between roars of merriment. Someone suggested we should be quieter, as the Germans—and 'Mon . . . les salauds!' shouted Madame as she bore an omelette to the table.

I never saw her downcast, even at the worst moments. She was always ready to house and feed soldiers and slap them on the back and tell them they were heroes when they felt more like lost dogs. She was, as I say, the type of the Resistance, and her grandeur of character bore a classic hall-mark: she was not conscious of being remarkable. After the war I visited her to get her to fill up a form which would enable her to receive the King's Medal, and as she placed a hand on my shoulder, fairly weighing me down where I sat explaining the details, 'Mais non!' she broke in, rolling her blue eyes, 'Voyez—ça n'est pas pour moi, c'est pour les militaires—ça.' There was no affectation. I asked her what had happened to her after our departure.' 'The Boches were always round the house,' she said. 'They guessed all right. So one day I called out to their sergeant: "Hi, you," I said, "are you looking for billets for your men? Come in here. I have plenty of room and plenty of hay." They went.' I can imagine how she uttered that invitation.

There were many such gay stout-hearted women in the Vosges, but I must not allow an impression that such beings were a majority, or that , though these merry-makers were the strength and the spring of defiance, the nightmare was anything but insupportable. Fear was a daily companion. It is difficult even for a soldier to imagine the intensity of such unremitting drawn-out ordeals of fear which French people suffered for five years; the fear of death in battle is little compared to what is engendered by the helplessness of immobility and remorseless hostile scrutiny. I know of two women of the Vosges who went mad. I know of another who nearly went mad, but was able to save herself by the same strict self-discipline by which she had quelled to great purpose five years of fear.

Mlle Bergeron was the antithesis of Madame Rossi: a severe, conventional, serious, middle-aged spinster who kept a small farm out in the country. The Germans knew she was frightened and suspected that she was working for the Maquis and us. I think they hated her more than the others because she seemed so much more easily within their power. She was the principal message-bearer of the whole Maquis organization, and there were few things they wanted to know that she could not have told. She never gave in. They heaped every humiliation on her to break her spirit, to break the spirit of this obviously terrified woman, and they failed absolutely. They made her house into a brothel, they beat her, they tortured her, without avail. This quiet, prim, very ordinary-looking well-dressed woman had the strength of a tiger. The final revenge on her was too disgusting to be described. The Germans dragged her old invalid aunt, who lived with Mlle Bergeron, from her bed, and as a result of their obscene fooling, the old woman died. It was after her death, after the liberation of the Vosges, and when the strain was relaxed, that this brave woman almost went out of her mind.

There was one 'ange de la résistance' in a nearby village

who, as I look back, seems almost to spoil my picture, seems to bring a touch of over-popular sentimentalism into the hard realism of my gallery of modern Joans. She was a young girl of eighteen, with bright fair hair, beautiful features, and for all her grace the strength of a man; she was, in fact, Joan of Arc much as popular fancy would have her, but such as an astute theatrical director might reject on the grounds that she did not fulfil the requirement of plainness. If Mlle Bergeron illustrates the darker, the more true aspect of resistance, this adorable creature may stand as a symbol for the occasional and no less real element which, as by a flash, illuminated the hateful scene at rare moments. I knew her by repute as she had guided a group of our men through the forests south of Baccarat and across the river Meurthe to join us in the Vosges highlands. Her beauty, her incredible endurance on the march, how she leaped down precipitous stream-beds from crag to crag, had often been told to me, so that when after the war I went to pay her an official visit of thanks, I was in much curiosity. Mlle Simone was exactly as she had been described, and when later she conducted me through the woods to a neighbouring hamlet, I followed with as much difficulty and as many falls as though guided by some intelligent wild animal.

She had lived as a Maquisarde for two years and had enjoyed herself thoroughly. She had crossed the lines (which after mid-September of 1944 were static and thus very difficult to get through), some five of six times. When military information was needed about German dispositions, she took the simple course of walking to the German lines and looking at them. She had only one grievance, namely that when the American Army at long last arrived in November they placed her under arrest for a few hours. I tried to calm her by explaining that as she was the only person left in her shell-shattered village when they arrived, and as the only explanation she could give them was that she wanted to see a battle, they were not wholly unreasonable in viewing her with momentary suspicion. But nothing could assuage her anger or stem her torrent of protestation. She was a strong and garrulous character.

Our meeting ended in a pleasing scene. I had been charged with a set of finely printed documents, formal letters of thanks from our Brigadier to French families who had helped us in the campaign, one of which was destined for Mlle Simone. As it was written in English, I translated it for her, without interruption until I came to a particularly solemn statement: 'Vos actes de patriotisme,' I read, 'en ce qui concerne nos opérations sont notés par le gouvernement britannique, et seront conservés dans les archieves de notre ministère de la Guerre.' At this she burst out, laughing outright, and unable myself to continue with a serious countenance, I handed it to her with the translation incomplete.

HOW YEO-THOMAS WENT TO FRANCE

By Bruce Marshall

Prior to the 1914–18 war Christian nations had required only armies and navies to protect them from the dastardly deeds of other Christian nations. (This is not a sneer at religion, but at our manner of practising it.) By the end of that war, however, science had so far outstripped morality as to make an Air Force an essential item in a nation's armoury; and in 1940 a fourth and not very easily classified form of warfare had been added: subversive activities or hitting the enemy behind his lines, but not necessarily below the belt.

The British organization for prodding the Germans in unexpected places had its headquarters, unsuitably perhaps from a security point of view, in Baker Street, where the ghost of Sherlock Holmes, driving past in a phantom hansom with Watson, might notice the variegated uniforms disappearing into the main entrance and murmur deductions in the doltish doctor's ear. Outside the door of Norgeby House a black *plaque* with INTER-SERVICES RESEARCH BUREAU engraved upon it in gold letters attempted to explain to a possibly curious public the number of Naval, Army and Air Force officers, British, American and French, constantly entering and leaving the building. Michael House, on the upper floors of which the high brass sat, pitched between heaven and Marks and Spencer, was slightly more discreet, because the admirals, the generals and the air commodores, with their not entirely misleading *Daily Mirrors* under their arms, entered from a lane at the back. Into both buildings, morning and evening, there also poured a stream of pretty secretaries, many of them, in the words of a popular lady novelist, 'with a subtle something in their eyes that swiftly roused the beast that lies in men'. Some of them, to judge by their literacy, might have been employed as a cover. There the pleasantry ends: in Special Operations Executive, known to its members as the Old Firm, even the sedentary were much too busy to have any time for dalliance.

For the purpose of S.O.E. was deadly serious, and men's lives depended upon its efficiency. The organization operated under the direct control of the Ministry of Economic Warfare, with tentacles reaching out to the Admiralty, the War Office, the Air Ministry, the Foreign Office and the algebraic M.I.'s. Its activities, as Yeo-Thomas says, were 'multiple, secret and complicated', and their purpose to harass by all means possible the enemy in his own country and in those which he had occupied. This was achieved, for the most part, by the infiltration of agents who alone, or with other agents recruited locally, disrupted the enemy's communications by blowing up railway tracks or hindered his war production by destroying pylons, electricity generating plants and machinery in factories. This form of warfare was both more accurate and benign than aerial bombardment. An agent insinuated into a factory could sabotage effectively and without loss of human life a piece of essential machinery which a squadron of bombers would be lucky to hit by chance. *Pace* Air Chief Marshal Harris, cruelty at a remove is, as the late George Bernard Shaw pointed out, still cruelty, even if the flight lieutenant who lets the phosphorus bomb drop doesn't see the baby catch fire.

For practical purposes and to maintain secrecy, S.O.E. was divided up into a number of water-tight compartments. Yeo-Thomas was sent to work in the Western Europe Directorate, commanded by Lieutenant-Colonel Keswick. Under this Directorate there were two French Sections, 'F' Section and 'R.F.' Section. 'F' Section, commanded by Major (afterwards Colonel) Maurice Buckmaster, was a purely British-operated section employing agents, French or French-speaking British, recruited by the British and not connected officially with any of the French Resistance Movements. 'R.F.' Section, commanded when Tommy joined it by Captain Piquet-Wicks, was a British-staffed section which worked in close liaison with General de Gaulle's Bureau Central de Renseignements et d'Action; it arranged the supply and parachuting of arms and equipment to the French Resistance Movements and the transport to and from France of agents recruited and employed by the Free French.

Colonel Passy, the head of the French B.C.R.A., deplores, in his *10 Duke Street, Londres*, the existence of 'F' Section, and, in conversation, Yeo-Thomas does not always refer to it cordially. The attitude of both is comprehensible. Passy, a loyal and very courageous Frenchman, did not like to see the British meddling in what he considered to be a purely French province; he forgot that if it had not been for Britain's example there would almost certainly have been no large-scale French Resistance Movements to encourage and arm. Yeo-Thomas, impulsive by nature but certainly understanding the French much better than many of his masters, was perhaps actuated by healthy rivalry; experience has shown that the competitive spirit, if carried only slightly too far, can make an Argyll and Sutherland Highlander hate a Cameronian in the same brigade much more thoroughly than the German whose misdeeds he only reads about in the newspapers.

There were, however, many good reasons for the existence of 'F' Section. The British wanted to be sure of having at their

Christopher Sykes

Bruce Marshall

Maurice Buckmaster

Photo. Basil Shackleton
Francis Noel Baker

Photo. Howard Coster
John Connell

F. Spencer Chapman

HOW YEO-THOMAS WENT TO FRANCE

sole disposal and under their sole control on 'D' day a number of small groups in French territory on whom they could rely to destroy military installations. The fact that these groups were small and had no communication with one another or with the larger French Resistance Movements increased their security, never a very strong quality of the French. There was also the uncertain French internal political situation to be taken into consideration and the prima-donna-ish vapours of de Gaulle, who would temporarily cut off all dealings with the British when he imagined that he had been snubbed by Churchill. In any case, the value of the work done by 'F' Section has been widely proved, and one of its heroic agents, Odette Sansom, has made its excellence known to the public.

This, however, is a polemic upon which I would not insist, and I mention it only because others have done so.

'R.F.' Section, in those days, 'lived out' at No. 1 Dorset Square, in a house in which, suitably enough according to the Section's critics in Baker Street, they had succeeded as tenants the directorate of the Bertram Mills Circus. It was here that Yeo-Thomas, running through reams of mostly supererogative courier from the field, had to learn to separate the essential from the useless and the possibly informative from the certainly nonsensical. It was here that he memorized the symbols of his colleagues so that he was able to act immediately when AD/E ordered him to contact D/R about the communication which MA2 had received from L/IF.

Yeo-Thomas had by now been promoted to flight-lieutenant to enable him to cope with his new responsibilities.

In between reading superfluous intelligence about German divisions on the Eastern Front which had been issued with women's knickers and brassières in mistake for Balaclava helmets, he had to equip and prepare the section's current operations. His work soon brought him in contact with his colleagues of the French B.C.R.A., with some of whom he was to work later in the field. He came to know and like the cool,

M

steely-eyed and efficient Commandant (later Colonel) Passy and his hard-working second-in-command Capitaine Manuel. He made friends with their assistants and agents, with Pichard, a slim young man with wavy chestnut hair, and with Ayral, and with other agents with whom he was afterwards to be intimately associated in the field.

1942 was a building-up period for the Free French and 'R.F.' Section, and the B.C.R.A. worked without respite. In spite of the protests of their commanding officers the best men available were selected from the French troops to be trained as agents. When they had been screened by the B.C.R.A. and M.I. they were sent to schools specializing in the functions for which they had been chosen. Radio operators and saboteurs and men to train agents recruited in France had to be instructed. Others had to be taught the difficult art of finding new landing and parachuting grounds in France and organizing reception committees to man them. These last were picked with special care, as many of them would ultimately be required to supervize all air operations in a large area.

By the autumn the section had grown to such importance that a lieutenant-colonel was appointed to command it. Colonel J. R. H. Hutchinson was a dapper little cavalry officer with a passion for tabbing documents with pink slips inscribed with the order: 'PLEASE SPEAK'. Under his instructions French was exclusively spoken at No. 1 Dorset Square and, as not all the staff was bilingual, liberties were taken with the language of Racine. An agent was once referred to as '*un vrai fil vivant*', and such literal translations as '*chanson de cygne*' and '*moi, mon vieux, si j'étais dans vos souliers*' enlivened the rooms where Bertram Mills had once contracted their clowns. 'Hutch', as he was inevitably called, was an enthusiastic and courageous soldier: in 1944, when he was more than fifty years old, he was dropped into France, where he valiantly conducted himself as a 'Jedburgh'.

Yeo-Thomas was now in charge of planning, and Johnson

had been recalled from Inchmery to supervize operations. But, although he no longer needed to waste time reading administrative irrelevancies about Polish and Czechoslovak officers being required to pay for the maintenance of their trusses, Tommy was not happy in his job. Perhaps the memory of a signal received from France in July helped to unsettle him: *Allez vous envahir avant le quinze août? Répondez oui ou non.* He felt guilty briefing men for dangerous missions when he himself had never been in the field, and he remembered the vow which he had made at the American Monument at Pointe-de-Grave. He made repeated requests to be sent to France, but all were refused on the grounds that his presence at headquarters was essential. At last, however, it was agreed that if a mission important enough to require his special knowledge could be found he would be sent to France. Yeo-Thomas quickly found himself this mission.

At that time the Navy was short of small craft for coastal operations. Tommy remembered that Captain Molyneux, his peacetime employer, owned a fast motor-yacht which was moored in Monte Carlo harbour. Thinking that the vessel might interest the Navy, he proposed that he should be entrusted with the mission of seizing her and making a dash for Gibraltar. This suggestion was finally approved and Yeo-Thomas was authorized to approach Captain Molyneux, who agreed to hand over his yacht without compensation. An agent called Charvet, recently sent to unoccupied France, was to provide a crew of three. Four hundred and fifty gallons of petrol, fifty of oil, food and two light machine-guns would be provided by felucca operation. Yeo-Thomas himself would be infiltrated in by the felucca or by parachute or Lysander operation. For this operation he was given the not very opaque name of 'Seahorse'.

To Tommy's disappointment the whole situation in the Mediterranean suddenly changed and the project was abandoned. He was, however, allowed to hold himself in readiness for another mission and on 29 November 1942 set off for the parachute school at Wilmslow.

When Yeo-Thomas returned to Dorset Square he found that the situation in France had become critical. The Free French agents working for the B.C.R.A. were in constant and grave danger. They were tracked and harassed not only by the Gestapo but also by the Vichy Police, the Groupe Mobile and Darnand's Milice. The weakness of the various Resistance Movements was accentuated by the fact that, largely because of their political differences, they were all working independently. In order to increase their efficiency it was necessary both to finance and to co-ordinate them. And if they were to aid the Allies when they invaded France, the paramilitary organizations of all groups must be welded into a unified Secret Army, working under a single Commander with an efficient staff. In particular, the activities of the Communist Party must be ascertained and their leaders persuaded to allow their combat units to join the united paramilitary branches.

It was therefore decided to send Colonel Passy and Commandant Brossolette to France to effect the co-ordination of the Resistance Movements in the Occupied Zone.

Passy, the head of the B.C.R.A., who had taken his *nom de guerre* from the métro station, was then thirty years old. Fearless, cultivated and intelligent, his real name was André Dewavrin. He had been educated in Paris at the Collège Stanislas, the Lycée Louis le Grand and the Ecole Polytechnique. In 1938 he had been assistant professor of fortifications at St. Cyr and in 1940 had fought in Norway. He had left France to join General de Gaulle on 18 June 1940. At the end of the war he was to hold the British D.S.O. and M.C. as well as French and Norwegian decorations.

Pierre Brossolette, still under forty, was small and thin. He had thick black hair with a bright white lock in front. Passy says of him: '*Brossolette fut, sans conteste, l'homme qui, parmi tous ceux que j'ai été amené à rencontrer dans ma vie, fit sur moi la plus forte impression.*'[1] Educated at the Ecole Normale, where he had taken his degree in history, he had, before the war, been a regular contributor to the Socialist daily *Le Populaire*. The Popular Front Government had appointed him an official foreign news commentator on the national radio, from which post he had been dismissed in 1938 because of his violently expressed disapproval of the Munich Agreement. After the Armistice in 1940, refusing to write for the collaborationist Press, he had purchased a small bookshop in the rue de la Pompe near the Lycée Janson de Sailly, whose pupils were his principal customers. He had arrived in England in April 1942, and had already been on a mission in France.

Passy felt, rightly or wrongly, that British agents making use of Frenchmen living in France often left them under the impression that they were working for de Gaulle, whereas in reality they were working only for the British. Suspecting, too, that British agents had caused trouble by contacting groups already linked with the B.C.R.A., he wanted to find out the truth for himself. This he proposed to do during his mission of co-ordination. But in order to avoid his report being regarded as biased he requested that a British officer should be sent with Brossolette and himself to make an independent report, both on this subject and on the co-ordination of the Resistance Movements. Because of his knowledge of France and of his perfect command of the language Yeo-Thomas was chosen. Security was increased by his retaining the code name of Seahorse. He was sent immediately to Beaulieu, where he learned the difficult art of sending messages in cypher.

On his return to London, Yeo-Thomas was given false papers in the name of François Thierry, whose story he had to learn by heart and make his own. He had been born on 17 June 1901, at Arras, and was a bachelor. Before the war he

---

[1] Brossolette was, without doubt, the man who, amongst all those I have met in my life, made the greatest impression on me.

had lived at 41 rue St. Ferdinand, Paris, and had worked as a clerk. During the war he had served with the 34th Batallion de l'Air and had been demobilized at Marignane on 27 August 1940. He lived now at 9 rue Richepanse, Paris, and had taken up his previous employment as a clerk. To support this story he was provided with a *carte d'identité* issued by the Paris Préfecture de Police on 16 April 1941, a *feuille de démobilsation* issued in Marseilles on 2 September 1940, and a *permis de conduire* issued in Paris on 12 June 1934. He was also furnished with a current French ration card issued in the name of Thierry.

Finally, Yeo-Thomas received his orders, which read:

SEAHORSE OPERATION ORDER

1. Seahorse to investigate with Colonel Passy ... the potentiality of Resistance groups in the 'Zone Occupée'.

This investigation will comprise:

(a) A thorough examination of the set-up, especially with regard to its effectiveness.

(b) An enquiry into the nature of existing groups and their relation to the present central staff, known as Etatmajor Zone Occupée.

(c) The consideration, in conjunction with the Forces Françaises Combattantes staff officers, of the means for establishing a system of joint control, firstly in France and secondly in relation to a future inter-allied command.

2. An especially important function, from the point of view of S.O.E., is to decide, as near as possible, the real capacity of individual organizations to furnish men and equipment, and carry out precise tasks or directives emanating from London but issued by local commanders.

On the basis of the above an approximate estimate of the requirements of these groups in the way of equipment, communications, arms and explosives will be furnished.

3. Special attention should be paid to the Communistic Organization, known paramilitarily as F.A.N.A., in order to ascertain:

(a) whether it is seriously willing to fall in with the F.F.C. plans for a local general staff, or, if not, whether use could be made of the organization on the basis of liaison rather than direct control;

(b) whether we may be able to implement the progress and action, especially on the side of training and ability.

Rather a tall order, don't you think?

In those days operations took place between the end of the first quarter and the beginning of the last quarter of the moon, preferably when the moon was at its fullest. Yeo-Thomas calculated that he would be leaving between the 17th and the 28th of February. As the day approached he was surprised that he did not feel frightened. Instead he found himself thinking of José Dupuis, the school-teacher friend to whom he had sent a postcard on leaving Pointe-de-Grave. Sure that she at least was loyal and hoping that she listened in to the French news from London, he sent her a message by the B.B.C. '*De Tommy à José. Nous reboirons bientôt du bon vin de Chignin.*'[1] During holidays before the war he had drunk this wine with her in the village near Chambéry after which it was named, and he was confident that she would understand the message if she heard it.

Meanwhile plans had been slightly changed. Brossolette had already left for the field and Passy and Yeo-Thomas were to follow him.

On the morning of 24 February Tommy was warned that the operation would take place that night. He had a farewell lunch with Barbara, who by now was a civilian working for the B.C.R.A. At three o'clock he left Dorset Square for 10 Duke Street, where he picked up Passy. They were driven through the cold misty countryside to Tempsford in the Midlands, where they arrived about five o'clock.

After a cup of piping hot tea they went through all their kit under the vigilant eyes of an accompanying officer. The clothing which they were going to wear in France was examined for tell-tale English labels and the pockets turned

[1] 'From Tommy to José. We'll soon drink again good Chignin wine.'

out to make sure that they did not contain any forgotten bus tickets or British-stamped envelopes. No objection was made to the Countess Grabbe's sachet which Yeo-Thomas still wore round his neck. When they had changed from their uniforms into their civilian suits they put in the now secure pockets their false French identity papers, their money, their benzedrine tablets and other appurtenances. In case of sudden need Yeo-Thomas placed his cyanide tablet in his waistcoat pocket while Passy concealed his inside a small signet ring with a swivel top. They were dined by the C.O., who produced a bottle of excellent burgundy.

The two agents then put on their strip-tease suits, rubber helmets and spine pads. An outer thigh pocket carried their revolvers and other special pockets their compasses and knives. To their already cumbersome gear they attached their parachutes. With all their armour on they were driven out to the waiting Halifax bomber whose shape loomed up eerily through the mist. The accompanying officer wished them luck by saying 'merde'. They climbed clumsily into the aircraft, because the hole was not very large and their parachutes made ingress difficult.

Inside there was not much room for them to sit because of the packages piled up all around. Each package was protected with sponge rubber and heavy canvas and had its parachute attached. The packages, inside one of which were Passy's and Tommy's suitcases, contained arms, wireless transmitting sets and explosives.

The despatcher, a sergeant, busied himself upon last-minute jobs. The engines started up, the aeroplane vibrated and began to move slowly forward. Because there were no windows or openings, Yeo-Thomas could not see out, but he could feel that they were taxying up to the end of the runway, where the aircraft would turn into the wind. The aircraft stood still. The engines broke out into a roar and then quietened down again. The pilot opened the throttle, and the great Halifax began to move forward once more, gradually going quicker and quicker. Soon a light, thin feeling beneath his legs told Yeo-Thomas that they were airborne.

In those days there were two nights in the world, one which we believed to be the right kind and the other the wrong kind. It was from the right kind of night to the wrong kind of night that Yeo-Thomas was going, so that the wrong kind of night might again become the right kind of night. A thought similar to this occurred to him as he sat there among the packages unable to talk to Passy because of the noise of the engines. He was wondering what it would feel like to be surrounded by Germans, to walk in familiar places and to know that all around him were enemies, the constant perception of whose presence might lend an appearance of rectitude to their purposes.

About half an hour later they were over the French coast. Soon the bursts of flak could be heard above the drone of the engines. The pilot took avoiding action, mounting, diving, swerving. Suddenly there was silence, the machine side-slipped wildly, and for a second Yeo-Thomas thought that they were going to have to bale out. Abruptly, however, the engines roared into life again and the aircraft went steadily on. Shortly afterwards they began to circle and Tommy knew that the pilot must be looking for the pinpoint and the lights of the reception committee. But although they kept there, there was still no sign from the despatcher, and at last the circling stopped and the sergeant came forward and shouted in Tommy's ear:

'Low cloud over your pinpoint. Pilot can't find it. We're going home.'

Yeo-Thomas passed the message on to Passy. Angry at the anti-climax, they sat in silence. They passed through searchlights and more flak as they recrossed the French coast, but both of them were too dejected to feel afraid. At 4.30 a.m. they were back in Tempsford, so short a distance separated the wrong from the right sort of night. Tired out, they went to bed and next morning, on instructions from headquarters, returned to London.

On Friday, 26 February, they made another attempt. The aircraft took off shortly after midnight in the pale light of the waning moon. Apart from a little flak over the French coast, the flight was uneventful. At about 3 a.m. the despatcher came to tell them that they were over the pinpoint, which was near the Lyons-la-Forêt in Normandy. He opened the hatch, round which he had already arranged the packages, ready to be pushed out after the agents had jumped. Passy and Yeo-Thomas climbed over and hooked up the static lines which would pull open their parachutes as they fell through the hole. (In operations over France the drops were too low to permit the use of self-opening parachutes.)

Passy, who was to jump first, got into position with his back to the engine and his legs dangling through the hole. Tommy sat opposite him, ready to swing in as soon as he had jumped. Below him he could see the lighted torches of the reception committee, twinkling like an incandescent necklace. The red lamp went on. Seeing his companion stiffen, Yeo-Thomas edged nearer the hole. The despatcher's arm went up, the lamp turned to green and Passy disappeared. Surprised at his own fearlessness, Tommy swung his legs into the hole and gave a push. He felt the rush of air in the slipstream and then the slight jerk of his parachute opening out as he started to float down.

Slightly to the right and underneath him he could see the monster flower of Passy's parachute shining in the moonlight. The air was crisp and cold. The light of the torches came rushing up to meet him. He touched the ground, rolled over, undid his harness, stood up and drew in his breath. He had fulfilled the vow which he had made in 1940 in front of the American memorial at Pointe-de-Grave. He had returned to France.

THE TRAINING OF AGENTS

By Maurice Buckmaster

It was evident from the outset that the success of our venture would depend to a very large extent on the value of the men and women who were recruited to perform these tasks. It was equally obvious that the decision to adopt this hard and solitary life must be a voluntary one on their part; there could be no compulsion, no drafting of recruits into this branch of the service. We decided from the beginning to give our candidates every facility to retire without loss of dignity if they wished to do so. Indeed, it was made clear to them initially that if they were 'returned to their units', such failure to qualify for our arduous service would cast no slur whatever on their military careers nor imply any reflexion on their courage. We merely asked them to make up their minds definitely before their final briefing, and we engaged them upon their honour to consider themselves bound at all times by the Official Secrets Act in respect of anything they had learned during their training period.

It was our object to speed up the last weeks of training and briefing as much as possible. Nothing is so sapping to morale as an indefinite wait before action which demands the highest degree of pluck. In the event, only one group failed us, and, although from time to time individuals notified their intention of reverting to more normal employment, the numbers who did so were infinitesimal in relation to the whole.

By arrangement with Free French Headquarters, Frenchmen and Frenchwomen who arrived in this country from abroad, whether as refugees from France or from a French colony or elsewhere, were automatically debarred from joining our organization: like Frenchmen already resident in the United Kingdom, they were called to Free French Headquarters, where their future was decided. My only available sources for recruitment were therefore non-Frenchmen, and this amounted, in the early days, only to men and women holding British passports. However, as the war went on, we were proud to include considerable numbers of Canadians (whose French, however, was often insufficiently metropolitan to pass muster); the small British island of Mauritius, with its French-speaking population, distinguished itself by contributing more than a dozen officers to our service—an extremely high proportion of its total service population. South Africans who had lived in Madagascar, inhabitants of the Seychelles and Indo-China, swelled the numbers, but, by and large, we depended upon the products of our own land to make up our field organization. When, later in the war, our headquarters became fully integrated with that of officers of the U.S. forces, a score or more of Americans joined us and performed deeds of great valour.

Recruiting was, at first, rather a haphazard affair. From M.I. we received details of officers or other ranks whose language qualifications appeared, on paper at any rate, to justify investigation. We found that the phrase 'fluent French' was not by any means always justified as an attribution. Language was, naturally, the first and vital hurdle. Schoolboy French was definitely inadequate. Among the applicants, I remember, was the son of my former school French tutor, himself a Frenchman. Here, I thought, was a likely recruit. His French should be fluent enough. I was, however, obliged to reject him on account of the British accent which five years of English public school life had grafted on to his native tongue. Many keen and courageous candidates declared themselves perfectly happy to take the risks of their tongues betraying them. But that was not the point. Any organization of the kind we envisaged was only as strong as its weakest link, and we could not afford to jeopardize valuable agents through the inability of a colleague to speak the French of a Frenchman. It was necessary to exclude from the start all those candidates who failed to convince our examiners that they could be taken for Frenchmen by a Frenchman. This applied to appearance as well as to speech. It is true that, later in the war, we modified these strict requirements in certain cases where an officer could be sent to a maquis group in which he was unlikely to come into contact with either German or, worse, French officials, but at the beginning we were adamant.

Those that survived the language test were next considered from the point of view of character. Now this is a difficult thing to assess. I do not know if I can do more than say that in the type of recruit we wanted, a rugged honesty and singleness of purpose shone in his or her face. We were not concerned with physique, for we knew that training could work wonders with even the most unpromising material, but we were vitally concerned with essential guts. Now, whatever the psychiatrists, whom we rudely referred to as trick-cyclists, averred, we were more ready to back our own judgment of a face and a manner than to accept the scientific appraisal. It was probably quite wrong of us, but it worked. We may have been grossly unfair to the psychiatric gentlemen, because we were unable to tell them, for reasons of security, just what we wanted these men and women to do. We really did not mind very much if the psychiatrist diagnosed a mother fixation or a lack of leadership. It was interesting, but not conclusive, for we could probably supply a French foster-mother, and we did not always want leaders. We wanted people who would obey instructions, blindly but intelligently; people who could be inspired with confidence and passionate belief; people who would carry on, however hopeless perseverance seemed to be.

The essential difference between the successful agent and the successful junior officer seems to me to lie in the fact that the agent has to rely entirely on himself, with only a tenuous and terribly dangerous clandestine radio link with his headquarters, which might fail him at any moment.

The percentage of candidates accepted after the 'character' interview was small. We had to be absolutely certain of our envoys. It was not until they had been assessed in this manner that we introduced the subject of the job. We told them that they should not lightly undertake it, that it meant continuous strain for perhaps years on end. No holidays, no home leave, no local leave, no Sundays nor bank holidays. All the year round pitting their wits against the *Abwehr* and the French *Milice*.[1] Very few took the opportunity we then afforded them for backing out. We told them that they would have to undergo an uncomfortable and arduous period of training before they would be of any use. This they accepted without demur.

We used to try to impute motives to our candidates. Did they come to us, we asked ourselves, out of boredom with their own jobs, or from motives of pecuniary gain (quite misplaced so far as our service was concerned, for we paid the pay of the rank plus a trifling extra for 'talent')? Or did they seek escape from a nagging wife or a financial embarrassment? Or were they impelled by sheer love of adventure and glamour? Or did they just drift into it? Or—and these were the interesting cases—did they come to us because they felt that only in this or similar work could they achieve their maximum contribution to the war effort?

It was sometimes difficult to tell, but it was only this last class that interested us, and it was only they who made a real

---

[1] Pro-German French Militia.

THE TRAINING OF AGENTS

success of the task. Of course, we had to guard against infiltration by enemy agents, who were quite clever enough to simulate this motive, but we had our protection against these.

We were aided in our recruiting by the advent of men and women vouched for and recommended by existing members of the service. One family contributed three brothers, another a brother and sister and cousin. It was quite a family affair, but for security reasons we seldom allowed relatives to work together. From about the beginning of 1943 we had another windfall. It was agreed that, where a Frenchman living in France had served his apprenticeship as a contact with one of our envoys, he might be sent back along the escape routes to England for training and then depart for the field again to establish a new circuit, carrying the rank of a British officer. But even so, we were, at nearly all times up to the spring of 1944, terribly short of wireless operators, essential to the building up of a circuit.

In all, during the period March 1941 to July 1944, we recruited over 460 male and forty female officers for work in the field. It has always seemed to me surprising that there were so many British or Dominion subjects, whose French was faultless, willing and anxious to undertake such supremely dangerous work. They were in no way conspicuous; the last thing we wanted in them was eccentricity. We denied them glamour, in their own interests; we made them look as homely and unremarkable as we could. In the words of one of them, they were 'just ordinary people, not particularly brave'.

Training was a lengthy and complicated affair. A party of recruits of both sexes was summoned to report at our London headquarters; the men who were not already commissioned in a unit were given the rank of second-lieutenants on the General List. The F.A.N.Y. Corps who, throughout the whole war, co-operated with the greatest readiness and efficiency with our somewhat curious organization, devised a preliminary course for the girls, at the end of which they emerged, a trifle breathless, but full of F.A.N.Y. zeal, as ensigns with raspberry insignia on their shoulders. The party, thus constituted, and under the all-embracing eye of a Conducting Officer, made its way to a remote country-house in Surrey. Here, under the fatherly care of a former officer of the Guards' Brigade, school life began again. It was very much like the old classroom affair, except that the language spoken was invariably French. The grounds of the country manor re-echoed to unfamiliar explosions, which disturbed the wild duck and snipe, but the village seemed to pay little attention, dismissing the queer goings-on at the manor as just another example of War Office eccentricity.

A close but not an offensively meddling watch was kept over the activities of the students. They were offered strong drink and their reactions under its influence were studied. Did they talk in their sleep? If so, in what language? Did they give evidence of any unmistakably English mannerisms or habits? What did they do with their knives and forks after they had finished a course? Did they indulge in a flow of reminiscence, or did they maintain a reserved aloofness? Were they perhaps too aloof? Discreet observation of these and kindred matters helped the Commandant to make his weekly report on the party. Written reports were supplemented by meetings: either the Commandant would come up to London or one of us would make a flying visit to Surrey.

We got to know the members of a course very well. We shared their training and exercises whenever we could. We watched them shoot, and we took part in their demolition practice. We spent evenings with them round the fire in the mess ante-room, and then hurried back to London to get on with the paper-work. It was possible, therefore, at the end of a three-weeks' training course, for the Commandant to form a fairly accurate judgment of the potentialities of the candidates, and for us to agree with him rapidly in his recommendations. We rarely found ourselves at variance, and although

J. H. WilliamsRichard Usborne

sometimes it was necessary, for overriding reasons of shortage of specialists—particularly wireless operators—to stretch a point in favour of a candidate, we lost no time in reaching a decision.

After this preparatory course came the toughening school, which was situated in Scotland. The party, less any rejects, went up to the west coast of Scotland to train their bodies to withstand fatigue. They walked, they ran, they swam, they bicycled (and how useful a bicycle was going to prove to them in Occupied France!), they learned to avoid skylines, to move silently through undergrowth, to use the natural background of rough country to get, unobserved, from one point to another. They scaled crags and cliffs, they stalked game, they practised rifle, Sten-gun and Bren-gun firing, they blew things up, they ambushed other parties, in fact they lived the life that the Maquisards of France were going to endure. Tired men and women were asked to pull out that extra bit of energy which might make the difference between life and death. And all the time the Training Officers were shaping them unconsciously for the possible line of retreat across the Pyrenees, with a fast-moving trained Spanish guide as their unrelenting cicerone. Undoubtedly this course of intense physical training saved lives, when lives depended upon the physical ability to walk thirty or forty miles a day up and down steep hills.

The gentle art of poaching was a favourite pastime, much encouraged by the training staff, and regarded with suspicious horror by the professional ghillies whose help was often enlisted. The climax, I think, was reached when, in the icy waters of a mountain burn, a charge of gelignite stunned the grandfather salmon who was the familiar of the local fishermen. The Londoner who perpetrated this unforgivable outrage later earned the D.S.O. for his courage in demolishing an enemy headquarters. The salmon died in a noble cause.

Three weeks of mountain air sent the party back to the south with ravenous appetites and a feeling of physical well-being.

As a contrast, the successful candidates proceeded next to a secret destination in the New Forest, where the art of living behind enemy lines was carefully taught to them. But, first, another weeding-out process took place. Each member of the party was asked whether, upon reflexion, they wished to go on with a career which would lead them to a task of such lonely and unabated hardship. It was the first time that they had been told the exact nature of the work. Curiously, none of the 500 men and women who attended these courses took this chance of dropping out.

A further process occurred at this point. During the course in Scotland, elementary practice in sending Morse signals by radio took place. Those who showed aptitude for this work were segregated and invited to become wireless operators. If they accepted, they were sent to a special training centre in the Midlands, where for six weeks or more they were immersed in the technicalities of their craft and in practising its rapid execution. Before leaving the W/T School they were required to pass a test of their ability, not only to transmit and receive coded Morse signals, but also to install and repair the midget sets with which a beneficent government would supply them, complete with camouflaged suitcase, for work in the field.

In the New Forest, lectures and practical work were interspersed. Candidates learned to pick out individuals in a crowd from an oral description, to pass messages in a crowded place without being overheard, to transmit and receive discreetly notes and documents without alerting bystanders. They were given secret codes which they memorized.

Meanwhile, their physical condition was not neglected. Courses of P.T. took place every morning, and exercises were frequent.

At the end of the course a trial problem was set, which took candidates to the far ends of the country on some difficult task. It might be to find out the size of a new vessel building in a closely guarded port, or it might be to bring back an object

THE TRAINING OF AGENTS

from the entrance to the Severn Tunnel, where Security police swarmed. Only in emergency were students permitted to hand over to the police an envelope in which their mission was described and explained. To do this was to admit failure. It was a hard test, but a very sound one. Upon his return to headquarters, worn out perhaps by the effort of a cross-country journey undertaken illicitly by cadging lifts or jumping trains, the student was grilled by officers specially selected for their ability to simulate bullying methods. The confidence gained by those who had the power to resist was of the greatest value to them. We did not judge too harshly the actual results, but we watched the mental reactions of the students, which provided a guide as to their ability to withstand interrogation.

The finishing course normally lasted about three weeks, but it generally proved necessary for the student to spend at least another fortnight receiving special tuition in one aspect or another of his work. The schools did not like being rushed, and it was perfectly true that assimilation of all the details took a considerable time. In one or two cases the training was speeded up without harm, but these cases were exceptional.

One type of training which could not be hurried was the radio school. Owing to the lack of radio operators, the country sections at headquarters were always bringing pressure to bear on the school to speed up their training. The Commandant rightly took the view that any skimping of instruction jeopardized the life of the operator unnecessarily, and possibly endangered other lives as well. We never succeeded in getting the course shortened.

At the end of the normal training courses the student was pronounced to be ready for the field, but it almost invariably happened that further specialist courses were prescribed, either in arms instruction (if the student was destined to be an instructor) or sabotage or commando training. The sabotage school was a terrifying place to visit. You might be pretty certain, when you pulled up your chair to the table in the mess, that you would cause some minor explosion, in the form of a booby-trap set by the enthusiastic students or even the irrepressible directing staff. If you looked out of the window on a summer's evening you might well see the C.O. of the school disappearing in a strange-looking craft beneath the waters of of the lily-pond. If you opened a window, a detonator might explode. When you pulled the chain in the lavatory, almost anything might happen. For it was in this school that the more advanced and delicate types of destruction were taught. Students were encouraged to calculate with a nicety how much explosive was necessary to bring down a chimney or derail an engine, without doing any consequential damage to neighbouring buildings. It was, in fact, a testing school for the competent saboteur.

The training period was hard but interesting. It was astonishing to learn to what a great extent our officers, male and female, attributed their success in the field to the soundness of their preparatory study.

FLOOD IN THE DESERT

By Francis Noel-Baker

THIS happened eight years ago, in the summer of 1945. I was in the army and in Cairo at the time, waiting for a posting. G.H.Q. was in no hurry to decide what to do with me next, and life was dull. It was also very hot.

One day, when I was beginning to get really impatient I ran into a friend of mine who was a major. We met at a little Greek eating-place in that round *midan*, the one with a palm tree in the middle of it, where the tremendously fat proprietor gave one a good, Balkan kind of meal—meat on little spits, olives, resinated wine and so on—for not too many piastres.

My friend Alex was always an enterprising person. And he found me in just the right mood with his plan for spending three or four days on the Red Sea coast, swimming and fishing. He could easily get away for this expedition, he said, and as I'd been waiting about for so long and had no orders to report anywhere at any particular time ('just keep in touch' I had been told, 'till we fix you up'), I decided I could take a chance and go with him. Alex's wife, who wa sworking in G.H.Q., would come with us, he said, and he could get his driver to take us the 80-odd miles down to the coast, drop us there, and pick us up four days later.

That journey would mean driving across the Eastern Desert. Earlier in the war, it had been used as a training ground for troops and tanks. But now the whole area between the Nile valley and the sea was completely deserted again. Nobody lived there—except possibly a few wandering shepherds—and nothing much grew there. It was just a great rolling mass of sand and rock and smallish flint-like stones, with the huge cliffs of a distant escarpment running along to the south, and here and there a shallow valley—a *wadi*—going down towards the sea. But down on the coast itself, Alex told me, there was wonderful swimming, beautiful wide beaches, and, he added, all sorts of fascinating fishing. For all I know, he may have been perfectly right about this. But we never found out. For we never actually saw the Red Sea at all.

I believe that Alex himself had been to the coast once before. At least, he certainly knew parts of the Eastern Desert. So I left most of the preparation to him. He decided what route we should go by, when we should leave and what gear and stores we should take with us. I remember that they included a strange collection of captured German concentrated food, some American K-rations, two or three jerry-cans of water, and an odd assortment of automatic weapons the possession of which was probably highly illegal.

Anyhow, I left all that to Alex. And it was he who guided us out into the desert early on Sunday morning, past the New Zealanders' Camp outside Maadi, and headed the truck along a track leading east. The desert grew gradually wider and emptier. The sounds of the camp and the Nile valley receded into the distance and it was very quiet. I found myself thinking that it wasn't really so very surprising that men who get lost in the desert often begin to have fantastic hallucinations after a short time. For, in the morning light, that rock over there on the left really *did* look just like a tent; those others, on the skyline exactly like advancing tanks. And surely that patch of rough stones really *was* a plot of vegetables growing in the sand. Well, of course, they were nothing of the kind. But even

FLOOD IN THE DESERT 183

in the early sunshine, the shapes and colours were often weirdly misleading.

For several hours, all went well. We stopped briefly for breakfast, and then drove on again towards the East. Here and there, Alex told the driver to branch off down a side track, or to skirt round some *tell*—some little desert hill—we had been travelling about forty miles before we noticed something strange. Though that desert looked about the driest place anyone could imagine, and anyway it was the middle of the summer, it seemed clear that there must have been some heavy rain out there during the past few weeks. At several points, the track we had been following had been washed out. And a few miles further on, it became clear, that we should probably run right off our route altogether if we tried to travel any further East. Besides which, frequent stops had slowed us up, and our driver had to get his truck back to the depot by that evening.

So we decided, after a short confabulation, to change our plans. We agreed that we would stop at the first suitable spot we found, and just camp out there in the middle of the desert. We should not be able to swim (or so we thought) and we shouldn't be able to fish. But, in spite of its emptiness, it was oddly intriguing country. Soon we spotted an old gnarled tree in the middle of a *wadi*. It was about sixty yards from a small hillock, from the top of which one could see for miles across the surrounding desert. There we stopped, unloaded the truck, lit a fire (using pieces of the tree for the purpose), gave the driver a mug of tea, and sent him off back to Cairo. He was sure, he said, that he could find his way back to the depot, and would come and collect us on the following Thursday.

So there we were—though none of us knew exactly where it was. Maps of the area were highly unreliable, and during the days when the tanks had been training here, they had made so many new tracks that there was very little way of telling what went where. However, we felt pretty pleased. The tree's gnarled branches and scraggy leaves—like dusty green feathers—gave quite good shade. And although the sun was very strong, the air was crisp and dry: a welcome contrast after the heavy dampness of the Nile valley, and the dust and dirt and flies of Cairo. And the Eastern Desert itself was a fine sight. Very different from what I had expected because there was an infinite variety of shape and colour in the surface of the sand and the distant hills. In the particular valley where we were, there was also some minor vegetation; a few odd little shrubs and thorns. And, away in the distance, loomed the vast blue-yellow cliffs of the escarpment.

Apart from the tree, the shrubs and ourselves, there were few other living things about. We saw some small yellow lizards darting among the stones, and occasionally heard the sounds of sheep and dogs and donkeys in the very far distance. But otherwise—for as far as we could see in any direction—we had the place entirely to ourselves.

We started to settle in. I was appointed cook for the first day, and got busy organizing a fireplace and thinking about the evening meal. Alex and his wife went for a short walk. It was late afternoon, and already starting to get cooler, though the sun was still high and bright in the sky. Then, suddenly, without any warning, we were startled by a dull, reverberating crash coming, as far as we could tell, from some miles further up the valley. It was followed by another and another and another; each one getting louder and more dramatic. Then we began to see great flashes of purple lightning in the sky. And soon we were in the middle of one of the most powerful and exciting thunderstorms I had ever seen. Great zig-zags of burning electricity and a noise like nothing one can imagine. And, while this was going on, a few drops of rain fell: but so little that it only lasted ten minutes or so and seemed to evaporate before it had even damped us. Then the raindrops stopped, and a little later—perhaps after half an hour—so did the storm. It was terrific while it lasted; but once it had ended, we had soon forgotten all about it and were settling down hungrily to our evening meal. Then the sun set, the first stars started to gleam in the evening sky, a nearly-full moon came up, and, after sitting round the fire talking for half an hour or so, we decided to turn in, I one one side of the tree, Alex and his wife on the other.

I suppose that it was about 11 o'clock that night when we woke. I was sleeping fairly heavily and couldn't make out at first what Alexis' wife was talking about. She seemed to be telling him something about water. I assumed she was asking for a drink, and turned over to go to sleep. Then, I heard them speak again. And as I listened I too thought I heard, in the far distance, the vague sound of swishing, lapping water, and behind it, as it were, a low rumble.

We got up and the noise got louder. Water it unmistakably was—and a very great deal of water at that. And it was obviously coming towards us—fast. In fact, the whole valley was flooding and what amounted to a considerable river was rushing straight down it towards our tree. By this time the low rumble had become a sharp, roaring noise as the water ground the stones on the bottom of the valley against each other.

We decided it was time to move. We grabbed our blankets and clothes, some of the food and a couple of jerry cans, and made off to the hill. As we walked towards it, we saw the water distinctly for the first time. It was an extraordinary sight. There we were, standing in the warm, parched sand, and there, hurtling down towards us was this rushing grey river ... or rather, half a river. For behind us the desert still lay dry and silent just as it always was. By this time, the front of the water—the lip of the river one might call it—was nearly a foot high, and travelling towards us at speed.

We dumped our loads on the hillock, left Alexis's wife in charge of them, and turned back to the tree again. This time, the water had come level with us, and was now flowing past us down the valley. We had to wade through it up to our shins with the stones twisting and slipping under our feet. The tree was already surrounded. We pushed two more jerry cans and some boxes up into its branches, picked up the remains of our stores, and staggered off back through the river. That journey was alarming. For by now the water was up to and over our knees and running with considerable force. However, we reached the hill, and found Alexis's wife right at the top standing surrounded by our stores, and looking out rather forlornly across the rising flood, which now filled the whole valley with swirling water, turning the hill itself into an island. For a moment, we wondered whether it, too, was going to be submerged. But by midnight the level had stopped rising, and left us ample room to settle down once more to sleep.

Next morning, the early light showed us that though our tree was still more than half under water, the floods had subsided to a moderate-sized stream—perhaps thirty feet across and two or three feet deep—with here and there some deeper pools where we were later able comfortably to bathe. In fact we came to the conclusion that, on the whole, the river was a distinct—if unexpected—improvement to our camping site.

That day, Monday, was hot and sunny like the day before. No sign of disturbed weather till, once again, exactly as on Sunday, another tremendous thunderstorm shattered the quiet of the desert for thirty minutes in the late afternoon. And then, later on that night, the floods rose once more, the water began raging down the valley, our hill became an island, and the night was filled with the sound of grinding stones. But this time, of course, we were already safely on the hill, able to watch the advancing tide at our leisure.

That night was the last time it happened. Next day, we again had a moderate stream in our *wadi*, the day after a little brook, the day after that a thin trickle, running between muddy potholes, and finally, on the sixth day, just a few puddles in the sand. Meanwhile, the most astonishing green patches of grasses and little fresh new plants had suddenly covered the valley where before there had been only the stunted shrubs. That was on the sixth day. Which was odd. It certainly surprised us. For it was on the morning of the fifth day, Thursday, that the truck should have come to pick us up and take us back to Cairo. It failed to arrive. On Friday there was still no sign and we were beginning to run a little short of food, though we had refilled our jerry cans with slightly muddy water from the potholes. We wondered whether, perhaps, our truck was lost. And we decided that someone was going to have to take a walk to Cairo—across some sixty miles of desert to fetch a rescue party. By a two-to-one vote, it was eventually decided that it should be me.

Actually it would have been a fairly easy walk. For we still had some K-rations and (as we later saw) there was quite a little water lying about in odd puddles in the desert. It was simply a question of heading due west and keeping going until, somewhere or other, one hit the Nile valley. But I was saved the trouble. For those storms which we imagined to be purely local, had in fact caused big floods in the Cairo area too. Several villages had been washed out, some people drowned, and a friend of Alexis's who knew where we had gone, had set out to find us three days before. But his truck had bogged down in the sand, and he had been dug out and towed back to Cairo by the New Zealanders. There he had proceeded to panic. With the result that, on Thursday, half a dozen Wellington bombers were sent out to scour the Eastern Desert from the air (we did in fact see some aircraft), and patrols of jeeps set out to search the area by land.

Four of these jeeps appeared over the horizon behind our hill on Saturday afternoon: the day before I was due to start my walk to Cairo. They came with stretchers, water, food and brandy, and seemed—perhaps naturally—a little disappointed not to find us either half drowned or dying quietly of thirst. But their concern was nothing to ours, when we noticed that out of the fourth jeep stepped three burly and determined-looking military police. And our first reception at G.H.Q. was far from friendly. But that's another story. It, too, had a happy ending. Despite our misdemeanours in the desert, seven or eight weeks later I was back in England and Alex was a Lieutenant-Colonel. But we still don't know much about fishing on the Red Sea coast.

ARAB RADIO STATION

By John Connell

SHORT-WAVE radio listening is a game which nowadays I don't often play. Yet twiddle the dial a bit among the higher frequencies, and suddenly—away from the torrents of operetta-like Italian, away from the throaty and arrogant mutter of German, clear above the merely atmospheric squawks and growls—you may hear the high, plangent, characteristic and utterly unforgettable cry of an Arab *taqht*; hold it for a minute, let its fierce, forlorn melodies flood as they will into your spirit. Do you recall a night when you strolled away from the billet or the rest-camp down a dim-lit side-street, down another—narrower, muddier, more odorous—boys and men, nightgowned, alien, and curiously unconcerned, shuffling past you in the dusk, shuttered windows, the croak of bull-frogs and, then round a corner, a café from whose recesses blared or moaned or whined this sort of music?

Across a widening gap of years as well as across many thousands of miles you hear the sounds, you feel the sharp joys and sorrows of your own youth: the prickle of sweat, the cool reassurance of newly-laundered khaki drill, the tilt of a beret, the taste of a brew-up... all sorts of memories and images surprisingly and stirringly evoked. For me, I must confess, the sound of Arab music has an extremely poignant significance; the recollection of some of the most exciting and enterprising months of my life is steeped in it. You have only in my presence, of a winter evening, to twist the dial of a radio, and I relive urgently and fully the life I had ten or eleven years ago.

I founded an Arab radio station—perhaps, the very one to which you have just been listening, el Mohattat el Sharq el Adna, the Near East Arabic Broadcasting Station. Nowadays it is an imposing, professional affair, with a distinguished board of governors, a large staff—both technical and artistic —a faithful listening public and correspondents in all the bigger capitals. It began a little more than eleven years ago with a memorandum of mine, scrawled on two and a half pages of foolscap and read aloud, one hot evening in Jerusalem, in the presence of a senior staff officer.

I was myself then a junior staff officer and a very inexperienced one. I was concerned in an obscure but enthusiastic fashion with the morale of the population of British-mandated Palestine. I was as fecund in ideas as I was barren of knowledge. I put forward plausible schemes with the utmost zest and as much persuasiveness as I could muster; and when one was turned down I thought of another. A week or so before, I had indeed put one of my ingenious little proposals on a piece of paper which, somehow or another, had reached the desk of the General Officer Commanding Palestine and Transjordan, a formidable and famous soldier known—outside his hearing—as 'Jumbo'. My suggestion, couched in the cheerful and informal manner of my civilian calling, was that it would help to improve local morale if some tanks—a couple of dozen say—could parade through the streets of Jerusalem, Tel-Aviv, and Haifa. The period was midsummer, 1941; and I daresay the G.O.C. Palestine and Transjordan was a good deal more keenly aware of the real state of the armour in the Middle East than was a newly-arrived staff captain. His comment on my happy notion was, I have been told, majestic: 'Well, it'd send up my morale if I could see *one* tank going down the street outside that window.'

. . . .

My radio proposal, founded as it was on just as inadequate knowledge and experience as my tank-lift, met with much better fortune. Also—though this was perhaps fortuitous—it bore a much closer relation to reality. The Axis Powers, at the peak of their career of aggression that summer, controlled all Europe with the exception of that small scrap of territory known as Turkey-in-Europe, and one or two other small fortresses like the British Isles, Malta and Gibraltar; Rommel and his Afrika Korps were on the offensive in the Western Desert. The Arabs have a notable admiration for and inclination towards the winning side. The Axis propaganda services quite naturally cashed in on this characteristic.

From their radio stations at Berlin, Bari and Athens they poured out, day after day, hour after hour, a flood of sulphurous stuff; after the failure of the abortive rising in Iraq and the Allied occupation of Persia, they had at their disposal the greatest Arab figure of the time, the wily Haj Amin el Husseini, the self-styled Mufti of Jerusalem, who nowadays—discomfited but never finally discredited—is a refugee in one of the member-States of the British Commonwealth, Pakistan. In 1941 Arab nationalism was a potentially explosive element in the Middle East situation which the Axis Powers were eager to exploit. We on our side—since, after all, we had made very good use of it in the 1914–18 war—were just as eager to turn it to our advantage. Various organizations, branches of Intelligence and quasi-Intelligence, had sprung up and were still springing up all over the Middle East for just this purpose. My proposal—and I repeat that I was a junior officer with no experience of the Arab countries, no experience of broadcasting, and five words of kitchen Arabic as my vocabulary—was simple and forthright: to set up a short-wave station, run by Arabs and for Arabs, but on our side, and thus to act as a counter to Berlin, Bari, and Athens. This ingenuous little suggestion acted as a catalyst (though at the time I was far too ignorant to see how) for the ambitions, plans, and hopes of many who, in various fashions, were involved in Middle Eastern politics and diplomacy.

Ignorant as I was, however, I had one great advantage—cash. The particular Intelligence organization of which I was then a member was rich, powerful and much in favour; its funds were lavish and not subject to ordinary Service scrutiny and accountancy (my salary indeed was paid monthly into my London bank in notes, delivered in a sealed envelope by a despatch rider, a proceeding which I considered most romantic); and its mysterious affairs were presided over by a secret committee of Cabinet Ministers.

The senior officer to whom I expounded my scheme was impressed—far less, I have come to realize, by its sketchy and bouncingly optimistic details, or by the hocus-pocus with which I was surrounded, than by the money of which I might have the disposal. 'Go and talk to your bosses in Cairo,' he said. 'Get them to back it.'

I did. I had three steamy, turbulent days in Cairo, arguing, pleading, touting my now rather soiled and tattered sheets of foolscap around from one mandarin to another, propounding a monthly balance-sheet, an establishment, and a list of technical and administrative requirements which lengthened rapidly and alarmingly. I drank huge quantities of *Limoon*; one of the mandarins offered me a whisky and soda from his private ice-box; another took me to dinner at the Turf Club. The organization's expert Arab adviser was called in; he was a red-headed Irish scholar who had turned Moslem, lived in Old Cairo, drove a large car almost as big as King Farouk's, wore a tarbush and talked nineteen to the dozen and with obvious authority. He frightened the life out of me. Nevertheless, on the evening of the third day I had what I wanted. I could go back to Jerusalem and found my radio station; I had the money and the backing. The expert Arab adviser flung a momentary flicker of alarm across my natural exaltation by saying in the accents of one who brooks no denial: 'You'll have it on the air for the first night of Ramadan, of course.'

Ramadan, I should explain, is one of the months of the Islamic calendar, and of especial sanctity, during which the faithful are bidden to fast all day and every day, and during which they feast, sing, play music, tell tales and fire off artillery salutes every night and all night.

'When is the first night of Ramadan?'

The expert Arab adviser did some rapid mental arithmetic. 'Three weeks and three days from now,' he announced.

'We'll have it on the air for the first night of Ramadan,' said I.

When I think of my youth, I think of these full and frantic weeks as its climax. I enjoyed myself, I suppose, more than I have ever done; I worked harder than I had ever worked in my life—far harder than I had conceived possible. My small, remote, and mildly mysterious office (it was on the top of Jerusalem's only sky-scraper, and it had from its windows a view of breathtaking beauty across the Judean wilderness to the mountains of Moab) buzzed with activity. Next door to me there was another official—a member of the I.C.S. on loan to the Government of Palestine—who was almost equally busy. He was Mr. (now Sir John) Strathie who was engaged on the task of devising an income tax system for the inhabitants of Palestine, a factor in contemporary life of which, untii the stresses of war compelled it, they had lived in happy ignorance. Let it be a warning to fiscal pundits that my achievement still stands, while Sir John's has long since been blown away on the winds of withdrawal and the abdication of authority.

No defeatist fears oppressed me then. I had a formidable responsibility and a fairly impressive opportunity. I seized both eagerly. My Arab staff—Mr. Nejib Khoury, my confidential clerk (who was respectable, Christian, and came from Nablus), and Mr. Mahmoud Khyami, his not-so-confidential deputy (who was a twinkling, wily, naughty Damascene with a high and delicious giggle)—were whirled into ceaseless labour. I acquired a friend, supporter and co-founder, a brother-Scot named Robert Mason, who masked quicksilver intelligence, gaiety, and tolerance beneath a racial aspect of grim and Calvinistic severity. He is now Her Majesty's exalted and careworn diplomatic and consular representative in a high and important country in equatorial Africa; he had then just reached the rank of Major in the Intelligence Corps. Since we worked for different departments, and since I was the junior officer and controlled the cash, friction and intrigue might have been expected. Instead we were a zestful and happy partnership; and we shared—and still share—a unique claim to fame: we are the only two entirely ignorant amateurs who have ever put a fully-working broadcasting station on the air inside three weeks and three days.

We knew nothing at all about the technical aspects of radio transmission. Robert, before the war, had done a little work for a Continental commercial radio organization. In December 1940, I had attended a week's course on radar, at which exasperated electrical engineers strove to teach 200 Royal Artillery subalterns all electrical theory and practice in one week; the only effect of this instruction was that I was apt to make jokes about Ohm's Law.

We were without staff, equipment or site. Our knowledge of Arabs and Arabic was—to put it mildly—elementary. Our enterprise was, it had been decided in secret at the highest official level, to be sited in Palestine and the Palestine Government and Palestine Army H.Q. knew nothing about it—until we, two junior and lately-arrived officers, told them about it. One senior official smiled at me, his expression an odd mixture of scorn, pity, and bewilderment, and said, 'But, my dear boy, it takes *two years* to put a broadcasting station on the air. First you draw up the plans, then you get out the estimates, and then . . .'

I said, 'Thank you very much, sir. We've got to be on the air on 23 September.'

Was there a single branch of Palestine H.Q., or a single department of the Palestine Government from Security to Agriculture and Fisheries, that we did not fluster in those exuberant days, on whose toes we didn't tread? I learned about official protocol by shattering it. To be an officer of a secret organization was, I admit, an asset which I employed unscrupulously. If anyone refused to let me have, through the proper channels, anything I needed—from steel for an aerial to padding for the walls of the studio—I went out into the black market (or rather I sent Mr. Khoury) and bought it. And if after this display of ill-gotten wealth there was still a lack of co-operation in the proper channels, I sent a signal to my Cairo chiefs. This simple and undisciplined procedure got me almost everything I wanted: the site for the station, in a fierce hot little Arab town on the edge of the Plain of Megiddo, called Jenin; an aerial; my technical staff—an R.A.F. sergeant who knew everything about radio and feared no man and no institution, and two lamentably ignorant, conceited and plaintive Poles; my programme staff, whose recruitment from the ranks of nationalist and patriotic-minded Arabs gravely disturbed the C.I.D.; furniture, cables, power, even three juvenile delinquents to keep the studio clean and make and distribute the constant cups of coffee without which no Middle Eastern enterprise can prosper. But ten days before we were due to open I still had no transmitter.

This was especially galling because my secret organization did, in fact, possess a transmitter, a small $1\frac{1}{2}$-kilowatt affair, which, at the conclusion of the campaign in Vichy Syria, we had lent to the Free French, to replace—for a month—the equipment of Radio Beirut which (said the Free French) the R.A.F. had wantonly destroyed with their bombs. My crude, tough efforts to get my department's property back, after the period of the loan had been extended for three weeks, precipitated a major diplomatic *bruhaha*.

In a hot little room in General Catroux's headquarters in Beirut I argued with a wrathful, almost hysterical French press officer to whom I—stocky, sweating and stubborn—was the personal embodiment of perfidious Albion; all the Anglo-French grievances from Agincourt to Oran poured out over me; the Spears Mission sought to intervene soothingly; a thunderstorm raged in the mountains behind the city; the press officer wept, tore his fine blond hair and beat his expensively-tailored breast; in the courtyard outside a band blared the Marseillaise in evening salute to General Catroux and the glories of tragic, splendid France.

'I've got a lorry and four men waiting to take my set away,' I said woodenly.

'*Your* set!' screamed the press officer. He invoked the august shades of Louis XIV, Napoleon, Joffre, and Foch to witness the treacherous insolence of England. '*Your* set! Do you seek a battle, Captain? We Frenchmen may be beggars, Captain, despicable beggars, but we can still fight and die in defence of our rights of free speech.'

It is only fair to say that after and in spite of all this eloquence, my R.A.F. sergeant reached an amicable agreement—on the sheerly technical, as distinct from the diplomatic, level—with his French equivalent; and early next morning the transmitter was lashed down in my lorry, and we set off southwards for Jenin: and we had had no battle.

Somehow the set was got into working order. Somehow the programme staff was assembled and trained in the elements of its duties. My organization's expert on Arab affairs arrived for the opening, accompanied by a blind Egyptian Koran chanter of extreme holiness, whose services he had hired for us at an enormous fee.

On the first evening of Ramadan—according to schedule, that schedule which no one had believed we would fulfil—my station went on the air.

'Good old Shark,' said the R.A.F. sergeant who had coaxed miracles out of the battered and unimposing transmitter. During the first three-quarters of an hour there was a long recital of the Koran, which mounted in splendour and fervour until the whole studio seemed to throb and quiver with the vast bodiless clamour of sound which poured from the mouth of the blind singer. Much of the evening was a confusion. There was endless shaking of hot, damp hands, endless patting of backs; there were orgies of courteous greeting. The lintel of the station's door was sprinkled with the blood of a newly-killed sheep. A majestic feast was prepared in the back quarters. Robert Mason and I went for a stroll down the dark, quiet road out of the town. Up in the Samarian hills the hyenas and the jackals called.

'We've started something, you and I,' said Robert.

Back at the station there was a comforting glow and hum in the transmitter room. In my haversack I had a bottle of champagne which I had bought that morning at the King David Hotel, in Jerusalem. The sergeant produced some tin mugs. The champagne was warm and sweet. But with some solemnity we three toasted our new Arabic station which, we hoped, was that night for the first time being heard in Iraq, in Bahrein, in Muscat, along the windswept edge of the high plateau of the Hadramaut and in the distant Spice Isles.

That was eleven years ago. The political shape of the Middle East is strangely changed. But still, after many vicissitudes, that station is on the air. Achievement, when you come to think about it, is a funny, perplexing business.

NIGHTMARE JOURNEYS

By F. Spencer Chapman

[A hitherto unpublished manuscript recounting the
experiences of the author of *The Jungle is Neutral*]

AFTER two years behind the Japanese lines in Malaya I joined, on Christmas Day, 1943, John Davis and Richard Broome who had got into the country by submarine.

After some months of comparatively comfortable living in their camp I set off, accompanied by a single Chinese, to try and get in touch with another Englishman who was supposed to be living with the Sakai (the little aborigines of the Malayan jungle) further north. Unfortunately I was caught by some Chinese bandits and the day after escaping from them I was taken prisoner by the Japanese. I escaped again but it was several months before I at last got back to Davis's and Broome's camp.

The following pages describe some of my privations on the journey home.

We left the pipe-line early next day, 16 June 1944. I was delighted with Ah Sang, my new companion. He was a typical Straits-born Chinese, well mannered and quietly efficient, brave without being foolhardy, and very easy to get on with. Even in the jungle he contrived to be well turned out, kept his

NIGHTMARE JOURNEYS 199

nails carefully manicured, his hair smoothly brushed, and always smelt of scented soap. He could speak a little English, but preferred to talk Malay. As he was a town-dweller and not acquainted with the jungle, he was accompanied by an older man who rarely spoke but seemed to know everybody we met and acted as scout, guide and porter. I was provided with a battered felt hat, shapeless with age, which I could pull down to hide my face. Unfortunately, I could not borrow a razor, and with my ragged beard and torn clothing, felt very self-conscious beside my dapper companion.

For the first few miles we followed the pipe-line down river with the old man and another Chinese far ahead to spy out the land. The pipe, which was four feet wide, crossed the river, went through deep cuttings, and was carried over gorges on crazy scaffolding. With the night's dew still on it, the pipe was so slippery that although there was a rickety hand-rail in the dangerous places we had to remove our shoes to prevent us from falling off it. At last we struck off to the right through the jungle where we passed unseen so close to some Sakai houses that we could hear the men talking. We now came out into some young rubber and were so near the edge of the jungle that we could see the plains with the red scars of cultivation and the huge grey limestone outcrops that are so typical of the Ipoh district. In the afternoon we kept out of the jungle, travelling through innumerable manioc (or cassava) plantations, wading down sandy river beds, and occasionally making uncomfortable detours through bamboo thickets and secondary jungle to avoid Malay or Chinese houses where there were known to be informers. In this district, indeed in all the country in which I spent the next two months, every Chinese family seemed to be concentrating its energies on growing manioc, crushing the roots in a hand or treadle machine, washing it, spreading the residue out to dry on what looked like hard tennis courts, and turning it into flour which was sent in to the towns to make gruel dumplings, biscuits and cakes. Innumerable pigs were kept on the refuse; and the smell of these, combined with the sour odour of the rotting manioc, was most revolting.

We saw numbers of Chinese working in the manioc plantations and were sometimes unable to avoid being seen by them. Once we passed within a few yards of a party of about twenty barefooted girls—some of them young and looking most attractive in wide black trousers, gay coloured blouses with scarlet scarves round their shoulders, and enormous sun-hats. I felt very self-conscious, but they took no notice of me at all—as if, two and a half years after the occupation, it were an everyday occurrence to meet a gaunt and haggard Englishman in filthy ragged clothes and with a month's beard on his face.

Outside the jungle it was terribly hot and oppressive; all day I had felt ill and had been going very badly indeed, especially uphill; but Ah Sang had been very patient and had had to stop frequently to wait for me. In the afternoon I could hardly travel at all and every step was an effort: all I wanted to do was to lie down and go to sleep—which I did whenever we stopped. Nor was I able to eat when we halted for a short time at the tiny hut of a Chinese squatter; but Ah Sang insisted we should go on as it was unsafe to stop the night there. When we set off again, I was in a very bad way, indeed, I was only half conscious, and no one but a Chinese—who are in some ways quite inhuman—would have allowed me to go on travelling in such a state. I could not close my mouth properly and was unable to prevent the saliva dribbling down at the corners of my mouth; I could not focus my eyes correctly, and consequently was continually falling down and having to be helped to my feet again. All I could do was to stagger on with my arms stretched out in front of me like a blind man. Ah Sang at last realized that I could not go on much longer like this and we turned aside to a large Chinese house among the manioc. The moment we were inside I lay flat on my back on the earthen floor and lost all consciousness.

When I woke up, I looked around the house, and recognizing its six inhabitants, found to my horror that I was in the very same house near Tanjong Rambutan that I had entered exactly a month ago when I had emerged from the jungle! All I had done in that long and hideous month was to carry out an enormous and abortive circular tour in search of Sakai— merely to satisfy my pride and sense of independence in an attempt to get myself home without the assistance of the Chinese guerrillas.

I felt much better now and, my appetite having returned with my recovery, I finished off several bowls of sweet-potato mixed with rice, and some dried fish and cucumber. Then I had a bath in the stream, combed my hair and beard, and felt ready for anything.

While I was eating, two young men came in who were obviously from a guerrilla camp, and when they set off carrying loads of manioc, Ah Sang and I accompanied them. We started towards the small hut where I had sheltered before, then turned north and followed a stream through a series of clearings to its source, crossed a low pass, and followed another stream down a similar valley on the far side. This journey took several hours and we were in cultivation practically all the time. Steep fields of hill paddy led upwards on either side to the summit fringe of bamboo or jungle, and in the bottom of the valley was a succession of large plank- or bamboo-walled houses with *atap* roofs, each surrounded by gardens containing vegetables of every description. But the whole valley was deserted; only a few meagre cats had remained and they came running to us, mewing piteously, thinking their owners had returned. Apparently the Japs had ravaged the place some weeks before and those Chinese who survived had taken to the jungle and had not yet returned. The rice was ripe for harvesting and the pumpkins and cucumbers rotting on their stalks. Some of the houses had been burnt down and in others the whole of the interior had been torn down and scattered in the looters' search for hidden money and valuables.

I found that I could get along well enough on the level, but went slower and slower uphill. Most of the time we walked actually in the stream, as there was no other path, and as we had already done this much of the morning my feet were getting very sore indeed. If I went barefooted my feet were cut by the sharp stones, and if I wore my rubber shoes the sand would get in through the many holes and would rub away the skin, especially on the tops of the toes which were red and bleeding. Later on I was able to sew some bits of cloth into bags and to tie these outside the shoes to prevent the sand getting in, but they did not last long and I had to patch them whenever we stopped.

Towards evening we turned up a side valley which ran far into the jungle, and here there were a few Chinese, though they were in a terrible state of nerves. Ah Sang spent a long time in earnest conversation with a tall girl with very pronounced Mongolian features, who seemed to be the liaison officer with the nearby guerrilla camp. She then led us up the bed of a tiny stream into the jungle until we came to an *atap* shelter piled high with bags of paddy. Here we made a fire and roasted a number of maize cobs and drank quantities of hot water which the girl had brought along in a kettle.

The two young men had returned to their camp, but it appeared that as I had no credentials, neither Ah Sang nor the girl would take the responsibility of letting me accompany them. In fact, although I had actually trained a sister and two brothers of Ah Sang's in the Slim camp and he knew all about me, neither he nor the girl would take the responsibility of providing guides and arranging my journey home without permission from a higher authority, and I was given pen and paper and told to write my requests to Perak headquarters.

I wrote a long letter to Itu, explaining what had happened to me and apoligizing for the trouble I had caused. Now my only object was to get home and I asked him to ask Davis to send me quinine, M.B. 693, and money, and to pass on all my news to him.

The girl disappeared with this letter, and Ah Sang, refusing my request to spend the night in this hut on the grounds that my presence was too great an embarrassment to the demoralized Chinese, insisted on setting off at once for the hide-out where I was to stay until permission came for me to proceed, which I thought would be at least a month. By this time I was only just able to walk, but the knowledge that this was the last lap of the journey and the prospect of a month's rest and good food kept me going, and Ah Sang was extremely patient and sympathetic, pushing me from behind when we had to go uphill. We retraced our steps to the top of the deserted valley, then turned east up an old timber-hauling track into the jungle and followed it to an isolated clearing where there were two huts: the lower one packed with a dozen or so youths, who appeared to be semi-guerrillas and who were engaged in clearing the jungle and planting paddy, and an upper one at the head of the clearing where a young Chinese was growing vegetables.

I stayed in the upper house on the very edge of the jungle, but one of the guerrillas stayed with me each day, so that if the Japs suddenly appeared he would be able to take me to a small hide-out in the jungle. The vegetable garden seemed to be owned by an old man who appeared now and then from the 'town'—presumably Tanjong Rambutan, worked solidly all the time he was there, and disappeared again. The son suffered very badly from malaria, having shivering fits each morning, but as he was 'wanted' by the Japs he had to stay here. Ah Sang was away most of the time, but would sometimes return in time to have supper with me and give me the news.

The food was excellent. Each morning and evening I would have two large bowls of sweet-potato and rice with salt or dried fish and a vegetable—beans, brinjol, marrow, or cucumber. A feature of the *cuisine* here was that there were always two large bowls of sauce on the table, one of black soya beans and curry, and the other of chillis, and both so hot that the contents of the bowls seemed to last indefinitely. My only lack was the absence of any reading material. While I was here I shaved off my beard with a rusty cut-throat razor. It was the first time I had ever used one and it took an hour to hack away a month's growth. Fortunately the razor was very blunt or I should have cut myself severely. I always think that the lower one's morale is, the more important it is to keep oneself clean and look after one's personal appearance, not only to impress other people, but to impress oneself.

The hut was a typical Chinese squatter's dwelling. It was twenty feet square with a doorway, which could not be closed, on each side. There were no other windows. The walls were of bark and plaited *atap*. In one corner was the cooking oven of baked mud with two hobs for a large and a small cooking pot. There was a plank table with log seats, a shelf for salt, bottles of cooking oil, bowls, chopsticks, and spoons, and in the corner opposite the oven a bicycle, piles of manioc and sweet potato, bags of rice, and a few tools. Over half the floor was a loft made of split bamboo with a ladder leading up to it. On this were a few grass mats and blankets and a mosquito net. There was a small and smoky lamp which burned oil distilled by the Japs from rubber. All refuse was thrown outside the door, and for sanitation one took a hoe outside and dug a hole in the jungle edge. In the garden were rows and rows of sweet potatoes, also millet, long beans, pumpkins, sweet and bitter cucumbers, brinjols and various kinds of leafy vegetables so much prized by the Chinese.

On 19 June, after I had been here only three days, Ah Sang appeared with a large, self-possessed, tough-looking

Chinese in khaki called Lau Ping, and we sat till far into the night discussing the latest war news. According to the Jap newspapers the Germans had got a new weapon (the flying bomb) and this was proving highly successful, especially in attacks on London. Japan had been bombed by Super-Fortresses from bases in China, and of course Russia was doing wonders. The local news was that the Japs had caught a Chinese who knew the small guerrilla camp nearby and that this area was no longer safe. Lau Ping had come to take me to a much better hiding-place only a day's journey away.

I was quite sorry to leave this pleasant sanctuary and sorrier still to say goodbye to Ah Sang, who was a delightful companion. I was still not sleeping well, but I was already feeling much better for my few days' rest and good food, though I did not feel ready for more travelling. However, there was nothing else for it, and on 20 June Lau Ping and I took the road. I insisted on setting off at earliest dawn, as I knew I could not go fast, especially uphill. As the next day was one of the most unpleasant I ever remember, I will quote the account of it that I wrote in my diary as soon afterwards as I had sufficiently recovered to do so.

20 June. A ghastly nightmare of a day. Away at six, the moment it was light enough to travel. Followed stream down the way we came, then cut across south on a path through thick jungle to meet the small water-pipe just above the manioc house. Here Ah Sang left me and handed over to Lau Ping and two young guerrillas. We set off along a cart-track towards the plains with our advance party out in front to see that there were no wandering loonies (from the Tanjong Rambutan asylum) about, though they say that the Japs have reduced their numbers to one-tenth by deliberate starvation. After an hour Lau Ping left us—to follow an easier route outside the jungle which was unsafe for me, and, turning south, we went up and down the steep rounded hills of a rubber estate for an hour. As usual the trees had not been tapped or the undergrowth

cleared since the occupation. There were signs of pig everywhere. We then waded across the wide thigh-deep Kinta river, and for the next two hours followed tiny paths through *lalang* grass, which traversed along the sides and circled round the heads of steep little valleys where manioc was being planted. Every single family seems to be growing manioc and making flour out of it. What would this country do without manioc?

The two guides went like hell; they carry their gear in a rice bag balanced most awkwardly on one shoulder. We saw the red-tiled roofs of Tanjong Rambutan only a mile or two away to the west and several grey limestone outcrops with jungle growing on top. We passed through another rubber estate, then came down on to a ten-foot-wide tarred road with two telegraph wires and a pipe-line running inland to the Kinta intake works. A third of the road was spread with chips of manioc drying in the sun. We crawled in thick *lalang* grass until we were near the road, then raced across it and up the open ground on the south side. Two old Chinese saw us and ran into their house—usually they take no notice. I was panting and wheezing. For the next two hours we followed a rough cart-road south-west, right up the side of a long valley. Below us all the way were Chinese villages, all making manioc flour, and steep clearings running up to jungle on each side of the valley.

At the top of this pass we stopped for hot water—though they called it tea—where two old Chinese were scraping the outer skins, but not the thick peel, off huge manioc roots with a tin scraper. We had now been going for eight hours, flat out, and I was beginning to fail, especially uphill: and though it was good to be out of the jungle, it was terribly hot and airless in the bright sun.

Next came half an hour of the worst going in the world—across a newly felled clearing where no path had yet been made. This involved tight-roping over fallen timber, and I fell often. Now we crossed an old tin-mining area with little cliffs of red laterite, small streams, and ochre-coloured sandy detritus, broken pipes and rusty machinery, all overgrown with Straits rhododendron, bracken and sometimes a claret and white orchid. The red *kerengga* ants were very bad here: they get on your clothes, then climb up and bite the back of your neck.

Now we entered the real jungle—what relief to get out of the burning sun!—and a clayey path led up two long steep hills beside a derelict pipe-line. Last night's rain had not yet dried and the path was as slippery as ice, and I had to take my shoes off. The next three hours were beyond description. The path did not seem to have been used since the pipe-line was abandoned—years ago—and I had to fight my way through thickets with bracken clawing my face, legs, and clothes, and continually pulling my hat off. Thank God I carried no gear bar a *parang* (jungle knife) tied round my waist with rattan and a few odds and ends in my pockets. We were still following the remains of an eighteen-inch pipe-line and once we had to use it to cross a gorge about forty feet up—and no rail of any sort.

I went slower and slower, and at one stage started to stagger and thought I was going to collapse, but my guides would not let me rest or we should have had to sleep out—and this was against orders! At last we left the pipe and the path went downhill and was even worse. We had to go on hands and knees under thickets, and wade through wide swamps.

Suddenly in the V of the valley I saw some huge limestone outcrops just in front of us and we left them on our right. They were most awe-inspiring, running up almost sheer for 1,000 feet of grey cliff and covered with an acre of thick jungle on the summit, completely unclimbable I should say as the rock is so rotten. The path improved now and showed signs of having been used from this end. Once, when we stopped, we heard a hissing growl in the grass beside the track. A tiger—or panther! One of the guides pulled a Luger automatic out of his shirt (I didn't know he was armed till then) and we all clapped our hands and heard him no more.

There was a wide, sandy cart-track now and we passed just at the foot of the limestone outcrops. In one place a series of crazy wooden ladders led several hundred feet up to a cave—presumably to collect bat guano. A few bushes and then trees clung to the cliffs at fantastic angles. We were going faster than ever, but one could at least stand upright. Now we crossed a large river (the Sungei Raja) and there was a most lovely sunset behind the outcrops. It was really beautiful now, with a sort of lost-world enchantment. At the bottom of the valley were thatched houses surrounded by palms, banana and *papaya* trees, and vegetable gardens; then there were the level sky-reflecting squares of swamp paddy, reminding me of Bali; then smooth verdant green of paddy or *lalang* slopes up to the foot of the vast precipices of grey limestone stained with orange and red. The guides said we had still two hours to go.

We now walked for some distance along a four-foot pipeline skirting the village of Ambang where all the Chinese had been massacred in May 1943 for harbouring guerrillas. My guides told me the Japs bombed it twice, shot up anybody they saw—men, women, or children—then looted and burned the houses. They say a thousand Chinese were killed. The survivors had returned, however, and as usual did not seem the least surprised to see me. I was glad I had had a shave and I smiled and saluted them, although I felt like death.

We still went very fast. I walked automatically now and was revived, as usual, by the cool of the dusk and the utter beauty of the scene compared to the jungle. At last, at eight o'clock, we reached a very large manioc house where forty or so Chinese lived, each family having its own 'loose box' round the sides and down the centre of a single large *atap* shed. It was lovely to see women and children again, and they were very friendly. Lau Ping was already here (he came by bicycle) with a large Mauser sticking out of his belt.

We had travelled for fourteen hours, flat out, with less than an hour off for rests, and must have covered more than twenty miles—though the effort equals about sixty English miles—quite apart from my miserable weakness: I must be four stone under my normal weight. I saw my face in a large glass here and was horrified.

THE GREAT ELEPHANT TREK

By J. H. Williams

THE foothills to the west of Imphal Plain are treeless. From where we started there is a graded mule-track up to about two thousand five hundred feet, as far as Tamelong. Only one person saw us off on our departure: an R.A.F. pilot in a Harvard Trainer, who damned nearly stampeded the whole party of elephants, just as they were descending a very steep bit of the track. Whether he was just verifying the direction in which we were starting off, or whether he thought we were a horde of Japs, I can't tell. But he made off as quickly as he came, possibly because he realized how disastrous to us his presence would be, or possibly because he saw a few rifles being aimed in his direction! If our curses had any effect, he would have had a forced landing on his trip back.

We were a most extraordinary collection. I went ahead, with an armed vanguard of Karens, and when I looked back, down over the serpentine track, the collection looked like the 'Lame Host', and we were strung out to such an extent that it seemed possible that the first of the elephants would reach his destination before the last of them got started.

Our total strength was forty-five elephants, forty armed Karens, ninety elephant-riders and attendants, sixty-four refugee women and children, and four officers in charge. From where I was watching them, the elephants looked like slowly moving moles, followed by a trail of black ants. The cheerfulness of the Burmans was a great encouragement, and, provided that we escaped being attacked by Japanese patrols, we felt confident we should make the Surma Valley sometime and somehow.

Our first halt was the Iring River, after we had crossed the first watersheds. There was good water and ample fodder for the elephants at that halt. Half-rations were issued to all, and even the lamest of the lame ducks got into camp before dusk. That first evening, however, we were overtaken by the first echelon of six hundred Pioneers. They were carrying ten days' hard rations, and it was obvious that chaos, if not tragedy, was going to mark the whole of their route, as they could not cover the distance in that time.

I was, anyhow, anxious to get my party off their track as quickly as I could. I did not at all relish the company of seven thousand eight hundred Pioneers, and could visualize my elephants providing them with a most welcome supply of fresh meat if we remained with them. We were out of touch with any further orders, and had only one remaining duty—to visit Tamelong and send off a signal from there.

We therefore arranged that White and I should continue as far as Tamelong, and send off the signal, while Browne and Hann should proceed due west to Haochin, where we would rejoin them. However, we were still two marches from the point where we planned to part company, and during those two days I thought we should get an idea of what we might expect on the trek.

The women and children found the marches very exhausting, but on the whole they were marvellous. When we started off in the morning there would be three women and about four children riding on elephants, owing to various ills. When we got in at night ten to fifteen would be riding, the oozies having taken pity on them, although pity was a luxury we could ill afford, since the elephants were already overloaded with rations and kit, and were making very severe marches. A few elephants showed signs of feeling it. These had to be nursed, by giving them lighter loads, which, in turn, meant that the others had to be still further overloaded. However, although every day the elephants would become more exhausted, every day we were eating a portion of their loads. That would make quite a difference after a week of marching. Before White and I separated from the elephant party, I gave orders that they should on no account delay during their march to Haochin, and any rest and reorganization of loading that might be necessary should take place after they had left it. For we were by no means out of range of Japanese patrols. I was to learn later that the very day on which the elephants left Haochin, a strong enemy patrol arrived in the evening and occupied the village, murdering a Political Officer, named Sharpe, who was following in the tracks of our party.

Tamelong was in the state of chaos which I had expected. A very young Political Officer, named Young, was in charge of thirty rifles, with one Indian officer. The fact that Sharpe did not arrive led eventually to a second tragedy.

The Pioneers were straggling deplorably. All the lame, the blind and the halt were just sitting there, and showed no disposition to push on. Young seemed to have been forgotten in the general confusion elsewhere, and was trying to manage against very heavy odds. I got a signal sent off, giving my intended route, and adding just what I thought of the Pioneer echelons marching out. This led to the departure of any further echelons from the Imphal Plain being stopped, and to an air drop of food for the stragglers stranded there.

White and I rejoined the elephants, as planned. The night after that we had to camp for the first time on a ridge, where there was only a trickle of water for the elephants. But it was just enough.

From Haochin onwards we had to face the unknown and

travel due west over whatever was in front of us, until we reached the Surma Valley. The point nearest us on the map was marked Baladan Tea Estate, high up on the edge of the valley. We made jokes about it, and decided we should find a bungalow with a very old tea-planter living with a very lovely young wife, and there would be buttered toast and a telephone. Then, slapping my Labrador, Cobber, on the flank, one of us added that he was quite sure that this ideal couple had a very elegant Labrador bitch who would appreciate him.

We were by this time five thousand feet up, which is high above any normal 'elephant line'. In fact, we were as high as Hannibal was when he crossed the Little St. Bernard. The great beasts were painfully slow in climbing, and Browne had had difficulty, owing to some of the older animals nearly collapsing. It was magnificent scenery, which made a great deal of difference to us four officers, in spite of the hundred and one worries which continually beset us.

So far there was no doubt that there would be sufficient fodder for the elephants and, provided we could cross over a watershed each day, we should be able to find sufficient water for them at lower levels.

I had been given a compass by an Australian War Correspondent, who once spent a night at Elephant Camp, Tamu. It had originally been given to his father by Sir Alan Brooke, and it proved invaluable to us on that trek.

The cold, at the altitude we now were, brought on attacks of malaria amongst the women, and we soon had a number of fever patients to look after. There were heavy falls of rain at night, which made their lives miserable. In addition, there were cases of sore feet, dysentery, pneumonia and abscesses in the breasts. Some of the elephants were in need of first aid as well. But we could not let our invalids rest and recuperate; we had to push on. Every day we marched from dawn till after five o'clock in the afternoon, always in fear of a Japanese ambush.

From Haochin onwards we had to organize track-cutting and digging parties, each officer in turn starting off with a party, to clear the way ahead of the elephants. When, in climbing up from a creek or river, I had fixed on our reaching some particular point on that ridge from which to drop down into the next drainage area, I had to make certain that the leading party kept their direction to that ridge and did not drop into a side creek. Unfortunately game-tracks were non-existent, as there was very little or no game in those hills. Any small villages marked were usually non-existent also. This was because the people are nomadic agriculturists who move to new areas as they are cultivated for hill rice—and the land can be cropped only once in three years. When new areas are cleared in rotation the village moves on. The villages marked were, however, a guide, as we always found the headstones of the graves at the village site. The dead remained, though for the time being the living inhabitants had moved into another valley.

As we ate our rations, we could afford to carry more of the children, who had by this time quite lost their fear of the elephants. The mothers soon found that they need not walk beside the elephant, constantly expecting to have to catch a falling child. For the oozies were very good at looking after the children, and I rewarded them for their work with an extra cigarette ration. Thus the mothers were able to make an early start with the vanguard of path-finders. Many of the younger women even lent a hand with jungle-knives, clearing bamboos. I was constantly badgered by everyone for a day's rest. Then, on the ninth day of consecutive marching, the country decided the question for me.

We had reached a large creek with good fodder, far off the beaten track. It had been my day with the vanguard, and, as I reached the site for the camp a long while ahead of the elephants, I crossed the creek and went part of the way up the next ridge, so as to see what it was like for our start next morning. The map read as though there were a fault or escarpment running north to south, parallel with the creek, and on the west bank of it. The ridge I was climbing seemed the most likely to provide a way up to the top of the escarpment. I struggled up for about two miles of very steep climbing, through dense bamboo jungle, which would mean a very slow and exhausting climb for the elephants. Then I suddenly came out against a sheer rock face escarpment, three or four hundred feet high. My heart sank. I turned south and followed the foot of the cliff for a mile. There was not a single place where I could have possibly climbed it myself. There was no question of an elephant climbing a perpendicular cliff. I then came to a patch of old and very large bamboos, some of which had obviously been cut with a knife possibly a year before. This looked to me like the work of a Chin villager, who must have been there at some time, and who was more likely to have come down the escarpment, particularly as the map showed a deserted village on the ridge to the west of it.

Before I retraced my steps to camp I found a place where there had been a landslip in the escarpment. It looked a possible way for men to come down, but not at all the kind of place for elephants to go up. I marked the place with a large blaze on a tree, and went back to camp, exhausted. There could be no question of our turning back.

When the elephants and our party came into camp I was forced to announce that we would stay in camp for two days. The evacuee women and children actually cheered, and practically all the clothes they had on were immediately washed and hung up to dry, before the sun went down. I explained that there was a lot of hard work and serious trouble for us ahead. This was not because there was no path—we had not been following a path for many days—but because it was impossible to go on, until we found a place which it was possible to climb, and then dug a path up it. Next morning I sent Browne, White and Hann, each with a separate party, to explore the foot of the escarpment. Browne was to attempt to get up at the place I had found, Hann was to follow the escarpment to the north, and White to the south. I stayed in and provided food for the party by blasting fish with grenades.

Much to my surprise, Browne was back in camp by noon. As I watched him crossing the creek I remembered his return to Elephant Camp at Tamu, after two attempts to reach the elephants at Mintha. Then I saw that among his party were two Chins, armed with spears, and I wondered if he could possibly have got up to the ridge. It was not long before I heard his story. He had climbed up the place I had found at considerable risk. It was, apparently, the route by which the Chins had gone up or down some time ago. But it developed higher up into a narrow ledge, with sheer cliff above and below it, until the top was reached. He knew how I hated heights, and said that I should have to be taken up blind-folded. He said also that he thought that unless White or Hann found something better we were stumped. He had, however, reached the main ridge above, and found the village marked on the map. On the ridge was quite a good path, which ran due south to join the Bishenpur track. This, however, was just the place we wanted to avoid, as, until we had crossed this path to the west, I thought there was quite a good chance of our running into a Japanese patrol. I wanted to keep out of trouble, not to look for it.

It was evening before White and Hann got back within half an hour of each other. They had found no place nearly as good as Browne's.

The only decision I made that night was to cut rations down still further. The strictest watch was set on our food dump. In fact, we officers slept on it, and I posted a guard over it during the day.

We spread the red parachute over some boulders in the bed of the creek, though we had seen no aircraft up to this time.

Hann reported having heard a Harvard Trainer during the afternoon, but we had no wish to see our old friend again.

We agreed that the following day we should take our two head elephant-men to see the way by which Browne had got up. It was easy to understand, from the signs made by the two Chins, that there was no alternative route.

I was not actually blind-folded, but I preferred to crawl a good part of the way on all fours! I made sure of my hand-holds, knowing my feet could look after themselves.

Except for the one narrow and dangerous ledge round the face of the cliff, we considered that we could make it possible, with two days' cutting and digging. Fortunately, it was sandstone. The question was whether elephants would face it. In some places it was so steep that the elephants would almost be standing on their hind legs.

Po Toke, who was not my head Burman, but in charge of a group of seven elephants, which included Bandoola, surprised us all by saying as we returned: 'Bandoola will lead, and if he won't face it, no other elephant will. He knows how to close his eye on the khudside, and won't put his foot on anything that will give. Moreover, if he should refuse half-way up, he can back all the way down, as he has eyes in his backside!'

Bandoola was a magnificent tusker, but with a bad name as being dangerous.

I don't think he really believed half what he said, but I took care not to give him an opportunity for retracting. All of us agreed what a marvellous elephant Bandoola was, and we left it at that.

Apart from the narrowness of the ledge, or shelf of rock, and the occasional, almost impassable, outcrops of rock, the whole of the inner wall of the proposed track had to be cleared of jungle-growth. This would widen it as a path, and was in any case necessary for the passage of the pack carried on the elephant's back. White went ahead to the village with the two

Chins, hoping to raise a party of men to help in bamboo-cutting. He brought a dozen, all with good jungle-knives, and they started work from the top that afternoon.

Every fit man and woman in the camp, oozies included, was at work on that road by dawn next morning. We divided our labour force into four parties, each working on a different section. I took charge of the one nearest camp, so as not to be working where I might get giddy and fall over!

The good humour of even the evacuee women in tackling what was more than a full day's hard work helped enormously. In the evening I went up again. Far less crawling on all fours was necessary, and a lot of the jungle-growth cut from the inner wall had been piled up on the outer edge, so as somewhat to hide the terrifying drop below. One day's work had certainly made a vast difference. All the same, I rather doubted if we could do it. I knew, however, that there was no possibility of turning back.

We continued work throughout the following day, and by evening the head Burman and Po Toke were satisfied that we could not improve it any more. If we could not do it now, we never could. There were two particular danger spots, where the track was only about three feet wide, with a wall above, and a sheer drop on the outside, with nothing to blind it. I could not help wondering whether the whole of this ledge might not collapse under the weight of forty-five elephants passing along it.

I had worked up old Po Toke to the pitch of thinking he was practically in charge of the whole adventure, and that all our chances of success depended upon his elephant, Bandoola.

I arranged that all the refugees were to wait until the last of the elephants had gone up the track. Needless to say no women or children were to ride, and invalids who were unable to walk would have to be carried up later. There was to be no talking among the oozies. Po Toke was to lead the way on foot, in sight of Bandoola.

I myself had pushed on ahead of everyone as soon as all the elephants were loaded up.

Only those who know how silently a train of elephants can march can imagine what an eerie start we made that morning. From half-way up, where I turned to look down into the valley, I could hear nothing but the burble of the water of the creek rushing over its boulders far below, and at intervals the distant thuds of gunfire, coming from the direction of the Bishenpur track to the south.

I sat and waited for two hours on that ledge, and thought over many things. Before I left Imphal I had given a scribbled note for my wife to a Spitfire pilot, who was flying to Calcutta. In it I merely said, 'Starting to march tomorrow'. I knew that this would set her wondering, now that the news of the Japanese offensive on Imphal was coming through.

I had stopped just two hundred yards above the most dangerous spot, at which we had actually cut a series of steps in the sandstone, each just big enough to take an elephant's foot. Once I saw Bandoola pass that, I intended to push on up the next stretch.

I thought that Po Toke would never appear—nor, in fact, did he. Bandoola's head and tusks suddenly came round the corner below me. He looked almost as though he were standing on his hind legs. Then up came his hindquarters, as though in a slow-motion picture. The oozie was sitting on his head, looking down, and seemed to be directing the elephant where to place each of his feet. Then he had passed that worst place. I caught a glimpse through the elephant's legs of old Po Toke following. Without a word I pushed hurriedly on. We had got Bandoola up at least half-way. I just prayed for good luck, but had no faith in success.

It was more than two hours before I saw Bandoola again, and then he was practically at the top, and all danger of his slipping or refusing was over. He was up, at all events, and my relief and excitement cannot be expressed in words.

Behind Bandoola came Po Toke, and after him a female elephant. As he passed me, Po Toke behaved rather like a pall-bearer at a village funeral who unexpectedly gives one of the onlookers a wink. He was intensely solemn, and did not utter a word, but he gave me a queer fleeting look, that was as good as saying: 'Don't you worry. They'll all follow now.'

He was right. They all did. I waited, and ticked off forty-five adult elephants and eight calves at heel go by. The back legs of some of the animals had been strained to such a point that when they halted they would not stop quivering.

Much as I hated having to camp on a ridge, where there was a well-worn track to the south, up which the Japanese might come, there was no alternative. It was dark by the time we had got the last of the refugee women up to the top. No day ever seemed longer.

I learned more in that day about what elephants could be got to do than I had in twenty-four years. Po Toke's intuition had been perfectly right, and I am certain that we should never have done it if we had led with any animal except Bandoola.

Our camp on the ridge that night was the last one where I put out pickets. From there onwards I felt no fear of the Japanese.

Our next move was down to the Barak River. The descent was almost as steep as the previous day's climb up to the ridge, but there was no escarpment or ledges of rock to follow. Again we had to have a day's rest, as the elephants were feeling the strain, and had to be allowed to recover.

From there we followed the course of the river; our obstacles were mud and swamp, and very dense bamboo, through which we had to hack a track. We should never have got through if we had not been using Siamese-pattern gear on our elephants. It is much stouter.

Time was now our enemy, and my chief worry was whether our rations would last out. We still had a long way to go, but from the map it looked as though we should move into better country once we had reached the Digli River. It was quite obvious that our trek would last twenty days at least, and not the fifteen I had allowed for. By that time we had two cases of pneumonia among the refugee women, as well as other things. The only food we four officers were getting, on which to do a day's march, was chappattis made by the refugee women, jam and half a cigarette-tin of rice in the evening. As might be expected, our tempers were getting a bit short. Cobber, my dog, enjoyed himself more than anyone, but even he found the food dull. The Burmans were down to half a cigarette-tin of rice a head per day, and were feeling the pinch. They eventually petitioned me to increase it. But I refused, and told them that it was my job to get them through this march alive, and that I was determined to keep three full days' rations as a reserve, in case of some miscalculation. About this time we came to a Chin village, and had some trouble over a pig. Po Toke paid forty rupees for a village pig, but it escaped to the jungle just before he killed it. It was obvious that the villager would get it back after we had gone, as these pigs are left free to roam during the day, and come back to their pens at night. Po Toke naturally asked for his money back, and, just as naturally, the Chin villager refused to give it him. The dispute was therefore brought to me to settle, so I handed Po Toke a rifle and told him to go and shoot a wild one tomorrow instead. Before we left camp he had bagged two. Of course, I knew they were not wild ones, but it did at least settle the argument in favour of my men.

Before we moved on that morning the headman of the village came and asked me for compensation for damage done by the elephants to banana-trees during the night. He had actually got his bill down on paper, and brought with him a boy of seventeen, who could speak a few words of English and claimed that he had been educated. It was he who had put the headman up to this ruse to obtain money. I told White, who could speak Hindustani fluently, to deal with him. It did not take him long!

But from my point of view the incident was the first sign that we were reaching civilization again. However, as we were not going south to link up with the Bishenpur track, but west, it turned out there was a very long stretch of uncivilized country still to cover. Nevertheless, we had by this time at least left the mountains. In place of precipices we struck jungle swamp in which the animals got bogged. In trying to cut across country above the junction of the Digli and its tributary we were forced to turn back and follow down one river-bed to the confluence and then up the other river. It involved eight miles in water, knee-deep, with semi-quicksand bottom. It was just as slow going for the elephants as for the humans. All the children and the majority of the women had to ride, but the younger women were quite game to carry on. A few dropped out, and we had to send elephants back to pick them up.

Following elephants along a creek with a patchy quicksand bottom is an experience which thoroughly tests one's endurance and one's temper. It amounts to floundering along and continually losing one's balance, as one is always taking a step that meets with no resistance—as though one had stepped into a hole. It is next to impossible to carry anything, and the Gurkha girls soon discovered it was equally difficult to wear anything. It was not a time or place for false modesty and they were quite beyond caring about such matters. So they just handed up their garments, one after another, to the oozies and floundered on, naked, unimpeded and unashamed.

It was quite impossible to travel along the banks or to keep near them, as the dense jungle not only came down to the water's edge, but bamboos and canes grew right across. These had to be cut to allow the elephants to pass, and the sharp, twisted masses that resulted were awkward obstructions for those following.

I estimated that we covered only ten miles between 5 a.m.

and 5 p.m. that day. Everyone was dead beat when we arrived at the confluence. It was an amazing sight to see the refugees sorting out their few wet rags of clothes on an open patch where we had decided to camp.

That last desperate day of floundering down the river had brought us, I reckoned, to within one day's march of the tea estate. But we agreed that to arrive there with our entire party might not be popular, so I decided to take the really sick along with me, on nine elephants, and to leave the remainder of the party camping as near the tea estate as we dared. I had the astonishing experience of walking right out of the wall of dense jungle into the open plain of the tea estate—an ocean of green tea, as far as the eye could see. I had come out exactly where I had planned on the map. There were doves cooing. I felt a lump in my throat, and could hardly believe my eyes. About a mile away was a large bungalow, typical of so many planters' bungalows in Assam. I went ahead to introduce myself to the old planter and the lovely young wife whom we had imagined.

It looked a homely bungalow. As I approached it I could see a figure in a white shirt on the veranda, for the bungalow was built on high ground, above the level of the surrounding tea bushes.

Before I reached it I was hailed by a man, speaking with a strong Scotch accent, 'What is the hurry? What about a cup of tea?'

OUR SECRET SERVICE

By Richard Usborne

I HAD my first instruction in Secret Service work at my mother's knee. She was a keen player of *L'Attaque*. *L'Attaque* was a board-game that worked on a mixture of the principles of chess and Pelman Patience. On a board that my mother kept remarkably steady on her lap, we arrayed our armies, all with their backs to the foe, all our pieces mobile except *Le Drapeau*. The object, if you were in an aggressive mood (my mother was always aggressive, and her defence was bad), was to probe around for the enemy *Drapeau*, and say '*Attaque!*' If you attacked in sufficient strength, and with the right pieces to get through the minefields, brigadiers and rivers, you might be lucky and bump the enemy *Drapeau* before your own got bumped. *L'Attaque* was a good game and, by my mother and myself, cleanly played. Why our armies were French, with French terminology, I don't know.

One man in each army was in mufti, *L'Espion*. He was a very valuable piece, and I think he could only be annihilated by the other *Espion*. I have long since forgotten the details and the features of the other ranks. But *L'Espion* remains clearly in my memory. He was standing in high grass, which, like a bird-watcher (perhaps he said he *was* a bird-watcher if challenged), he had slightly parted to get a better view. He had an expression, again like a bird-watcher, of mixed calm and cunning. He was a man used to working alone. He was not afraid of seeming to be afraid. If a platoon of enemy *sapeurs* had bicycled past, he would have drawn the grass together in front of him and lain doggo. He would not have sprung out and offered battle. If he carried incriminating papers, he was prepared to eat them. If he was caught, he died with the same calm, cunning look on his face, refusing a bandage round his eyes. You loved your own *Espion*, hated your opponent's.

I doubt if any mere writer, of fact or fiction, has improved on that picture. Many have complicated it. Some have amplified it. But for the war-time spy, the cardboard *Espion* of my mother's favourite game is the pattern. The complications and amplifications begin when the brave (or, if he is on the other side, devilish) gentleman has to operate in peace-time. Since authors must live between wars, so must their spies.

The fact is that, in romantic fiction, espionage in peace-time is Not Done. When peace breaks out, the brave Englishman, lately an *espion*, must make do with being a *contre-espion*. The hero should be the saviour, not the disturber, of peace. If the clean-limbed Englishman goes on perilous journeys, it is not to plant a bomb in a palace, or to steal the Secret Treaty. It is to dish the devilish Ruritanian who is preparing to plant a bomb in Buckingham Palace, or, by stealing the Treaty, is pushing England into war.

The terminology changes. 'Spying' and 'The Secret Service' begin to sound pejorative terms, even in an armchair in the 'Rag'. The word for your own side now is 'Intelligence'. ('Intelligence' in war-time is such a wide service that there is no glamour in the word, unless you speak it in French.) When peace begins, ostensibly, England draws in her pickets and pensions off her war-time agents (venal foreigners) abroad. Official Intelligence in peace-time comes home to roost in Whitehall, and is an office job.

By all accounts there are a lot of Army Colonels in peace-time Intelligence. They can be tired men who live cheaply in hotels off the Cromwell Road, or spruce men who have chambers in the Albany. It depends on their private means. There is no real money in the job. There is still a little glamour, and some foreign travel. The work has to go on. But there are no D.S.O.'s gazetted on vague citations. Civilian clothes are no longer an intrepid disguise. The man who is caught is not shot at dawn. It is no longer a matter of life and death. It is, most of it, an exchange of files between the Foreign Office, the War Office, and Scotland Yard.

In *Greenmantle* and *Mr. Standfast* Germany was the declared enemy; there was a war on, and the boundaries of Tom Tiddler's Ground were clearly defined. Since nations were fighting against nations, and the broad principles of enmity were not in doubt, Buchan could at moments even make his enemy villains (Von Stumm, Hilda Von Einem, Moxon Ivery and such) human; indeed, in their patriotism, almost noble. But in peace-time the villain tends to become a stateless, probably Jewish, venal personal menace, a bad man disturbing the peace for his own pocket or to increase his own sense of power (Medina, Castor, d'Ingraville).

There is generally, in conditions of world peace, one nation which can be fairly safely suggested as having villainous intentions towards England at the period of writing. But it is seldom more than a suggestion, and the easy-going author prefers to leave the villainous nation vaguely defined or pseudonymous. Russia has been a good stand-by for daring authors over the peaceful periods of the last seventy-five years. Russia was the threat on the North-west Frontier in Kipling's *Kim* and *The Man Who Was*. Russia was the threat in Buchan's *The Half-Hearted*. Russia was the threat in almost all Sapper's Bulldog Drummond books.

But you will notice that the pointing of fingers and the naming of names in these books is, even so, rather discreet. The extent to which a nation in peace-time can be called a villain even in fiction depends to some extent on the distance by which it is separated from England geographically; but largely on the pulse-beat of international affairs of the moment of publication, and the candour of the author and his publishers.

In peace-time, then, nations and national ideologies tend to recede in the plot of thrillers, and personal villains come forward. Only the best authors can play The Game against such a drab backcloth of peace. And they have to pile on the personal devilishness of their foreign villains to make their capture, by the heroes, seem worthwhile. If the chase is confined to the English scene, it has the air of a drag-hunt rather than of the real thing. The English police, that fine body of men, are immanent, at least in the reader's subconscious, to help and protect the Right. It pays dividends in action to send the hero abroad to get his man. Abroad there are ravines and dungeons. Abroad the police are mercenary, and few and far between. Abroad there is reason to let the Bentley blind, the Rolls rip. The war-time *espion* may have, for the sake of The Code, to become a *contre-espion*. But there is nothing against his going into the badlands to do his stuff.

Perhaps we ought to define the term 'Secret Service', even at the risk of rubbing some of the romantic bloom off it. I take it to be a phrase never officially used, but fully understood, by the governments of such sovereign states as bother about national defence at all. A State may be said to have a Secret Service if it spends secretly any funds on the collection of secret information about another State, with the object of discovering that other State's secret doings or intentions. Ruritania may collect some such information about Bessonia's secret agents inside Ruritanian territory. That could be called counter-espionage. But if the money Ruritania spends on its sleuth-work is public money deceptively accounted for, then the operation comes under the heading Secret Service.

The sanction of Secret Services is war, or the preparation in case of war, or the prevention of war, or the prevention of severe damage to the State by any means just short of war. If the British Treasury sets its sleuths to rumble the forging of British banknotes by a French gang, that is not strictly Secret Service in the best and most glamorous sense of the word acceptable to us readers of thrillers. But if the French gang is encouraged by the French Government, and the basic purpose of the French malfeasance is national, with the intent to wreck England's economy, and thus soften England up for a possible future attack in war, then it is up to the British Secret Service to get to work. At a lower than national level, and with no threat of war on the horizon, the counter-measures may be given to a Special Agent to handle, and by any Whitehall Office. If it is a national peril, then the Foreign Office or the War Office, or both, will put their Dick Bartons on the job; and the Dick Bartons then will be Secret Service men.

I never did quite understand what Medina's purpose was in Buchan's *The Three Hostages*. Although no war seemed to be threatening England from Medina's machinations, Medina was apparently heading a group of anti-British agents whose object was not their own personal gain so much as the softening up of England. So the planning of counter-measures came into the province of Lord Artinswell (Foreign Office and Secret Service proper) as well as of MacGillivray (Scotland Yard).

I wonder whether Switzerland, Iceland and Panama have Secret Services. Do they have agents abroad, ostensibly busimen or charwomen or waiters in cafés, but coming home in the evenings to mutter coded messages into radio transmitters? Does Luxemburg have its Ciceros photographing secret treaties in the Chancelleries of Europe? How big or important does a sovereign State have to be before it starts secretly buying information? Does it, when it is small, rely on Big Nation A giving (not selling) its scraps of secret information about the secret machinations of Big Nation B? Do neutral countries such as Turkey and Portugal like, in war-time, being full of Hannays, Arbuthnots, Standishes, Ashendens, Von Papens and Canarises, to say nothing of hosts of their eager juniors? Is there then a premium on the price of valets (who are good photographers), *concierges* (who can read any foreign language, albeit coded, blurred and upside down, on blotting pads), *femmes fatales* (who can slip a Top Secret document out of the pocket of a coat on a bedrail) and waiters (who can intercept glances and interpret sharp intakes of breath?) Do their prices go up, and does their country prosper on its exciting *entrepôt* trade?

During the last war I was briefly in Syria and Lebanon. It was the first time I had had to use extensively my preparatory school French. When asked by Arabs what my job was, I said '*Intelligence*' with all the French accent I could manage. What my prep. school hadn't taught me was that the French equivalent for our Army 'I' was *Service de Renseignements*, and that when I said '*Intelligence*' it was the accepted French for the dread British Secret Service. The sharp intake of breath by Arabs who had read their *romans policiers*, and knew the omnipotence, omniscience and ruthlessness of the British Secret Service, was flatteringly audible. Some Arabs instantly asked me if I was a lord. Others came snaking round to my hotel room after dark, desiring me to take them on as highly paid agents. Others, more sophisticated, suspected that my alleged job with the British Secret Service must be a cover for something else, and they paled beneath their tan wondering what. Long afterwards, when my French improved and the penny dropped, I looked back, nostalgically, to those days of false glory, of gazelle-shoots with Emirs and of baffled looks from Free French officer allies; and I wondered how many other English officers were blissfully making confusion worse confounded in the Near East with their schoolboy French.

I only once met a man who, to my certain knowledge, was a career officer in the British Secret Service. Appropriately, he wore a monocle. It was during the war, and we met in one of the countries that changed hands and was liberated by both sides. I had some work to do which in this one instance necessitated my being in the picture about this man's activities and background. And I had to tell him I knew. Spoon-fed on Buchan and Sapper, I ought to have had the right sophisticated words with which to convey the information. Perhaps I ought to have imitated the hoot of an owl or the bleat of a snipe before entering the man's office. As it was I blushed and tittered, 'You, I gather, are in the—er—Secret Service.' He sized me up pityingly for the sort of man I was, i.e. spoon-fed on Buchan and Sapper; and he said, 'My dear chap, my job is simply to buy information.' His eyelids were a little weary. Perhaps he had been trafficking for strange webs with Eastern merchants that morning. I know he had had a tiring game of golf that afternoon with the Inter-Nuncio from the Vatican. There was presumably little information on sale that evening, so we sat and drank tea in his office while he told me of his difficulties.

'It's all right in war-time, and for you chaps,' he said. 'But I was here five years before the war, and, unless I'm lucky, I shall be here for five years after it's over. The military barges in, with no thanks for the information I had sweated to collect for them in the previous five years. Their damned Security boys imprison half my best agents, and employ the other half for their own dirty work without telling me. And when the war's over, they'll clear out, leaving everybody handsomely brûlé. I've got to work to get things organized now so that we can go on doing our job after the war. It's hell. Have another cup of tea.'

If that is the problem—the enduring qualities of the basic Secret Service against the temporary and *ad hoc* war-time alarums and excursions—it is justification for the Secret Service's use of Hannay, Drummond and Mansel whenever possible for its active jobs of derring-do. They are free-lance. They are brave and will not count the cost. They do not have to be given the complete picture. When the job's on, they cannot give the whole thing away under torture. They are men of means; so that, when the job's over, they will not come whining around asking for salaried office jobs to keep their mouths shut. They are mobile, but they can usually be contacted at their West End Clubs.

In war-time the heroes are in uniform, and can be taken out of the front line, bravely protesting, and sent off through Switzerland in bowler hats. It is practically an order. In the period between the wars Whitehall and the career Secret Service has excellent free-lance helpers.

BIOGRAPHICAL NOTES

AMERY, Julian. Born 1919. Educated: Eton and Balliol College, Oxford. War correspondent in Spanish Civil War. Served as Attaché to British Legation in Belgrade and in R.A.F. as sergeant. After transfer to the army served in S.O.E., being landed in 1941 on coast of Montenegro by submarine. Parachuted into Albania in 1944. Later on staff of General Carton de Wiart in Chungking. Returned as Conservative M.P. for Preston since 1950. Publications:
SONS OF THE EAGLE—A STUDY IN GUERILLA WAR.
Volume four in THE LIFE OF JOSEPH CHAMBERLAIN.

BUCKMASTER, Maurice. Born 1902. Educated: Eton. Pre-war work with J. Henry Schröder & Co., Bankers, and Ford Motor Co. Ltd. Served with 50 Div., France, 1939–40 and 'A' Force, Dakar. Joined 'F' Section, S.O.E., 1941, and remained with it until the end of the war. O.B.E.; Chevalier, Légion D'Honneur; Croix de Guerre with Palm; Officer, American Legion of Merit. Mentioned in despatches 1940. Now Public Relations Officer, Ford Motor Co. Ltd. F.I.P.R. Publications:
SPECIALLY EMPLOYED.

CHURCHILL, Peter. Born 1909. Educated: Malvern and Caius College, Cambridge. Ice Hockey International. Served in S.O.E. during the war, going twice to France by submarine and twice being dropped by parachute. Captured April 1943, and after return from solitary confinement married his courier in the Resistance, known as Odette.

Lecturer and Member of the Stock Exchange. Publications:
OF THEIR OWN CHOICE.
DUEL OF WITS.
THE SPIRIT IN THE CAGE.

CONNELL, John. Born 1909. Educated: Loretto and Balliol College, Oxford. Leader-writer on *The Evening News*. Six years war service, partly with Royal Artillery, partly with S.O.E. in Middle East, India and Italy. Book critic, novelist and journalist; Deputy Mayor of St. Pancras 1951–2. Fellow of The Royal Society of Literature. Publications:
LYNDESAY.
WHO GOES SAILING?
DAVID GO BACK.
TOMORROW WE SHALL BE FREE.
THE HOUSE BY HEROD'S GATE.
MIDSTREAM.
W. E. HENLEY.
THE RETURN OF LONG JOHN SILVER.
TIME AND CHANCE.

DAVIDSON, Basil. Born 1914. Pre-war journalist, often in Southern and Eastern Europe. Served 1940–45 with S.O.E. in Balkans and Near East. Parachuted into Yugoslavia and Northern Italy. M.C.; twice mentioned in despatches; United States Bronze Star. Since the war on the staff of *The Times*, *New Statesman & Nation*, and *The Daily Herald*. Publications:
PARTISAN PICTURE.
GOLDEN HORN.
HIGHWAY FORTY.
GERMANY: WHAT NOW?
DAYBREAK IN CHINA.
REPORT ON SOUTHERN AFRICA.
THE AFRICAN AWAKENING.

FIELDING, Xan. Born 1918. Educated: Charterhouse and New College, Oxford; and Universities of Bonn and Munich. Served in S.O.E. in the war. In Crete under enemy occupation, and then parachuted into France. Awarded D.S.O. Publications (in addition to several translations):
FIVE POEMS.
THE STRONGHOLD.
HIDE AND SEEK.

FLEMING, Peter. Born 1907. Educated: Eton and Christ Church, Oxford. Grenadier Guards (Supplementary Reserve) 1930. Served in Norway 1940 (mention); Greece 1941 (wounded); and S.E.A.C., 1945. O.B.E.; Order of the Cloud and Banner (Chinese). Commanded 4th Battalion Oxf. and Bucks. Light Infantry (Territorial Army) 1951–54. High Sheriff of Oxfordshire, 1952. Publications:
BRAZILIAN ADVENTURE.
ONE'S COMPANY.
NEWS FROM TARTARY.
THE FLYING VISIT.
A STORY TO TELL.
THE SIXTH COLUMN.
A FORGOTTEN JOURNEY.

HOWARTH, Patrick. Born 1916. Educated: Rugby and St. John's College, Oxford. Pre-war journalist in Poland. Served with S.O.E. in Middle East and Italy. Press Attaché H.M. Embassy, Warsaw, 1945; Home Civil Service, 1948–53; Publicity Secretary, Royal National Lifeboat Institution. Publications:
THE YEAR IS 1851.
THE DYING UKRAINIAN.
A MATTER OF MINUTES.

BIOGRAPHICAL NOTES 235

MARSHALL, Bruce. Born 1899. Educated: Edinburgh Academy, Glenalmond, St. Andrews and Edinburgh University. Served with Royal Irish Fusiliers in 1914–18 war; wounded and taken prisoner. Between the wars lived mainly in Paris as accountant and writer. Served on staff of S.O.E. during the last war. Publications:
   THOUGHTS OF MY CATS.
   ONLY FADE AWAY.
   THE FAIR BRIDE.
   EVERY MAN A PENNY.
   GEORGE BROWN'S SCHOOLDAYS.
   ALL GLORIOUS WITHIN.
   YELLOW TAPERS FOR PARIS.
   FATHER MALACHY'S MIRACLE.
   THE WHITE RABBIT.

MILLAR, George. Born 1910. Educated: Loretto and St. John's College, Cambridge. Pre-war journalist. Served in the Rifle Brigade and taken prisoner by Afrika Corps in 1941. Escaped, joined S.O.E. and was parachuted into France. Chevalier, Légion d'Honneur; Croix de Guerre with Palm. Publications:
   MAQUIS.
   HORNED PIGEON.
   MY PAST WAS AN EVIL RIVER.
   ISABEL AND THE SEA.
   THROUGH THE UNICORN GATES.
   A WHITE BOAT FROM ENGLAND.
   SIESTA.

MOSS, W. Stanley. Born 1921. Educated: Charterhouse. Served with Coldstream Guards and with S.O.E., landing in Crete twice and in Macedonia, and being parachuted into Siam. Author and journalist. Publications:
   THE HOUR OF FLIGHT.
   ILL MET BY MOONLIGHT.

BATS WITH BABY FACES.
A WAR OF SHADOWS.
THREE PLAGUES.
WARPATH.

NOEL-BAKER, Francis. Born 1920. Educated: Westminster and King's College, Cambridge. Served in war in the Royal Tank Regiment and Intelligence Corps; and in S.O.E. as liaison officer for Middle East with Greek Forces. Mentioned in despatches. Returned as Labour candidate for Brentford and Chiswick, 1945, and for Swindon, 1955. M.P., Foreign correspondent, magazine editor and broadcaster. Publications:
GREECE—THE WHOLE STORY.
SPANISH SUMMARY.
THE SPY WEB.

QUAYLE, Anthony. Born 1913. Educated: Rugby. Pre-war actor. Served with Royal Artillery and S.O.E. during war; parachuted into Albania. Play producer and actor. Appointed Director, Shakespeare Memorial Theatre, October 1948. Publications:
EIGHT HOURS FROM ENGLAND.
ON SUCH A NIGHT.

SETON-WATSON, Hugh. Born 1916. Educated: Winchester and New College, Oxford. Served in S.O.E. in Bucharest and Belgrade 1940–41, and in Middle East 1942–44. Fellow and Tutor in Politics, University College, Oxford, 1946–51. Appointed Professor of Russian History, School of Slavonic and East European Studies, University of London, 1951. Publications:
EASTERN EUROPE BETWEEN THE WARS.
THE EAST EUROPEAN REVOLUTION.
THE DECLINE OF IMPERIAL RUSSIA.
THE PATTERN OF COMMUNIST REVOLUTION.

SPENCER CHAPMAN, F. Born 1907. Educated: Sedbergh and St. John's College, Cambridge. Pre-war schoolmaster and explorer in Greenland, Lapland and Tibet. Awarded Arctic Medal. Trained Commandos in Scotland, Australia and Malaya, and then in S.O.E. Spent three years in charge of stay-behind parties in Malayan jungle. Lieut. Col., D.S.O. and bar. First headmaster of King Alfred School, Plön, 1948–52. Headmaster Elect of St. Andrew's College, Grahamstown, South Africa. Publications:

NORTHERN LIGHTS.
WATKINS' LAST EXPEDITION.
LHASA, THE HOLY CITY.
HELVELLYN TO HIMALAYA.
MEMOIRS OF A MOUNTAINEER.
THE JUNGLE IS NEUTRAL.
LIVING DANGEROUSLY.
LIGHTEST AFRICA.

SYKES, Christopher. Born 1907. Educated: Downside and Christ Church, Oxford. Before the war on staff of H.M. Embassy, Berlin, and H.M. Legation, Tehran; author and journalist. Served with the Green Howards, from 1940–43 with S.O.E. in Middle East; 1943–45 with 2. S.A.S. Parachuted into France. Appointed Deputy Controller, B.B.C. Third Programme, 1948. Publications:

WASSMUSS.
INNOCENCE AND DESIGN.
STRANGER WONDERS.
HIGH MINDED MURDER.
FOUR STUDIES IN LOYALTY.
THE ANSWER TO QUESTION 33.
CHARACTER AND SITUATION.
TWO STUDIES IN VIRTUE.
A SONG OF A SHIRT.

USBORNE, Richard. Born 1910. Educated: Charterhouse and Balliol College, Oxford. Before the war in magazines and advertising. Served with S.O.E. in the Middle East. Since the war Assistant Editor of the *Strand* and the *Leader* and in advertising. Book critic and broadcaster. Publication:
CLUBLAND HEROES.

WALKER, David. Born 1907. Educated: Ampleforth and Christ Church, Oxford. Pre-war journalist. Served as war correspondent in Greece, Belgium, Holland and Germany, and also with S.O.E. Foreign Correspondent, U.S.A. 1945–6, Australia 1947–8, Europe and Middle East 1951. War Correspondent, Korea 1950. Publications:
EAT, DRINK AND BE MERRY.
RELIGION IN THE REICH.
DEATH AT MY HEELS.
THE GREEK MIRACLE.
CIVILIAN ATTACK.
WE WENT TO AUSTRALIA.
I GO WHERE I'M SENT.
DIAMONDS FOR MOSCOW.

WILLIAMS, J. H. Born 1897. Educated: Queen's College, Taunton. Served in First World War from the age of $17\frac{1}{2}$. Between the wars worked for the Bombay Burmah Trading Corporation, mainly in teak forest. Served with Royal Indian Engineers, 1942–46. Elephant Adviser to the 14th Army, and in S.O.E. O.B.E., mentioned three times in despatches. Now farming in Cornwall. Publications:
ELEPHANT BILL.
BANDOOLA.

WOODHOUSE, the hon. C. M. Born 1917. Educated: Winchester and New College, Oxford. Served with Royal

Artillery and S.O.E. In command of Allied Military Mission to Greek Guerrillas in enemy-occupied Greece. D.S.O., O.B.E., Officer of Legion of Merit (U.S.A.), Commander of the Order of the Phoenix with Swords (Greece). On staff of H.M. Embassy, Athens, 1945, and Tehran, 1951. Assistant Secretary, Nuffield Foundation, 1948; Fellow of Trinity Hall, Cambridge, 1949. Fellow of the Royal Society of Literature, 1950. Appointed Director General of Royal Institute of International Affairs, 1955. Publications:

APPLE OF DISCORD.

ONE OMEN.

DOSTOIEVSKY.

THE GREEK WAR OF INDEPENDENCE.

For Product Safety Concerns and Information please contact our EU
representative GPSR@taylorandfrancis.com
Taylor & Francis Verlag GmbH, Kaufingerstraße 24, 80331 München, Germany

www.ingramcontent.com/pod-product-compliance
Lightning Source LLC
Chambersburg PA
CBHW070559300426
44113CB00010B/1314